IMOGEN RACZ is Senior Lecturer in Art History at Coventry University. Her publications include *Contemporary Crafts* (2009), as well as many articles related to sculpture and object-based art.

ART AND THE HOME

Comfort, Alienation and the Everyday

Imogen Racz

BLOOMSBURY VISUAL ARTS
LONDON • NEW YORK • OXFORD • NEW DELHI • SYDNEY

BLOOMSBURY VISUAL ARTS
Bloomsbury Publishing Plc
50 Bedford Square, London, WC1B 3DP, UK
1385 Broadway, New York, NY 10018, USA

BLOOMSBURY, BLOOMSBURY VISUAL ARTS and the Diana logo are trademarks of Bloomsbury Publishing Plc

First published in Great Britain by I.B. Tauris & Co Ltd 2015
This edition published by Bloomsbury Visual Arts 2019

Cover design: Chris Bromley
Cover image: Michael Landy Semi-Detached – John & Ethel Landy 2004, Photograph,121.9 x 162.6 (48 x 64in.) Image © the artist.
Image courtesy of the artist and Thomas Dane Gallery.

A catalogue record for this book is available from the British Library.

A catalog record for this book is available from the Library of Congress.

ISBN: HB: 978-1-78076-200-5
PB: 978-1-50135-986-6
ePDF: 978-1-78673-998-8
eBook: 978-0-85773-868-4

Series: International Library of Modern and Contemporary Art, volume 5

Text designed and typeset by Tetragon, London
Printed and bound in Great Britain

To find out more about our authors and books visit www.bloomsbury.com and sign up for our newsletters.

CONTENTS

LIST OF FIGURES

ACKNOWLEDGEMENTS

I have loved writing this book. To go and really look at great art, read what artists and others have written, think about these things and discuss them with others, and then organise my thoughts into a text has been a privilege. Of course there have been the usual ups and downs of any large project, but I have met with wonderful generosity from many quarters: from the artists themselves, from curators, archivists and librarians. In particular I would like to mention the archivists and librarians at the British Library, the Courtauld Institute of Art, Coventry University, the Henry Moore Institute, Leeds, the National Art Library, University College London and Tate Britain. I would like to thank the directors and curators at the Henry Moore Institute, Leeds, the Ikon Gallery, Birmingham, the Serpentine Gallery, Tate Britain and the Thomas Dane Gallery. There have been many others who have also given their time and expertise, to whom I now extend my thanks.

I would like to thank the editors at I.B.Tauris, who have always been enthusiastic about this project and answered all my queries quickly and efficiently, but have also given me space to work in my own way. This trust gave me courage.

I am grateful to Coventry University for the sabbatical I received in the spring of 2010. This was a wonderful time that allowed me to rethink and develop ideas for my research, and to put together the proposal for *Art and the Home: Comfort, Alienation and the Everyday*. I am also grateful to my line managers John Devane and Kollette Super, and to Professor Martin Woolley, all of whom have supported me in various ways during this project.

I would like to thank Anne Tyson, Joan Gibbons, Mark Racz and Margaret Garlake, all of whom read chapters of this book and gave helpful comments. It was invaluable to have their eyes and brains engaged with the text, as it is all too easy to continue down a research groove. To all my friends and colleagues, I would like to thank them for being supportive when I have either enthused or ignored them at different times during the last few years. However, my greatest thanks go to my husband Mark, who has unfailingly encouraged, listened and helped in more ways than I can enumerate.

INTRODUCTION

A major theme in postwar art has been an engagement with the home, not only to explore our personal, social and cultural relationships with the spaces in which we dwell, but also to consider how homes and houses have been implicated in political and economic strategies. Artists as diverse as Gordon Matta-Clark, Robert Rauschenberg, Cornelia Parker, Rachel Whiteread, Grayson Perry, Emilia and Ilya Kabakov and Miriam Schapiro have explored different ideas within this theme using an array of materials, techniques and display strategies. These and most of the artists who will be discussed here make three-dimensional works that have stretched and challenged the traditional frameworks of sculpture's rubric, channelling deeply felt ideas and tensions from the real world into objects and installations that have the capacity to disrupt, redirect or extend conventional narratives.

Sculptural practice is of the world, and is experienced spatially, materially and in time. Sculpture is measured against the scale of the body, and the audience needs to move around it to engage with its material reality. Its physicality can act as a metaphor and stand in for other states.[1] Found and manipulated objects hold echoes of their previous existence both in function and material. This does not mean that sculpture, objects and installations are 'reality'; their staging is also crucial.[2] They act as mediators between art and life, and articulate the elusive boundaries between fact and the subjective values we ascribe to things.[3] As such, sculpture can enhance our perceptions about what it means to be in the world.[4] As Peter Schjeldahl has written: 'Sculpture's prerogative is to confront us with the fact of our material, physical, bodily reality, making that fact available to thought and feeling – and making it sociable, an open secret shared with others in a common space.'[5]

The home both contains us and is within us. The overall scale of the dwelling, its thresholds and internal spaces are all related to the scale of the body, the stride of the legs, the swing of the arms and the space above the head. Any alteration of these relationships is felt both physically and mentally. Related to the scale of the rooms is that of furniture that supports and comforts the body, and our objects that act as functional tools and are the ballast to our lives. We hold these material and physical memories within us, and so when viewing sculptures there is an instinctive dialogue with these internalised tactile, spatial and haptic knowledges. In addition, domestic objects are active in our value systems, and, like the spaces that contain us, are implicated in the relationships that have been developed within the walls.

The relationships that people have with their homes are complex. Recent Anglo-American research has explored what people find important about them.[6] Whereas the house is the structure, a home – especially one that is owned – tends to be a place that reflects back onto its owners, reinforcing aspects of pride and identity.[7] Unlike in many traditional cultures, Western urbanised people move quite frequently, so that the location and type of dwelling also changes according to needs at different stages of life and depending on circumstances.[8] However, the basic elements of what people describe as making a home – as opposed to a house – remain fairly constant. These include a secure material structure over which one has control; a place that one can modify according to desires and needs and that reflects one's status, ideas and values; somewhere permanent that gives a sense of continuity; and a place where one can develop and act out relationships with family and friends.[9] It is also a place where one's sense of identity is developed.[10]

Walter Benjamin discussed the repeated processes and habitual behaviours that are required to fashion a shell for ourselves, where the house and inhabitant become adapted to each other.[11] We choose objects and decorations, negotiate with others about these, make and mend, and gradually build a place that reflects the way we feel about ourselves. This repeated care and alteration lavished over time on spaces and acquired things is important for the materialisation of memory and feelings of continuity and stability.[12]

Indeed, the architectural theorist Andrew Ballantyne has discussed the way that gestures of cleaning are akin to grooming and stroking.[13]

All this implies that the home is always positive. Clearly there is evidence to the contrary. More recent scholarship has brought to the fore the differences of experiences related to gender, class, ethnicity, sexuality and social spheres. It argues that the home is not a stable concept, nor is it a place that is always a retreat or where identity is grounded.[14] The home can also be a place of resistance and oppression.[15]

Writing as early as 1992, Doreen Massey discussed the huge changes that had occurred in the Western world over the previous 20 years, including the changing patterns of capital across the globe, the move from a modern to a post-modern society and from industrial production to a post-industrial service economy. These changes have reshaped spatial and social relationships at every level, including those of the neighbourhood and within the home.[16]

The book is divided into seven chapters, each of which explores the way that the work of particular artists and ideas converge around a particular issue. It is not a chronological survey; rather, some chapters discuss how an idea is manifested in different situations over time, and some concentrate on the imbrication of particular ideas within a group of affiliated artists. Chapter 1, for instance, discusses art from different periods and on both sides of the Atlantic that articulates people's relationships to the enclosed spaces of dwelling, as well as introducing a phenomenological underpinning about the mental and physical notion of being in the world, which became important for minimalism and installation art. Chapter 3 concentrates on the feminist reclamation of the home as a place of female creativity in 1970s California, and Chapter 5 discusses how artists have engaged with the way housing has been used as part of political and economic strategies. In the former, I show how the artists initiated the deconstruction of the apparently seamless narrative underlying the gendered myths about the home by coming together, reworking aesthetic languages and critiquing traditional female roles.[17] In the latter, rather than concentrating on a group of artists working at the same place and time, I take the traditional idea of the ruin and explore how a number of postwar artists working across several decades and in different contexts have altered real houses to reveal and critique the results of urban policies, through cutting, casting and photography.

I have discussed particular works in more depth, choosing those that either bring together ideas already discussed or speak effectively about a particular issue. In Chapter 1, for instance, Michael Landy's *Semi-detached*, a life-size replica of the artist's parents' home installed in the Duveen Galleries in Tate Britain in 2004, is discussed towards the end of a broader consideration of what the enclosed spaces of a home mean and how they have been interpreted within art, as well as of the tensions between art and life. Chapter 7 concentrates on British artists who have made, appropriated and altered objects, playing with ideas of domestic display, subverting expectations of the 'decorative' and reminding us of the overlooked material world that surrounds us. Again, certain works, like Cornelia Parker's *Thirty Pieces of Silver*, are considered in more detail.

I am aware that there are huge gaps in the narrative constructed here, but this provides opportunities for the future. Most of the work that is dealt with is by postwar artists who live in or have produced work in America and Britain, although some chapters, like Chapter 2 and Chapter 6, have introductory sections that go back in time to introduce the origins of the ideas to be discussed. Also included are some artists from non-Western backgrounds like Mona Hatoum and Ilya and Emilia Kabakov, who, although originating from outside America and Britain, are now practising in the West.

The choice of America and Britain was made for a number of reasons. Although we now live in a world where art from different cultures is exhibited internationally and can be easily seen on the internet, this is a fairly recent development and would not have been relevant for the earlier decades of this discussion. The artistic, cultural, social and political dialogues between Britain and America have been rich and engaged since World War II, partly because the common language has meant that art journals, books and websites have been readily available on both sides of the Atlantic, partly because many artists from one country have travelled and gained exhibitions in the other, and partly because there is a historical, cultural and political affinity. Although the two countries are dissimilar, there is a real social and cultural understanding of the ideals underpinning the home and family.

These are important factors for the underlying theme of how everyday experiences have been translated into art. In postwar practice the means used, which include the appropriation and modification of objects, the juxtaposition of different genres of objects, the use of domestic techniques for subversive intent, the manipulation of scale, implied narrative, and many other strategies, all shine a light on the apparently 'natural' within our cultures. When combined with their staging either within or outside institutional confines, the dialogues become more complex. Some artists have chosen to use the traditional gallery space to frame their art, either as a subversive strategy or one that exploits the expectations of the viewers. Other artists have made work within the everyday world, and the geographical or historical situation of these interventions has been crucial to perception and interpretation. Most of these works have been temporary, so all that exists is their documentation, which is again a complex issue that will be discussed as relevant.

While each chapter is self-contained, in common with all art practice there are dialogues that run across the themes and between previous and contemporary practices, and that reconsider and subvert ideas and engage with issues within the social and political realm. What I intend is that by the end the reader will have an enriched appreciation of how different artists have drawn on the fundamental aspect of being human – that of dwelling – and represented this often overlooked area in ways that disturb, challenge and enrich the normal understanding of this phenomenon.

1

Enclosure

In his autobiographical work 'A Berlin chronicle' Walter Benjamin describes the childhood walks that he took around Berlin with his nurse and mother, and frequent visits to his relatives. To get to the apartment where Aunt Lehmann lived, he and his nurse had to climb up dark, steep steps and wait for his aunt's thin voice to invite them in.[1] The stairs were the transition between the outside world of cafes, parks and zoos and the inside, which sheltered her life and possessions. The essay describes in detail a range of episodes that he had unearthed and given tone to through returning to them repeatedly and mulling them over in his mind 'like a man digging', turning over the soil of his memories in search of collectors' pieces that he could arrange in the 'prosaic rooms of [...] later understanding'.[2]

This interrelationship between the mind and rooms, and the mental and physical link between the contained spaces of the dwelling and the individual, forms the basis of this chapter. A home develops over time and becomes part of the person, who, even when not physically there, can return mentally to revisit memories located within the walls. On a daily basis one moves around the spaces and knows them so well that conscious directing is not necessary. Homes are places of habits, rituals and movements, and when experiences are translated into installation and sculpture, these also require the audience to move around and measure the work against its own bodily and mental memories. This translation of the everyday into art and the relationship of these works with the spectator will also be an important thread running through this chapter.

INSIDE/OUTSIDE

When Baudelaire wrote 'The painter of modern life' in the mid-nineteenth century, he described a particular artist and traveller, whom he called M. G., as a man of the world. In his constant curiosity about the cosmopolitan world where he felt at home in the crowd, M. G. was more than a mere artist who remained in his district, 'tied to his palette like a serf to the soil'.[3] An avid idler and observer, M. G. was part of the throng; he was at home anywhere, and with his independent, intense spirit, he loved life and made 'the whole world into his family'.[4]

Baudelaire was writing at the time of Baron Haussmann's destruction and renovation in Paris, where new, broad boulevards were pushed through old neighbourhoods. For the first time the lives of people from different classes and occupations geographically overlapped, and it became common for people to move beyond the immediate warren of their close-knit communities, where all would have known each other and lived intermeshed lives. To be at home in the crowd, therefore, was a modern experience, and Baudelaire's writing suggested a heroic male who was unfettered by family and domesticity.

Walter Benjamin's demarcation between inside and outside and Baudelaire's insistence that the important life happened on the street are reflections of both the cultural and experiential ideas about public and private spaces that have underpinned Western culture since Ancient Greek times, in which men's ability to mix and argue politics within public arenas, regardless of rank, formed the basis of democracy. The home on the other hand provided shelter and was the area where women cooked and raised families, and while these things enabled public life, they were perceived as being bound to biology rather than culture.[5]

Baudelaire was writing at a time, however, when the middle classes were growing and sought to differentiate themselves from the working classes. The artists who followed Baudelaire's edict to paint modern life revealed the different classes on the street through occupations, visibility and fashion. The home in everyday life and in art also revealed class and gender roles. The middle classes fostered the ideal of the home as a place of retreat, quiet and family life, into which friends could be invited, rather than one implicated in the business of earning a living. As Griselda Pollock convincingly argued, dining rooms, drawing rooms, bedrooms, balconies and private gardens were the spaces where females were seen to act out notions of bourgeois femininity.[6] These enclosed spaces were areas of family life and refined leisure.

While this ideal has been manifested in different countries and across social strata in various ways, the notion of the home as the basis of family life, which provides security, warmth, rest and nourishment, still runs deep in Western culture. It is the 'core of place experience' and 'the realm in which we live, from which we move out into the wider world and to which we return.'[7] As such, the enclosed space, surrounded by walls, and secured by doors and locks, into which personalities, memories and identities are forged and revealed, is precious.

THE HOME AND SELF

The search for a space where the private world can be acted out within an atmosphere of permanence and away from the constraints of the outside world has been an aspiration in north-western European life for centuries, regardless of social and economic circumstances. Writing about Georgian England, Amanda Vickery painted a vivid account of this, saying that the desire for a demarcated area that one could control developed during the early modern period, and by the eighteenth century was firmly entrenched. If economic circumstances meant that there was not even a room one could call one's own, a lockable box where one could keep a collection of special things and harbour dreams and memories was sought.[8] All classes of society, even the very poor, have put a great premium on retaining a separate and independent state of habitation even into very old age.[9]

To cross the threshold from the public to the private world is one of the many transitions and rites that we unthinkingly perform every day. This physical movement creates a corresponding mental shift from being in the public arena, where the rules and threats are beyond our control, to being an area with which one is intimate. As a child visiting the homes of his relatives, Benjamin absorbed the nuances and understood the rituals and relationships that were enacted within the walls. It was because he was part of the family that he had access to these private places and understood the relationships between each of the inhabitants and those that they had created with their possessions as no one else could. His grandmother's home evoked memories of visits, feasts, smells and the sounds of piano music, and was a place where childhood memories were entwined with the material facts of everyday life. Benjamin described the 'heavy, faded-violet curtain' in the corner of his parents' bedroom where his mother's shawls, dressing gowns and housecoats hung, and the lavender scent of the linen cupboard.[10] The shadows, textures, scents and sounds that made up his experiences were not only a physical backdrop to private everyday life, but also the hooks by which the memories and experiences were felt and relived. Reflecting the fact that this could be both reassuring and stultifying, Benjamin wrote that his grandmother's home was 'so cosy by day, and by night [became] the theatre of our most oppressive dreams'.[11]

The contemporary video artist John Smith has explored the relationship between the self and domestic spaces in some of his films, including *Leading Light* (1975), *Home Suite* (1993–4) and *Blight* (1994–6). *Leading Light* is a short film that shows a room in which the light from the window illuminates particular things as the beam travels around it during the course of the day. The camera eye captures both fleeting in-between spaces and objects that allow for private moments – the bed, the shadow created by a pot plant, books and a chair.[12] *Home Suite* is a much longer film, in which Smith accompanies the audience around his home, which is to be demolished, stopping at different points to articulate the memories that are located at particular places. Like the text by Benjamin his memory of relationships and happenings are fused to the material world, so that carpets, the staircase and the texture of a wall trigger different recollections.[13]

In her photographs Mary Maclean has also explored the relationships that we have with particular places. Some images are uneasy, some meditative, but most focus on framing details and the spaces next to furniture and objects: the areas that one only concentrates on when one knows a place well. A group of photographs made for the Jerwood Artists Platform in 2002, like most of her work, suggest a presence within the empty room.[14] These pictures, like the text by Benjamin, create an intimate view, with details of furniture and a gaze towards the window and towards the inconsequential objects that surround everyone but to which meaning is attached.

This private space has widely been described as the place where we are most ourselves, and 'at home'. As Martin Heidegger has written, humans build homes because we are by nature dwellers. It is these places that we get to know intimately, both mentally and physically, so that we can walk around, anticipating distances and obstacles and reflecting on past experiences. Homes, he writes, are intrinsically interior and exterior.[15] In this he echoed the writings of the phenomenologists Maurice Merleau-Ponty and Edmund Husserl, who also examined the relationship between consciousness and the material world. For Merleau-Ponty the world was the setting for thoughts and perceptions, and he wrote that, when moving around his flat, he knew where he was and where things were instinctively and without conscious thought.[16] He also discussed how we project thoughts and feelings onto objects, landscapes and people, making our internal mental life integral with the world beyond, which becomes the 'homeland of our thoughts'.[17]

These philosophical ideas about the home have been borne out in studies made by social scientists, architects and anthropologists. In a study about people's priorities for the home, Juhani Pallasmaa identified three key symbolic elements. He found that the liminal areas of the entrance and hearth have deep unconscious, biological and cultural roots of meaning. Objects that relate to the lives of the inhabitants or are inherited help to anchor memories of events and people. Social symbols that give particular messages to outsiders are also important as they are signs of wealth, education and social identity.[18] By including these ingredients, and gradually working on the dwelling place, over time it becomes a site where one is literally 'at home'.

In art, the home and dwelling have been rendered in images by artists as diverse as Pieter de Hooch, Édouard Vuillard, Pierre Bonnard, Mary Cassatt, Spencer Gore and Richard Billingham. While Dutch paintings from the seventeenth century of the domestic sphere frequently contained moral and metaphorical messages, the paintings and photographs by later artists have tended to depict times of reflection or people attending to private tasks or engaging with family life. Just as in real life, the depicted furniture and decorative choices frame and articulate the circumstances and character of the occupants. This backdrop acts like the scenery in a play or the background details of a novel that are included to set the tone and enable the audience or reader to believe in and enter into the world of the depicted characters.[19] In the real world, ideally the home is the place that we decorate and inhabit, where we can build a sense of self and be who and what we are.[20] For the audience standing before the images, the links between these constructed worlds and the everyday become blurred, as the activities depicted are universal and ones towards which one can extend an empathetic understanding.[21] Like the memories of Benjamin, and the films and photography of Smith and Maclean, which have been translated through a web of nuanced language, these images map onto the memories held by the reader. In none of the genres are the results 'natural' or unmediated. As Smith has said, he works in the space where the viewer perceptually moves between realising that his work is a construction and becoming involved with the illusions and stories.[22]

The difference between the posed presence made by the artist for the viewer – as in many images by Edward Hopper – and that which has been captured by an insider is palpable. Vuillard repeatedly painted the home where he lived with his mother, depicting her going about her daily life: sewing, checking the table prior to the meal and doing other day-to-day bourgeois activities. It is an insider's view. In his journal of 1893, he wrote, 'Why is it always on the familiar places that the mind and the sensibility find the greatest degree of genuine novelty?'[23] The abstraction of the paint surface and the play with space however, act as a distancing mechanism, making painting very different from the photographic image, where there is the suggestion of reality and 'truth'. Richard Billingham, for instance, used his camera to capture the lives of his working-class family living on a council estate in the English Midlands during the 1990s. In spite of the depictions of drinking and poverty and the sense of unease and boredom, the home that they occupy is also a sanctuary from the outside world. The images reveal moments of tenderness, such as when a boiled egg is offered by his mother to his father, as well as showing her making a meal in the kitchen or being engrossed in a jigsaw puzzle.[24] These are scenes that would not have been available to an outsider, but because of Billingham's proximity and the ability of the camera to capture a moment quickly, there is an apparent naturalness in the capturing of the everyday.

Although I have been discussing ideas and art from different centuries and countries, there is a core of meaning shared by all of them. The quiet moments depicted within private, enclosed spaces, together with possessions that might or might not have great material value, are recognisable and precious to the owner. The home is the space that we make our own, giving the dwelling 'its psyche and soul in addition to its formal and quantifiable qualities'.[25]

MINIMALISM AND PHENOMENOLOGY

So far I have been discussing images whose spectator remains static and considers what is in front of him or her. Such images are framed and understood as suggesting a fragment of a larger world existing beyond the given parameters. However, of particular importance not only for this chapter but for much of the work discussed in the book was the development of installation, where the experience of the viewer became immersive, as he or she walked through spaces and engaged with art objects not only visually but physically and mentally, in a manner that echoed the experience of the home.

In defiance of the critic Clement Greenberg's notions of authorship, of critiquing the medium of paint, of hermetically engaging with the history of art and of the audience remaining static, the sculptural movement known as minimalism engaged with gallery spaces and encouraged the audience to move around and over its works.[26] As Donald Judd wrote in 1965, actual space is intrinsically powerful so that the various forms set within a gallery space should be seen as one entity that asserts relationships with walls, floors and ceilings.[27] Rather than being self-contained, objects were designed to lead viewers to consider aspects like material, scale and their own distance from the sculpture and the walls of the site.[28] While the scale of the images discussed in the previous section was important in their relationship with the world of the audience, the abstraction and physicality of minimalism forced a different engagement, one that was described by Michael Fried as theatrical. Not even allowing minimalism to be 'sculpture', he described it as 'non-art', as the meaning was situated less in the work than in the encounter, which changed as the gallery visitor moved around.[29]

In 1966 Robert Morris wrote 'Notes on sculpture', which was published in three parts in *Artforum*. These essays opened up a debate on how sculpture could be viewed in a gallery, which privileged a public encounter over the private contemplation of a self-contained work of art.[30] While clearly different from the ideas discussed earlier in this chapter about moving around domestic spaces and negotiating this private world physically and mentally, there are resonances that overlap. The large, repeated and simple geometric forms, for instance, that were installed in Morris' famous exhibition at the Green Gallery, New York, in 1964–5, were not meant to seduce the viewer through obvious skill, surface texture or accreted memories. However, each element set up relationships between itself, the surrounding architectural space and the viewer, and these folded back onto the viewer as he or she became aware of existing within the same space.[31]

The apparent simplicity of this work and those by other minimalist artists like Carl Andre, who, as part of his output, made sculptures consisting of industrially produced metal tiles arranged in non-hierarchical grids that the audience walked over, elides interpretation. Unlike the sentiment embedded within a home, these works were not carriers of meaning related to events or accrued bodily knowledge related to the spaces of dwelling. For Andre, sculpture does not contain meaning but exists in the 'phenomenological world', where the viewer engages physically with the art, and this encounter bridges the gap between mind and feeling.[32]

The phenomenological writings of Merleau-Ponty and Husserl became important during the 1960s for many avant-garde sculptors as well as for critics like David Sylvester and Rosalind Krauss in the English-speaking world. Merleau-Ponty's book *The Phenomenology of Perception* was written in 1945 and translated into English in 1962, and other essays of his were translated within the next few years. Building on the earlier writings by Husserl, Merleau-Ponty offered a way of viewing in which the world was not 'out there' but perceived through an interactive enmeshing of mind, body and immediate world. Although the minimalists were engaging with the ideas promoted in phenomenology – including a multi-sensory understanding of space, the notion that works were perceived over time and that the viewer changed his or her perceptual viewpoint as he or she moved around and across the sculptures – these were not the warm familiar things that surround one in one's dwelling, upon which one projects memories and values. The sculptures were geometric, industrial and cool.

Many of the artists whose work will be considered in this book can be seen against a backdrop of minimalism. However, as will also be discussed, this influence becomes tempered according to circumstances and contexts.[33] Likewise, I use phenomenology when relevant, and would argue that it provides a useful bridge between a real and sculpturally constructed understanding of the world.

ENCLOSURE, MYTHS AND PHENOMENOLOGY

The experience of the home has been described in phenomenology as multi-sensory, where there is a blurring of clearly defined boundaries between the subject and object. Husserl, who was one of the key initiating figures in phenomenology, described an intersubjective world, where the connection between consciousness and the real world is layered and interdependent. For him, the external world is reconfigured in our minds through memory and reflection, so that the consciousness and the outer world become connected and frame each other.[34] In *Ideas: General Introduction to Pure Phenomenology* (1913), Husserl illustrates this by starting with the premise that the immediate world is simply there, whether one pays attention to it or not. We experience it through sight, touch, hearing and other senses. However, one can also let one's attention wander around the room even when not there, mapping the features and pausing as the mind drifts across the physical things, remembering happenings and the emotional values attached to each.[35]

Transcending the individual homes that we have all lived in, Gaston Bachelard later wrote about the essence that permeates the understanding of what a home represents. He described the home as 'our corner of the world'.[36] It is the place in which memories are formed and which shelters our daydreams. It is through reliving these dreams that the place of dreaming stays with us.[37] His phenomenological writing – *The Poetics of Space* was the first of his books to move away from a psychoanalytical, Freudian standpoint and to use phenomenology as a means to articulate the relationship of humans to their environments – unites the physical and the mental. For Bachelard, this was not passive, but he passionately wrote about how one should explore experiences actively within the mind. Rather than perception occupying a linear aspect of time and memory, what Bachelard sought to explore was the imbrication of subject and object, in this case within the home.[38]

This embodied understanding of the home is encapsulated in the small sculpture of just a few cubic centimetres that Donald Rodney made in 1996 entitled *My Mother, My Father, My Sister, My Brother*. It consisted of a house made from the artist's skin, which was taken while he was having treatment for sickle-cell anaemia. This simple, frail building contains all of the fundamental elements that are necessary for dwelling: a roof, walls, a door and a window, providing ideas of shelter, withdrawal and fragile security.

A photograph, *In the House of My Father* (1996–7; figure 1.1), shows this sculpture held in the palm of Rodney's hand, suggesting both protection and the idea that the structure could be crushed without trace. The house's delicacy combined with the direct link between the body and the home underpins the difference between a house and home for most people. Over time the house becomes an extra skin into which we retreat and live out our private lives. For Rodney there was also the idea of the futility of living in a structure that was unable to sustain itself, while at the same time he shows a certain defiance in the face of his illness.[39]

This was one of a number of works that Rodney made for a solo exhibition at the South London Gallery entitled *Nine Nights in Eldorado* in 1997,

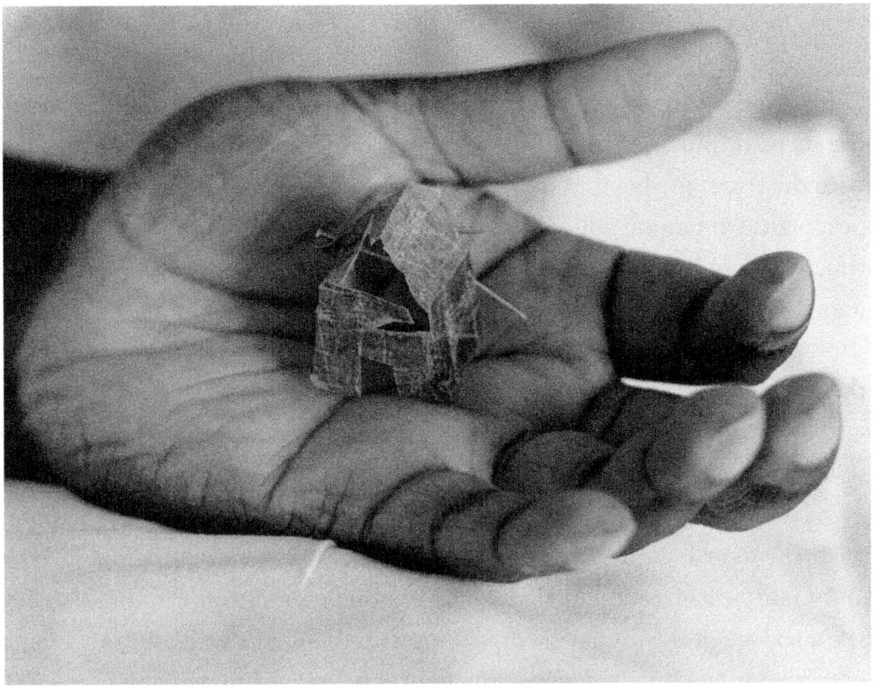

FIGURE 1.1 Donald Rodney, *In the House of My Father* (1996–7).

which was about him and the history of his family, and how they had come to Britain from the Caribbean with such high hopes.[40] Another work included was *Flesh of My Flesh* (1996), a photographic triptych with the outside panels depicting a greatly magnified knot of human hair, and the central one showing a large scar on the artist's leg after an operation.[41] Like much of Rodney's later work, *In the House of My Father* is concerned with living with the debilitating disorder that stopped him being able to do a great number of things, but the meaning does not stop with the immediate references.[42] It is also metaphorical, expressing something about the world beyond, as is the case with his works using X-rays, which show the progress of his illness but are also about the corrosive diseases of apartheid, police brutality and racism.[43] From a phenomenological perspective, *In the House of My Father* frames a particular embodied concept, which, through being cross-referenced in the viewer's mind, is not just the experience of Rodney, but empathetically comes alive for the viewers.

HOMES, TRANSITIONAL SPACES

Gilbert and George have made their house on Fournier Street in east London the focus of much of their artistic production. Frequently it is juxtaposed with the street life beyond the walls. Images of the interiors now reveal it to be a place containing collections of fine things, where much love, attention, time and care has been taken on choosing and displaying the objects. Their many portraits depicting them sitting at a table or on a high-backed settle show this to be a place of retreat, a hermetically conceived buffer against the outer world.

However, when Gilbert and George first owned the house they made several series of photographs of the two of them in the interior, including *Dusty Corners* (1975) and *Dead Boards* (1976), which were taken at the point when the wear and traces of previous occupants still remained, before Gilbert and George had accreted their own personalities into the rooms.[44] They show a place of possibilities, empty, but with sheltering walls, entrances and fireplaces intact. In *Dead Boards*, the floors are cracked through the repeated movements and habits of past occupants. Although Gilbert and George are shown posing in the enclosed spaces, where the scale of the rooms, windows and wall-panelling have been built to set up relationships with their bodies and pleasing proportions for the mind, the evident history etched onto the building sets these photographs apart from the spatial coolness of minimalist encounters. Only the living sculptures of Gilbert and George, posing in their immaculate suits, are complete. They create a fitting contrast between careful grooming and empty potential. As they were to say later:

> Us in nature or the empty house [...] we felt that ourselves as Living Sculptures was as much as we wanted to say to people. We were more shy of our own feelings, much less worldly [...] we still like the idea of the person in the house.[45]

The way that Gilbert and George articulated their ideas emphasises the overlaps for them between art and life. It is the 'reality' of photography that Gilbert and George liked. As they were to discuss, they wanted their works to 'become art' and 'say life'.[46] These overlaps were also evident in their arrangements of the photographs for exhibition. The different series tended to be shown in grids of four or more, with gaps between each group. The installation of *Dead Boards* in the exhibition *Arte Inglese Oggi* in Milan in 1976, for instance, had the photographs arranged in groups of six by six, with small gaps between each photograph, which suggested windows framing images of another world. As Husserl has suggested, there are strong inter-related layers of understanding between the 'rooms' of consciousness and external objects. In *Ideas* Husserl discussed this in relation to some paintings by David Teniers the Younger hanging in a room, suggesting that the frames around each painting demarcated the world to be entered, but also echoed the framed memories in our consciousness. These boundaries in art that correspond with those of mental states enable the viewer to experience the depicted world in a cooperative and empathetic manner.[47]

The artist Rachel Whiteread has also engaged with the empty spaces of abandoned homes. Eckhard Schneider has written that the core of Whiteread's *oeuvre* is the transformation of people's emotional and social investment in their dwellings into sculptural forms.[48] However, rather than including people, her casts of walls and floors show the memory of repeated actions of humans contained within the infrastructure of buildings.

Whiteread's sculptures echo some of the concerns of minimalism. Her floor pieces, for instance, call to mind those of Carl Andre. Echoing his installation for the Konrad Fischer Gallery in Düsseldorf, Whiteread's *Untitled (Bronze Floor)* of 1999–2000 was a flat sculpture made up of a grid of metal plates that the audience was encouraged to walk across.[49] However, unlike Andre's industrial surfaces, hers consisted of casts made from the original 1930s stone floor in the Haus der Kunst in Munich, where the repeated actions of people's footfalls had left marks that were captured in the casts, like fingerprints of previous usage. She covered the casts with a white patina, which in turn was eroded through further traces of human activity.

In *Untitled (Floor)* (1994) Whiteread made resin casts of the areas below the floorboards of a room in a house measuring roughly 3.9 metres by 2.75 metres. As Waldemar Januszczak said on viewing the grid of coloured resin forms, the room itself would have been very ordinary, at the heart of leisure time, and the floor would have supported the three-piece suite and a rack of old copies of *Woman's Own*.[50] The floor was worn through the habitual movements of previous occupancy, which were revealed in the cracks and wear imprinted in the resin.

Whiteread later made three casts from a disused synagogue in east London that was to become her home, one of which was of a staircase. Like the photographs by Gilbert and George, the building was between occupancy and function. However, unlike the rooms in their images, corridors and staircases function like the arteries of a home, places to be traversed in order to arrive somewhere else. Rather than suggesting the utility of those areas, Whiteread's staircase cast has been exhibited in different configurations and in different relationships to the gallery architecture, so that the notion of travelling up and down is no longer central to its meaning. When shown upright in the Serpentine Gallery, *Untitled (Upstairs)* of 2001 was played against the architectural space, but in Edinburgh, where there was less height available in the gallery, the cast was exhibited on its side.[51] As with encounters with the geometric forms of minimalism, the audience was invited to walk around and survey those of *Untitled (Upstairs)*. However, unlike minimalism, in Whiteread's works there are embedded memories of usage and the traces of traversing, the indexical links between the physical structure and the final sculpture that suggest lived human presence.

WALLPAPER

Wallpaper has long been the interior skin applied to the cocoon of space surrounding a house's occupants, which also encapsulates and frames their aspirations, social class and personalities. From being considered a background element, it has become something that many avant-garde artists have used as a foil for exploring themes of memory, home and identity.

The film *Blight*, made by John Smith in collaboration with the composer Jocelyn Pook in 1994–6, was concerned with the destruction of a street of houses to make way for the M11 link road in east London. Rather than being a documentary, the film, including its score, was created from the sights and sounds of the destruction and fragments of speech by local residents.[52] The partially destroyed houses reveal the interior walls complete with their wallpapers and murals. One image shows a large black-and-white mural of the film *The Exorcist* and some peeling lilac paper.[53] Other film stills show plain blue walls, white-painted walls, flowered papers, pink paper with large abstract prints and a blue paper with large circular motifs.[54] Each type of pattern can be located in time, but was also the result of choices made either by the residents or by others for them.

The voices of former residents recount their everyday lives in the street and their homes, but often their memories include references to interior decoration, including their wallpapers and the residents' emotional attachment to them. The hideous qualities of the red wallpaper, the woodchip or the sickly mushroom colour of a room are described, together with the fact that for many there had been no choice, as decisions had been made by others.[55]

Since the 1960s, when Andy Warhol designed his *Cow Wallpaper* (1966) and the wallpaper designer Vymura introduced novelty designs, including James Bond and, later, Barbie, wallpaper has left the bourgeois domain of taste and fashion, and become linked with art, film and broader popular culture.[56] Because of wallpaper's intimate relationship with the home, avant-garde artists have made unusual designs for domestic use, as well as incorporating wallpaper into gallery installations to act as a vehicle to consider ideas about the home, identity and childhood memories.[57]

The boundaries between real domestic wall covering and those that are art pieces have become increasingly blurred with the technological advances of reproduction and the increased interest in choosing paper outside bourgeois taste.[58] Well-known papers like Warhol's *Cow Wallpaper* can be ordered for one's home.[59] Designers like Deborah Bowness make cut-outs so that the purchaser can create collages of fragments of images like dresses hanging on coat hangers, or buy compete *trompe l'oeil* images to fit particular spaces.[60] Some artists and designers, like Abigail Lane, Brigitte Stepputtis and Bob Pain, have formed allegiances, in their case to create a company called Showroom Dummies in 2003, to make works for sale that confound any notions of boundaries between art and design.[61] One theme they pursued, the

Mexican Day of the Dead festival, manifested itself in skeletons walking across wallpapers and cashmere throws, and included skulls designed by Damien Hirst. Another design group, Timorous Beasties, has also designed many wallpapers and lampshades that counter the usual cosy, domestic vocabularies. *London*, for instance, is a wallpaper design whose pattern suggests a French toile, but on closer inspection reveals images of muggers attacking people, youths hanging out and drunkards lounging on park benches.[62] However, rather than discussing art and design made for the home, I want to continue by considering the use of wallpaper by artists within gallery installations as a means of commenting on dreams.

Wallpaper has been an important part of Robert Gober's installations, which tend to concentrate on uneasy domestic memories. He has said that it 'enveloped the room and [his] sensibility'.[63] His reproductions of basins and drains, together with his use of wallpaper, confound the industrial nature of most home goods and transform the installations into places that suggest the metaphorical and experiential. Through allowing familiar things to act as triggers, and through juxtaposing images and ideas, he sets up a train of thought that plays with symbolic language.[64]

Gober's art frequently relates to his experiences and to those that he reads about in the press. He often starts from a colour, image or overheard phrase.[65] Echoing the ideas of Bachelard, he suggested that it is a 'nursing of an image that haunts me and letting it sit and breed in my mind'.[66] Wallpapers are only one aspect of Gober's art, but they provide a shorthand for locating the works as domestic in origin. Repetition, which is a characteristic of the layout of wallpaper patterns, is used in his work to create hallucinogenic settings for fantasies, or to suggest the way that values become inculcated, which mirrors the usage of particular repeat patterns used in children's nurseries in Victorian times that were chosen for instructional purposes. The idea of the wallpapers enclosing the room and framing consciousness corresponds with the phenomenological view about the home becoming part of one's internal and external fabric of being.

Gober's wallpaper *Hanging Man/Sleeping Man* (1989; figure 1.2) was first shown as part of a three-room installation at the Paula Cooper Gallery in New York. In the first room, a metal drain was set into the wall at eye level. In

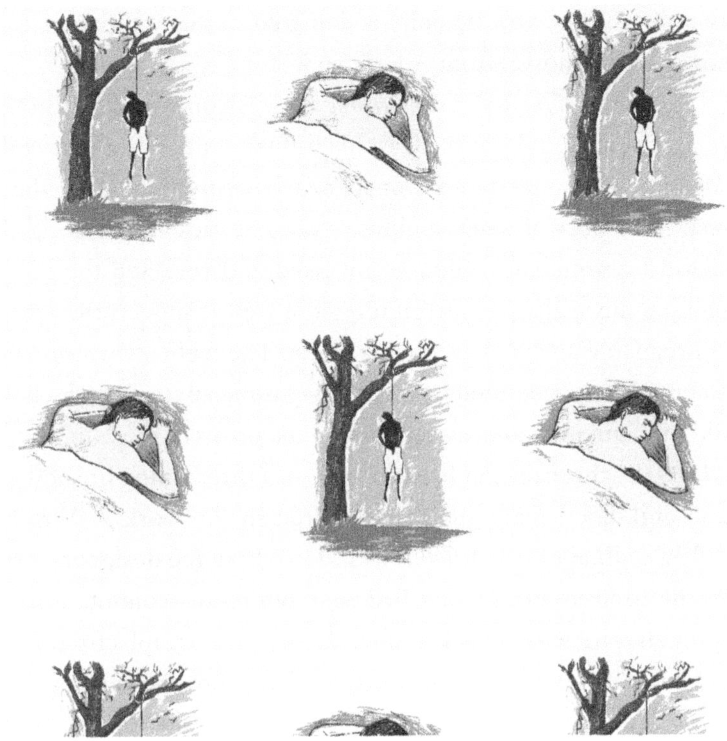

FIGURE 1.2 Robert Gober, *Hanging Man/Sleeping Man* (1989).

the second, a wallpaper with a repeated pattern of a white man sleeping and a black man hanging from a tree surrounded two painted plaster objects – a sack of cat litter and a wedding gown. In the third, the walls were covered with a black paper with what appeared to be crude scratched drawings of male and female genitalia, such as one might find on a toilet wall, together with drains set into the wall and a bag of doughnuts on a pedestal. The vocabularies of the two wallpapers were very different, with the former being a dream-like sequence in soft tones all over the walls.

Gober had already used the images of the hanging man and the sleeping man in other contexts, including on the cushion cover for a dog's bed in 1988. The incompleteness of the story and the suggestion of dreaming give an open-ended logic to the imagery.[67] Gober's work is concerned with exposing a social malaise in mainstream white, middle-class American society, one that accepts – even if unconsciously – stereotyping and discrimination.[68] While there is ambiguity in what actually is depicted in this wallpaper, it triggers uncomfortable memories from American history.

While Gober's *Hanging Man/Sleeping Man* is concerned with the internalisation of sexual and racist ideas, his forest scenes are about childhood fears. *Forest* (1991) suggested the imagery of picture books and the almost hallucinatory aspect of some children's fairy stories. Translating the fear engendered by some such tales, he inverted and reversed the imagery of trees, making the wallpaper surrounding the viewer suggest the appearance of an impregnable and claustrophobic forest. The feeling that is provoked is reminiscent of that generated by frightening nursery stories, which develop in a child's imagination and, as depicted in the prints of the Nursery Rhyme Series (1989) by the artist Paula Rego, take on a threatening life of their own.

These childhood fears are also explored in the work of Virgil Marti, who made a wallpaper titled *Bullies* in 1992–7. Like the designers Timorous Beasties, he used a pattern that had safe, bourgeois connotations, in this case a French toile with a flock surface. Using photographs from his school yearbook he transferred the images of 'bullies' onto the wallpaper, so that each was framed by ornate rococo flowers, and loomed out of the dark in fluorescent colours.[69]

Another artist, Matthew Meadows, has also used historical patterns in his wallpapers to confound expectations. His *Razor Wire Wallpaper* (2007) weaves together floral stripes from nineteenth-century patterns with stripes of razor wire, suggesting the contradictions of domesticity and comfort on the one hand and pain and confinement on the other.[70] Like Gober's and Marti's works, this paper suggests the influence on the mind of the public world, which is then brought back into the home. In this way, the enclosing walls of private spaces emulate the consuming nature of interior lives.

MICHAEL LANDY, *Semi-detached*

I would like to discuss Michael Landy's installation *Semi-detached* (2004; figure 1.3) in detail here, as it relates to many of the ideas that I have been discussing so far in this chapter.[71] As well as exhibiting a replica of the outside of his family home, he showed three films relating to his father's life, which reflected both the time and effort given to making the house into a home, and the private lives that take place behind the walls and net curtains of many homes.

Michael Landy built *Semi-detached* in conjunction with the Mike Smith Studio and Tate Britain as a result of obtaining the third Duveen commission.[72] It was a full-size replica of his parents' home and was installed in the signature galleries for sculpture at Tate Britain: the North and South Duveen Galleries. The original was built on the Seven Kings estate in Ilford in 1901 by the speculative builder Archibald Cameron Corbett. It was one of many houses constructed at the time to accommodate middle-income families who sought quiet respectability and separation from the poor masses.[73] Although there are some differences between the houses on the estate, fundamentally Landy's house was identical not only to those in Ilford, but to those across the sprawling suburbia that had developed around London.

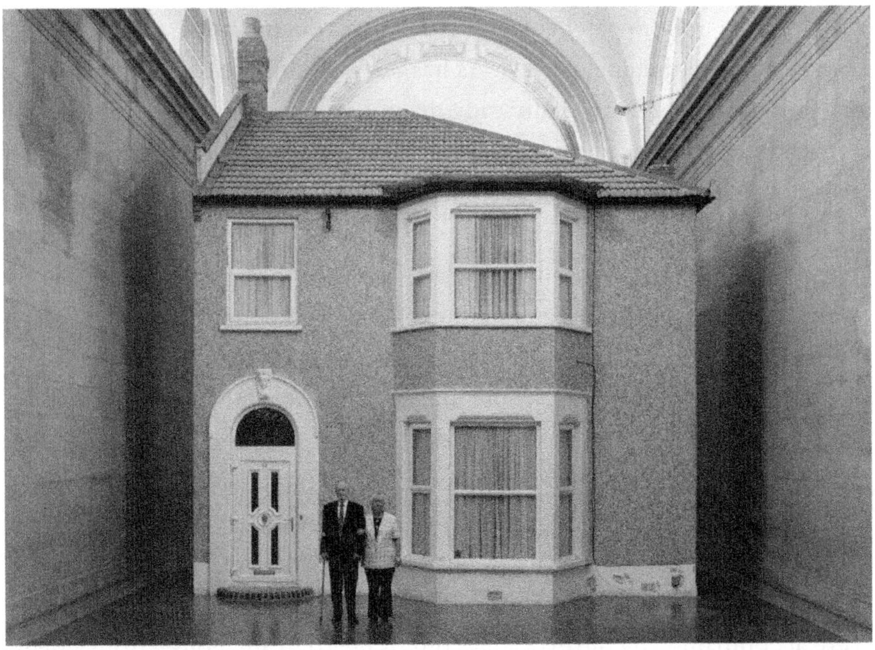

FIGURE 1.3 Michael Landy, *Semi-detached: John and Ethel Landy* (2004).

The sculpture was modelled in two halves, front and back, and rather than being open like a doll's house, the cut side of each half was covered with screens so that the interiors were invisible to the gallery-going public. Onto these screens three films relating to his father's life in the home were played, accompanied by real-time sounds. The installation filled the spaces, with the chimneys extending into the vaulted ceilings of the galleries and with only the minimum space allowed – 1.3 metres – on either side to enable viewers to move around.

The tension between representation and the everyday that was expressed in the films of John Smith or the photographs of Gilbert and George and Mary Maclean is obviously more acute when viewing a life-size replica of a house. All give the impression of a captured 'reality', but, in the case of Landy's installation, the viewer walked around the halves and experienced the scale of the house framed by the galleries. This was not a generic house, but a very detailed simulation of Landy's home. To achieve this, hundreds of photographs were taken and many plans and drawings made, so that everything, from bird droppings on the roof to peeling paintwork, from rusty nails in walls to patched pebble-dash, was documented, numbered and then realised in the final project. As has been pointed out by Gordon Burn, this forensic detail is normally only given to a place where there has been a macabre accident. The plans resembled those made in preparation for plastic surgery.[74] However, underlying this detail is the house that resembles so many others. Most people have seen a semi-detached, pebble-dashed house, have been through similar doors, have looked through double-glazed windows with net curtains and have expectations about the interior spaces. The empathetic engagement with a building like this, where there is a latent bodily memory of the scale, layout and surfaces, acts in much the same way that Merleau-Ponty described: it is the instinctive understanding of where the paths of personal experience intersect with those of others.[75]

Like the domestic paintings by Vuillard and the photographs by Billingham, the three films shown on the screens that Landy made from 110 hours of footage were an insider's view of his father's routines and possessions. These were accompanied by the everyday sounds heard in any house, from a plane flying overhead or the fridge coming on to his father whistling Irish ballads.[76]

Unlike the abstracting vocabularies of paintings, or indeed the play of reality and artifice used by Gilbert and George or in the installations by Whiteread and Gober, Landy's work confronted the viewer with an apparent slice of life. Many of the contemporary newspaper reviews of *Semi-detached* played on this tension, from questioning why one would want to travel to see a house that many people live in, to writing about the embarrassment of viewing the mundane and private, and of hearing the sounds of Michael's father whistling within Tate Britain.[77]

However, this blurring of art and life was the crux of the argument against the initial exhibition of Marcel Duchamp's *Fountain* in 1917, and since then this has been explored repeatedly by artists as diverse as Robert Rauschenberg, George Segal, Eleanor Antin and Gilbert and George. Unlike the objects in the installations of the two earlier recipients of the Duveen commission, Anya Gallaccio and Mona Hatoum, which were manipulated to suggest new dimensions of meanings, *Semi-detached* was, like Duchamp's *Bottle Rack* or *Fountain*, an apparently unmediated reference to the lived world, in spite of the many hours of labour taken to make it. The visual manipulation was in the editing of the films. Although the themes of the films were directly derived from his father's life, and their pace was likewise linked to the natural passing of time, the unusually intense focus on objects and occupations that are not normally contemplated made them appear unreal. The oddness was also emphasised by the 'framing' of the sculpture by the gallery, and in the lack of an adjoining house or of a surrounding garden and perimeter fence, which in the real world were designed to create a mental and physical distancing from the street. By showing the cut halves of the house alone, the house was decontextualised and therefore 'not real'.

Michael Landy's father John had broken his back in a mining accident in 1977, which left him unable to work and increasingly housebound. This was devastating both for John and the family, and so when Landy was approached by the Tate he knew that he wanted to do something about what had happened to his father.[78] The three films focus on his father's experience of living with the effects of this accident. Of most importance for this discussion is that they show the life of someone who had had a real passion for do-it-yourself – as many men had after the war – which, over time, contributed to turning the house into a home. Having become disabled, he was no longer able to do DIY. While being a personal story, Landy also wanted to consider the more universal social question about how the construction of identity is related to what one does, and what happens when this is derailed.[79]

After Landy had received the commission, he took some months to consider his options. In September 2003, the curator Carolyn Kerr went to see him.[80] He had not yet decided on the form of the exhibition, but had begun to film his father's daily routine of taking pills, sleeping, reading the newspaper, watching the television, smoking and eating, against the backdrop of the home and his objects.[81] Like the description by Benjamin of the interiors of his relatives' homes, the objects and memories were interlinked, and helped to situate and reinforce each other. The film *Shelf Life* concentrates on the shelves in John Landy's bedroom, where he kept his possessions. The camera eye pans inexorably and uncomfortably slowly across the objects: seed packets, barely used tools, family photographs and boxing videos. All are shown in close-up and only slowly are revealed as a photograph of John in the garden with a child, or of the garden with tomatoes ripening on the back windowsill, or of a squashed moth on the wallpaper. Only at the end is the whole ensemble shown.

In *No. 62* the camera eye remains still for periods of time, capturing normally overlooked, everyday things, like a piece of leaf caught in an old spiderweb, swinging rhythmically in the breeze, or a dead insect in a bowl. In one scene John Landy organises his weekly tablets in a dosage tray, trying to coordinate the movements of his fingers and hands so that elastic bands can be stretched over the lids of each compartment to keep them open. Rather than the focus being on the highlights of life, as in the photographs by Maclean and the films by Smith, the concentrated gaze is on the in-between, on the things one only notices when relaxing and taking time out. Landy wanted to show how everyday things, like eating or rolling a cigarette, had become tasks, or even small rituals within a constricted life. 'Because of the lack of activity even the background humming of the freezer, and ticking of the clock have an active presence.'[82]

The third film, *Four Walls*, is different. Landy had started this before Carolyn Kerr's visit, and it includes the sound of John Landy whistling Irish songs against fast-changing images taken from John's vast collection of DIY magazines that he had accumulated over the decades. These magazines reflected the growing market for DIY that developed especially after the Festival of Britain in 1951. By the 1960s it was recognised as an integral part of British leisure time, and was supported by television programmes, manuals, magazines and new retail outlets, all of which provided inspiration and advice on how to add value to one's property.[83] The selected images that Landy used in the film show people undertaking projects to solve problems, from condensation to broken guttering, which echoed John Landy's passion. While making these films Landy was thinking about how his father had, when he was still physically able, done a great deal to the house, but, after his accident, had been unable to perform such tasks, despite continuing to collect tools.[84] He wanted the footage in the films to suggest 'the wasted time, tools not used, tasks not done, [a] place where nothing happens'.[85]

For Husserl, one of the most important binaries is that between the external object and the internal concept of it, and how the two are perceived through each other, which cancels out their isolation from each other.[86] In *Semi-detached*, the films projected onto the dividing screens act as frames within the framed image of the house, so that the viewer can enter into the depicted world. The scenes are the everyday, and in Husserl's terms, as the viewer watches them they should, with reflection and reconfiguring, become absorbed into his or her consciousness, and linked with the narratives of his or her life. In the social sciences, personal narratives about lived experiences have been discussed as being important for the formation of identity, as well as the foundation of our understanding of time, memory and place. One of the ways of creating these identity-forming narratives is through the time, discussion and physical effort spent on large projects, like DIY, or indeed creating large art projects.[87]

The idea of developing a personal place where memories and stories are embedded echoes the writings of Bachelard, who believed that poetic thought helped the dynamic force of imagination. Through the confrontation between the self and the non-self a discursive and dynamic interrelationship between reason and reality is developed.[88] It is the ability of man to be gripped by something beyond him- or herself, where reality and the imagination act cooperatively, that helps enlarge the soul. These overlaps are relevant for considering the creation of a home as well as a large art project. In both, the commitment of the person who is imagining is such that what is actually there now is not a finally determining factor of what is possible.[89] Even if static in body, the individual's mind and roving eye can reflect and project. Landy's installation suggested a life captured, and the viewer was encouraged to engage with that overlooked and private world. The interpretation is left for the gallery visitor to consider through the overlaps of everyday realities and the poetic imagination.

2

Doors and Windows

This chapter will discuss art that is constructed around the liminal zones of the home, specifically doors and windows, which mark the boundaries between the outside public world and interior private spaces. This is a theme that has resonated throughout the history of art, from Renaissance portraits and seventeenth-century Dutch genre scenes to Romantic and Symbolist paintings, in which artists like Caspar David Friedrich depicted a figure lost in his or her own thoughts, looking out of a domestic window. As discussed in the previous chapter, the different spaces suggest the permeability between the interior mind and the external, material world, with the framed glass panes being the interface between the two.

The first section will introduce the philosophical relationship between eyes and windows articulated by the Ancient Greeks, reconsidered in Renaissance times and adopted by artists and poets from the late nineteenth century. There will then be a discussion about how this tradition was developed in American East Coast art from the 1950s and 1960s. The final section will be a discussion of more recent work that, while developing earlier ideas about the liminal zones of windows, suggests the denial of sight, and by extension a closing of the relationship between the mind and the world beyond.

BOUNDARIES

Boundaries are necessary to demarcate different areas of existence and to define interiority.[1] Doors and windows are the holes that puncture these walls, making connections between them, creating functional as well as symbolic passageways between the interior of the home and public space.[2] Just as the house has been repeatedly cited as a metaphor for the human body, the thresholds are its orifices. Linking with ideas discussed in the previous chapter, the interior room can be equated with the internal mind, with the material world stretching beyond.

In society doors are the crossable frontiers between custom and law and the private world.[3] They provide the mechanism to control who enters, and allow one to depart from the known place, secure it against intruders, and return later in the expectation that it has not been disturbed and that one's life can continue there as desired.[4] Although technology has brought the outside world into the private space through telephones, televisions, radios and computers, the front door is the physical and symbolic demarcation, which is frequently larger than necessary, embellished architecturally or with pots of flowers, and the step and mats that keep out the weather also help to emphasise its importance. Within the house, doors delineate different areas, separating those that friends or visitors see from those that are private, and dividing passageways from rooms. Each marks a change in emotional and physical engagements and habits.

While doors are clearly marked and shut out the world beyond when closed, windows are more fluid. They illuminate and air rooms, and add architectural distinctiveness to what would otherwise be an enclosing shell. They are weak points that allow sights, smells and sounds to permeate, but they are also symbolically important. Window frames help to define the limits of what is to be seen, to create different habits of looking and perception and also to reframe the viewer as viewing subject.[5] It is this framing of what can be seen from the outside looking in, and from the inside looking out, that has made the window such an important motif within art and literature. In art it has frequently been used to suggest the boundary between the interior mind and the exterior world, and to create a frame of the material world that changes according to where one is sitting or standing, 'producing eternal variety, the impromptu that is one of the great flavours of reality'.[6] In literature it has been utilised as a vehicle to reveal the lives of the primary subject or of others within the narrative, and to enhance the imagination.[7]

The word 'window' has its roots in the Old Norse 'wind eye', which was an unglazed opening in the roof of a hut. However, the linking of the gap between inside and outside to the eye through which the outer world is transmitted to the inside and vice versa goes back further. The eye as window to the soul was a topos in classical literature, appearing in the writings of Plato, Cicero, Lucretius and Sextus Empiricus. The first-century author Vitruvius, when writing about architecture, quoted Socrates as saying that 'the human soul should have windows and be open and accessible to study'.[8] When explaining Plato's ideas about art and the spectator, Robert C. Lodge wrote that 'if we consider, not merely the optical organ, the physical eye of the beholder, but the eye of his "mind", including the entire range of his experience, the scope of suggestion becomes very wide indeed'.[9] Leon Battista Alberti, the Renaissance architect and writer, suggested that in the art of painting, the canvas surface became the 'open window through which the subject to be painted is seen'.[10] His near contemporary, Leonardo da Vinci, saw the relationship of outside to inside as more of a dialogue. The eye was the 'window of the soul', which communicated the beauties of the world, especially light, to the mind. For him, the window was a metaphor for mystical illumination.[11] The eye as the primary organ for understanding the world, as well as the link between the spiritual interior and the external physical world, symbolised by the window motif, will form the basis of this chapter.

WINDOWS – ART AND POETRY IN THE LATE NINETEENTH AND EARLY TWENTIETH CENTURIES

With the explorations of space by the cubists and other early-twentieth-century artists, the motif of the window gained significance as both symbolic threshold and compositional device.[12] Many French avant-garde artists of the period aligned themselves to the poetic tradition prevalent in the nineteenth century, in particular the writings of Stéphane Mallarmé and Charles Baudelaire. Mallarmé's poems frequently suggest the creative struggle through metaphorical writing, as in 'Le pitre châtié' ('The clown chastised') (1864), in which the first verse starts with the line: 'Eyes, lakes with my simple passion to be reborn', and, after two lines describing the means used in different genres to perform the creative act, ends with: 'I have pierced a window in the canvas wall.'[13] In 'Les fenêtres' ('The windows') (1863), the window is the central symbol, with the pane of glass being the spiritual meeting point between one state of existence and another, between the exterior world and interior life.[14] Baudelaire saw windows as screens of imaginary transport and creative displacement, and that behind them, in 'that dark or luminous hole, life lives, life dreams, life suffers'.[15] These ideas influenced early-twentieth-century poets such as Guillaume Apollinaire, Pierre Reverdy and Blaise Cendrars, as well as many French avant-garde painters, including Pablo Picasso, Juan Gris, Robert Delaunay and Henri Matisse.[16]

Robert Delaunay read, discussed with other artists and took notes from Leonardo's notebooks, which inflected his writings and art.[17] His La Ville series of 1909–11 suggests a townscape seen through a sometimes curtained window, and his Les fenêtres series of 1912–13 used the reflective quality of glass to dissolve the representational elements into interactions of coloured marks.[18] Juan Gris, by contrast, in his Bandol series of 1921, used the transparency of the window to suggest the boundary between two states of being. In this series he placed a still life in front of a window and showed landscape beyond. In these, as in some of his later works, such as *The Painter's Window* of 1925, the subject was not just spatial, but the creative realm. Light was a metaphor for the illuminating power of artistic imagination. Emblems of the artistic life, like palettes, guitars and paints, were combined with traditional 'domestic' still-life objects, such as wine glasses and fruit bowls, and on the lake beyond was frequently a sailing boat suggesting the creative journey. The most spatially complex of this series is *The View across the Bay*, where the outside lines of hills, lake and clouds come into the room, and the guitar and music merge with the boat and water on the table, suggesting the interpenetration of material and mental lives.[19] These framing pictorial devices that separate different worlds were discussed by the philosopher Edmund Husserl and later by Gregory Minissale as prompts for the viewer to explore the interaction of frames within consciousness and the material world.[20] However, within the paintings by Gris they were only tactics within a self-consciously artistic depiction. The spatial flattening, painted surface and abstraction prevented the paintings from being 'realistic' depictions of the material world. As Gris wrote in 1921:

> No glass manufacturer would ever be able to make any bottle or water jug which I have painted because they have not [...] any equivalent in a world of the three dimensions. They only have an equivalent in the world of the intellect.[21]

POSTWAR BREAKS IN THE WALL – THE CREATIVE EVERYDAY

Speaking in front of his apartment window on Sixth Avenue in 1991, through which the sound of New York traffic permeated the room, the composer John Cage discussed his notion of silence. For him sound itself, unmediated and devoid of any intention, gave pleasure without having to mean anything. During this video, the camera alternated the focus between Cage and the sash window framed by houseplants, through which the noisy and busy urban environment was visible.[22]

In 1911, Umberto Boccioni painted his Futurist image *The Street Enters the House*, which depicts a woman standing on her balcony looking out at a city that is changing before her. Painted in bright fragments that jostle across the picture plane, the sounds and sights of the building construction enter her private space and consciousness. Urban noises and sights are ubiquitous, and for Cage this meant that the sound of traffic was equivalent to silence. Unlike music composed according to the composer's intention, using the traditions of rhythm and harmony, everyday sounds were about life and, like Boccioni's painting of urban development, were interesting in their own right.[23]

One of the ways that Cage brought the everyday into his music was through his compositions for prepared piano, the first of which was in 1940 for a performance in which there was no room for percussion instruments.[24] He experimented with adding found objects like weatherstripping and screws to the strings, which resulted in completely different tones. In some works he gives detailed instructions about how the piano is to be prepared. *A Room* of 1943, for instance, includes two 'long' bolts, two 'large' bolts, a 'bolt with rubber', a 'penny' and some 'weatherstripping', which were to be added at specified distances from the dampers, on certain notes and between particular strings.[25]

Cage visited Paris in the late 1920s and got to know the avant-garde artists there, and returned in 1949. As well as being conversant with the ideas of these artists, he also got to know László Moholy-Nagy, whose book *The New Vision* (1938) was very influential on Cage's ideas from the 1930s onwards. In this, Moholy-Nagy discussed the interpenetration of interior and exterior spaces through the glass walls of contemporary architecture, the different qualities of glass and how the loss of mass meant that in certain conditions a building could almost dematerialise.[26] Cage advocated the extensive use of glass in architecture, and indeed helped to build his own small home at Stony Point in New York in 1954, adjacent to that of his architect friend Paul Williams, with large windows that brought the outside woods into the space.[27] For him there could not be enough glass in architecture.

In Cage's lecture 'Experimental music' of 1957 he explored the spatial aspects of architecture, art, music and glass. Towards the beginning he discussed the act of listening, and by using the metaphors of doors and windows he described his idea about silence, which could be said to be '*opening the doors* of the music to the sounds that happen to be in the environment'.[28]

> This openness exists in the fields of modern sculpture and architecture. The glass houses of [Ludwig] Mies van der Rohe reflect their environment, presenting to the eye images of clouds, trees or grass according to the situation. And while looking at the constructions in wire of the sculptor Richard Lippold, it is inevitable that one will see other things, and people too, if they happen to be there at the same time, through the network of

> wires. There is no such thing as an empty space or an empty time. There is always something to see, something to hear. In fact, try as we may to make silence, we cannot.[29]

Cage and the group of American artists that were close to his ideals, which included Robert Rauschenberg and Jasper Johns, were influenced by the art and ideas of Marcel Duchamp, and during the late 1950s got to know him. While the exchange of ideas about the overlaps between the everyday and artistic practice was broader than the remit of this chapter, of particular interest here are two of Duchamp's works: *The Bride Stripped Bare by Her Bachelors, Even (The Large Glass)* of 1915 and a door that he installed in his Paris apartment that served two separate doorways, opening that of the bathroom while closing that of the bedroom. Refuting the French proverb that 'a door must either be open or closed', it was both witty and practical, combining the artistic with the cerebral and everyday. He had it photographed showing the spaces on either side of the door, and this became the cover for the catalogue of an exhibition: *Not Seen and/or Less Seen of/by Marcel Duchamp/Rrose Sélavy (1904–64)* (1964).[30]

Related to the words from Cage's 'Experimental music' quoted above, the transparent and reflective qualities of *The Bride Stripped Bare by Her Bachelors, Even (The Large Glass)* mean that the viewer simultaneously sees through the work and the shadowy reflection of him- or herself viewing.[31] Not only does one hear the sounds in the gallery, but beyond the work other people are framed as they move around the space. Within the *Large Glass*, different elements of sight and spatial play are articulated. The upper half contains the bride floating free and rendered two-dimensionally, similar to cubist constructions of artistic space. The lower half includes precise engineering drawings of forms that represent the 'bachelors', 'oculist witnesses' and a chocolate grinder, rendered according to traditional perspective – Alberti's window onto the world.

Revealing the cross-disciplinary and collaborative nature of the artistic group that surrounded Duchamp in New York, Jasper Johns made different elements of *The Large Glass* into transparent, inflatable stage sets for *Walkabout Time*, performed by the Merce Cunningham Dance Company in 1968. While

Duchamp was referring ironically to the concerns of avant-garde painters and poets in Paris in his use of materials, composition, subject and performativity, Cage's and Johns' ideas about the material properties of glass and the interpenetration of spaces were more closely integrated with life itself.

When, in 1948, Robert Rauschenberg enrolled at Black Mountain College in North Carolina, where he was to live and work on and off until 1952, he had already studied at the Kansas City Art Institute and attended the Académie de la Grand Chaumière in Paris.[32] However, it was at Black Mountain College that he met the legendary artists and teachers Joseph Albers and Franz Kline, and also got to know Cage, who was on the faculty, and Merce Cunningham, both of whom were to become lifelong friends.[33] The college was, to a large extent, a continuation of the Bauhaus, in the breadth of disciplines covered and because it had some of the same staff.[34] During the 1950s it became a centre where many New York artists, writers, dancers and poets worked, which ensured that not only was there a highly charged intellectual and creative atmosphere, but there was also a freedom and cross-fertilisation of ideas between the disciplines. In 1952, for instance, Cage organised at Black Mountain College an event that involved Rauschenberg's paintings, Cunningham's dance, David Tudor playing the piano, films, slides, records, radios and the poetry of Charles Olson and M. C. Richards recited from the top of ladders, and with the evening culminating in a reading of the performative lecture that Cage had given in the same year at the Juilliard School of Music.[35]

DOORS AND WINDOWS – FORMAL MATTERS

Photography was a fundamental and generative aspect of Rauschenberg's work and, as Walter Hopps has argued, vital for his 'aesthetic investigations of how humans perceive, select, and combine visual information'.[36] Rauschenberg posed his series of Black Paintings, which he made at Black Mountain, in front of, next to and against windows and doors and then photographed them so that the resulting images contained conceptual and material frames within frames. This created a grid of shapes, but also played with spatial and conceptual ideas similar to those of the prewar Parisian avant-garde, and which

Albers had developed in his coloured abstract paintings. In Rauschenberg's photograph *Untitled, Vertical Black Painting, Early State* of 1952, part of a large painting is shown next to a section of an open door, allowing one to see into the room beyond and through the window in the far wall. The cropping of the opening and painting, together with the placing of the black painting in line with the opening make the painting appear to be part of the building.[37] *Untitled Black Painting* of the same year is photographed partially blocking the door, with the door open towards the viewer. Here the painting is clearly a painting, but appears to float in space before the opening. *Untitled (Two Black Panels)*, also of 1952, continues this idea, but the two large black canvases dwarf the open door, and there is a large wooden stepladder posed to one side. These photographs are a documentation of his painted canvases, but the situating of the latter in front of the openings suggests that they also play with the equation of eye, window and creative act.

Although some of Rauschenberg's photographs are experimental, many are also of his friends and immediate surroundings. A theme that was clearly important in his work was the window. Sometimes this was suggested through implication, as with the shaft of light in *Quiet House – Black Mountain* (1949); sometimes through using the transparency of glass to show his friends within or looking through a car, as in *Untitled (Franz Kline, Black Mountain)* (1952), and sometimes he focused on the exterior view of domestic windows showing bare wooden frames and blinds, as in *Charleston Window 1* and *2* (1952).[38] These images suggest his different thoughts and references in relation to windows. In the first there are overtones of Renaissance religious paintings with the shaft of illuminating spiritual light. The second, while apparently spontaneous, was one of a number of photographs of his colleagues in cars; the one of Cage shows him ready to drive. In these the window is the barrier between contained space and the outside, between two different modes of being, where the viewer's frame in relation to the world is about to change. *Charleston Window 1* and *2* suggest a document about the area, but while the house itself is not portrayed, the lack of paint and the worn blinds act as a synecdoche for the poverty within.

One of the faculty at Black Mountain in 1952 was the photographer Aaron Siskind, whose work included details of textured and worn walls, peeling paint and other subjects that suggest the interrelation of humans and nature. He taught both how everyday things could convey personal and psychological effects, and how the photograph itself could stand in for the artist.[39] The textures created by torn paper and collage, which formed the basis of Rauschenberg's Black Paintings, and the capturing of worn buildings in his photography relate to the textures that Siskind captured in his abstract photographs.

DOORS – DOCUMENT AND MEMORY

Rauschenberg settled in New York in 1954, and found the juxtapositions, contradictions and surprises at every turn fascinating. There were exhibitions of Duchamp and Neo-Dada, including one at the Sidney James Gallery in April 1953, where Rauschenberg would have seen works like Duchamp's *Tu m'* (1918), which incorporated everyday things in front of the painted canvas, jutting into the space of the viewer. This exhibition along with others created great interest in the ideas of Dada and the different uses of the found object within art.[40] However, rather than developing the ideas of chance that informed both Duchamp and Cage's works, Rauschenberg liked to plan and consider how one area of a work referred to another. He allowed materials to act in ways that were natural to them, and thought of this as a 'friendly relationship with your material where you want them for what they are rather than for what you could make out of them'.[41]

From 1953, Rauschenberg started a series of red works in which he added soft, decorative elements that were, in some cases, loosely autobiographical. Many included photographs from the press, newspaper fragments, pieces of fabric and other found ephemera, knitted together by layers of paint that acted as background and that also dripped and gestured across the surface of the added elements. Like the prepared piano works of Cage, these brought-in elements were of the world and created an effect of improvisation.

Rauschenberg referred to works of this kind as 'combines'. Three such works from 1954 relate to the artist's past, and include windows and doors.[42] *Red Interior* has a semi-opaque window set into the top left with a pulley visible behind it, suggesting the high window of a lavatory, something that is also evoked in the type on the right-hand strip of material: 'Push', 'Toilet', 'Service', 'Deliver Goods in Basement'.[43] It has been argued that this work refers to his rural, childhood home. As well as playing with the positive and negative spaces of a window, he also includes fabrics and plastic. *Pink Door* consists of two linked halves, which harks back to the earlier photographs of his Black Paintings: on the right he includes a hinged screen door and wooden slats like those seen in the southern United States – Rauschenberg grew up in Texas – and on the left is a thickly textured collage and painted panel. However, unlike the earlier black-and-white photographs, the bright and contrasting colours mean that this panel cannot be read as a wall. *Untitled* (1954) suggests a window. The collage itself is square, with an illuminated stained-glass box at the top and a shelf at the bottom, and the painted area incorporates a mixture of materials, including part of a yellow crocheted curtain, which again references Texan home decoration of the 1940s.[44] In all of these works, the doors have become more than spatial elements, or direct references to a period and place. They also represent the doors that lead from the public world into the private home, and although decontextualised, nonetheless they relate to human actions.

Doors open and close with a clatter, are kicked against and, through re-establishing the original darkness and solidity of the enclosure, police the interface between inside and outside. Just as Cage asserted that everyday noises, sights and actions had values that could be incorporated into performances and art, so Rauschenberg also experimented with these ideas. However, unlike the impersonal art that Cage sought, these combinations also hint at his life and relationships.[45] Some, like *Interview* of 1955, in which he incorporated a found wooden door into a constructed shallow box that housed a range of found objects juxtaposed with painted panels, and *Self-made Retrospective* of 1954, a cabinet construction with hinged plywood doors that was hung on the wall and contained several small works that he had made, again suggest the continuation of the framing and interrelationship of contained, created and creative spaces and the material world.

Perhaps the most poignant of his combines from the mid-1950s is *Untitled* (1955), which is explicitly autobiographical and about the experience of domestic life. Although not including architectural doors, he arranged found and personal items on and in a structure resembling a cabinet with a door, and when considering the interrelation of contained spaces suggests the framing of consciousness and life that was outlined earlier.[46] Included is a clipping from a local paper announcing his parents' silver wedding anniversary, a letter in childish script from his son, an article about his sister winning a beauty pageant and some family snapshots. Rather than being labelled and identified, they appear like images stuck into corners and onto the walls of a home, which are there to act as reminders of events involving friends and family. However, although these images and cuttings suggest that this is a straightforwardly autobiographical work, they are set alongside others that appear to have no personal significance.[47]

Rather than the doors and other objects being positioned to suggest a stage set or a personality, as in the works by Eleanor Antin to be discussed in Chapter 3, in Rauschenberg's combines the syntax is less coherent. The everyday objects and doors culled from one arena and juxtaposed with loosely related items and painted elements cut across ideas of time, rather like an urban scoping vision or the fragmentation of memory. Rather than being a mesh of meaning, the implied narrative is less secure.[48] However, for Rauschenberg, this was part of the point. He did not want to be the one dictating the interpretation, and unlike Juan Gris in the earlier quotation, Rauschenberg did not want to create a hermetic art world.

Rosalind Krauss has argued that when looking at the range of material in the combines, with each refusing to be linked to others, each element becomes all the more present: the paint becomes a 'material image', the collaged objects embedded within coloured surfaces become material, and the free-standing objects become an extension of this, with their surfaces worn and pitted through use. Her argument is that the individual components' identities become less strong, united within the art context through being perceived as material.[49]

Like Rauschenberg, Jim Dine also made work that was evocative of his past as well as suggesting the domestic everyday. From the late 1950s, he created a number of works that brought together painting and objects to create abbreviated living rooms, or a bathroom that included a shower head in front of a painted canvas, as in *Four Rooms* (1962). As in the works of Rauschenberg, the painted and found elements cut across notions of time and syntax, but unlike their counterparts in those works the found objects are new and pristine. However, they are not meant to be read as items critiquing mass culture but, like the painterly gestures, are intended to suggest human presence through their actions.[50]

Others works suggest the open-window theme, as in *Studio Landscape* (1963), which has six painted vertical panels with a still life of real objects placed in front. Each panel is abstract, but one suggests clouds.[51] The objects evoke the domestic and are similar to those found in Purist still lifes, with bottles and glasses arranged on a small shelf. They are universal in form and non-symbolic, and are arranged to question the relationships between humans and the things they possess.[52] Unlike Duchamp's ready-mades, which transferred everyday items onto a plinth in a gallery, or Jasper Johns' *Painted Bronze (Ale Cans)* (1960), which questioned connoisseurship values through two cans being made in high-art materials and placed on a plinth, Dine places his objects on a shelf, in front of a painted canvas, thus extending the everyday into the constructed artistic world.[53]

As well as these general themes related to everyday life, there are others that are loosely autobiographical. Dine's grandfather had owned many tools and had worked as a handyman, and like his own father had owned a store. Dine worked there, and although he had no interest in continuing the business, these tools always fascinated him, not so much because of craftsmanship, but because of the way that they were displayed and related to each other, to the wall and to the floor.[54] The incorporation of tools into his two- and three-dimensional works is an important theme. In his etchings they are formally arranged as if for use, but sometimes become slightly surreal with overlaid textures, and brushes with extended hair. While making wrenches, hammers and saws poetic, he also made them appear poised for action or vaguely threatening. *Window with an Axe* (1961–2) is a three-dimensional window with an axe buried in the frame. The glass panes have been blackened, similar to the leather-covered windows of Duchamp's *Fresh Widow* of 1920. Like the stepladder, doors and windows in Rauschenberg's photographs, Dine's tools suggest human actions and everyday life, without actually including people.

WINDOWS AND DOORS – THE POETIC EVERYDAY

Like Rauschenberg and Dine, from the 1950s to the 1970s Allan Kaprow and George Segal explored the fluid interface between art and life, and in dissolving the divisions between the different genres of art and theatre sought ways of freeing themselves from abstract expressionism. Along with George Brecht, who studied with Cage and became a member of the Fluxus group, and Lucas Samaras, the photographer, sculptor and painter, they formed a group affiliated with Rutgers University in New Jersey that called itself the New Brunswick School. Unlike nearby New York, which inspired Rauschenberg by its constant juxtapositions and unexpected sights, New Brunswick at the time was drab, which the artists found attractive in its 'authenticity'.[55]

Allan Kaprow wrote about the two histories he perceived in art: that which was 'art-like art', which saw itself as separate from life and referenced themes and ideas from the tradition of art itself, and 'life-like art', which was connected with life and everything else. He perceived the latter – which included the Futurists, Dada and Fluxus artists – as one that mixed up the traditional binaries of Western traditions, like the body and the mind, the individual and people, civilisation and nature.[56] The 'Happenings' that he instigated and that the group were involved with blurred the distinction between art and life and between the different genres of art, theatre and dance. Instead of having plots, these events would enact everyday activities like cleaning teeth, telephoning a friend or shaking hands, activities that are nonetheless learned and cultural. By focusing on these normally unattended areas of life, he wanted to suggest the strangeness of these apparently natural rituals.[57]

It was through these Happenings, some of which took place on his farm, that George Segal became aware of an alternative way of considering art practice.[58] His early influences were the school of Paris and other artists shown in New York's Museum of Modern Art, as well as Hans Hofmann, who ran summer schools that Segal attended in Provincetown in Massachusetts between 1956 and 1959. Hofmann taught that the creative observation of nature should draw on all of the senses, as well as space and movement. He believed that an artist's inner vision should synthesise all the paths of communication between the environment and man.[59] During and after World War II, Hofmann explored these ideas in drawings and paintings that he made of scenes framed by his studio window depicting the outside world. In concept they were related to those by Gris and other avant-garde artists, but the spatial play was less constructed.[60]

The year 1958 was critical for Segal, as he began to explore a more sculpturally based language that would 'express the quality of my own experience'; he also had an exhibition at the Green Gallery in New York.[61] From then on, his work explored the lives that he saw around him, including those in his own home, which was unusual as domestic spaces were not considered important in the New York art scene at that time.[62] 'I started dealing with all the stuff immediately around me – the restaurants, the diners, the streets [...] Inevitably, I had to enter my own house.'[63]

While Segal found the work that the rest of the group was developing interesting, he felt that he could not follow it as he found it too mystical and built around the cult of Duchamp. For him, Duchamp's translation of found objects into art was ironic, rather than being related to feeling.[64] Segal's integration of overlooked everyday moments of life was also fundamental to the work of Kaprow and Rauschenberg, but he combined this with the idea of expressing an inner vision. In a statement from 1973, he wrote:

> I try to apprehend two realities: one high, quasi-religious, and the other low, made up of the banal and the unpretentious. I want to incorporate in my sculpture an intensification of my experience with my inner world and with the tangible world around me [...] My ultimate objectives are a feeling of revelation and of psychological truth.[65]

In *Man Sitting at a Table* (1961), which was his first portrait made by taking a cast of a figure – in this case his own – using impregnated plaster, we glimpse Segal through an old found window, sitting on a wooden seat at a worn wooden table, absorbed in his own thoughts. It is as much about our catching a glimpse through a window of another person's world as it is about artlessness. The cast taken directly from his body has a casual pose and the surface of the plaster has not been refined, but left with all its irregularities.

It is a genre scene, but without any of the formality and sanitisation of art. The window not only references the creative life that his teacher Hofmann suggested, but also defines the edge between the sculpture's space and that of the audience. They are on an equal footing, being at the same scale and in the same location, but the viewer looks through the window onto the supposed life of the artist in order to view the ordinary afresh.[66]

Unlike the plays of illusionism that were central to pop artists like Tom Wesselmann, this was apparently a glimpse of domestic reality. Wesselmann also included found objects in his domestic scenes, but typically they parodied the American dream and new affluence. *Still Life # 27* (1963), for instance, combined real elements with painted sections, playing with the boundaries between the real and artifice. There is a door on which are hung real coats on the left, and a radiator on the right. The other panels are painted, with the central one incorporating a Cézanne painting: *Madame Cézanne dans un fauteuil rouge* (1877). Above the radiator is a painted window through which there is an image of a Volkswagen Beetle. In contrast to the work of Segal – and indeed the images by Rauschenberg or Dine – the scene is of domestic order, where everything is newly decorated and clean, with ornaments arranged on the windowsill. Outside there is a symbol of wealth and success in the gleaming car. Without showing the occupant, her neat presence is palpable in this window onto her world.[67]

Although frequently discussed in conjunction with pop art, Segal was excluded from the large pop-art show at the Whitney Museum of American Art in New York in 1974. Responding to how he felt about this, Segal wrote:

> If we are talking about environments, facts, and objects – this is the entire territory that I inhabit. Of course, if Pop has to mean witty, ironic detachment, count me out. I make no bones about the fact that I am involved in the whole human situation.[68]

This is evident in the original version of Segal's *Ruth in Her Kitchen* (1964), which was the antithesis of Wesselmann's and other pop artists' output. Unlike in their highly polished works, here the cast of Ruth sits at her old, monumental wooden table, surrounded by a cacophony of her belongings.

Only in the final version does she appear at her table by a window, calmly seated in her thought world, but without her excess of debris.

Whereas in *Ruth in Her Kitchen* the window just lets in light, in *Gertrude: Double Portrait* (1972) the window becomes an active participant in describing the subject's character. Gertrude sits on her porch looking out at the passing world. To her left is a window, in which a film is played, which Segal shot using Super 8 film, showing the model living her everyday life: laughing, talking and daydreaming. The sequences portray her full-length and in close-up, from different angles and as if at the same height as the audience. Segal described how people accept the conventions of film and sink into its 'psychological language'.[69] However, more than this, the film in this sculpture asserts the idea of the window's framing sight, and creates the idea that we are looking into the building like voyeurs. The medium here supplies the viewer with prosthetic views of Gertrude, creating, like all films, an edited perspective on her life and world. It adds to the narrative, expanding and restructuring the perception of her that was provided by the already framed sculptural representation of Gertrude in her environment.[70]

In some works this voyeuristic gaze into the house and life is reversed, with the audience being in the same interior environment as the figure. In *Seated Girl* of 1967 the figure sits in a room, lost in her thoughts, while behind her the real window reveals the world beyond. However, in *Girl Sitting against a Wall I* and *II* of 1968 and 1970, the figures are again seated on chairs, this time against blanked-out windows. In the earlier work, the windowpanes are blackened and the chair painted red, which suggests a night scene within a home. In all of these pieces there is a sense of interiority and of waiting. The figures are not physically active, and are generic in form: anonymous actors in familiar situations. The blank setting with common furniture and windows, combined with the anonymity of the figures, means that the audience is free to project onto the scene its own thoughts. The 1970 version of *Girl Sitting against a Wall*, however, is totally white, so that the audience sees the tableau as just that: it has become a formal arrangement of shape and texture. The making of the cast, with the accidents of drips, edges of bandages and layering of the wrapping, makes the surface speak less of internal muscles pushing through the skin, or the manipulation of surface texture for concerted artistic effect, and more of exactly what it was, a covering that lets 'a person's inner set of attitudes come out in the plaster'.[71] The window has become part of a pattern within the roughly painted wall.

Doors also feature in Segal's work, in a way that evokes the poetic tradition of the door as the boundary between one world and another. While conceding this possible interpretation, Segal also described the door as 'cheap architecture, easily salvaged [...] an ideal anonymous foil'.[72] His *Woman in a Doorway II* (1965) shows the complete figure of a clothed woman, partly hidden behind a door, which she is opening, at the end of a short corridor. The audience is separated from her both by the stepped corridor and also by the outer doorjamb, with a second, fully open door. The off-white paint of the doors is old, the corridor a dark chocolate brown – all indicative of tenement buildings, although the room beyond is red, suggesting a warm private haven.[73] She is not welcoming, but hesitating, as one would expect when opening the door to a stranger in a poor neighbourhood.

The Corridor (1976) also includes a door, but the audience can move around and see the corridor from both beyond the door and within the corridor itself. Like *Woman in a Doorway II* it is painted in large, uninflected patches of colour. The door is yellow, the figure blue, the chair red and the corridor, with its ceiling light, black. Discussing this work later, Segal said that he made it after seeing a painting by Barnett Newman in the latter's studio after he had died, which was large and black with an upright yellow stripe an inch and a half wide. Segal decided to paint the door yellow, so that the stripe of the edge of the door could be seen as one moved around the work. Like Newman and Mark Rothko, he thought of colours as extensions of psychological states, so that while the sculpture appeared welcoming in gesture, he also wanted to hint at a 'passage of time and intimations of mortality', where he was trying to combine 'memory, formality, the literal and literary in a single piece'.[74]

In 1964 Segal wrote that the look of the figures was a mixture of the planned and accidental. He knew the emotional stance that he wanted to convey, but although he would ask the model to sit or stand in a certain way, after a while – plaster takes a while to dry – they would fall back into themselves.[75] Because each of the situations is everyday, the narrative folds back onto the viewer so that one not only questions whom one is looking at, but also who one is oneself. As Suzanne Delehanty has said, his figures and environments document common experiences, but without the usual film of familiarity, so that one can see the mysterious edge of overlooked life.[76] It is this aspect that links with the writings of Allan Kaprow, where the everyday can become strange, and that has led certain critics to call his works 'frozen Happenings'.[77]

From 1969, Segal experimented with making smaller environments that depicted fragments of a whole, where the framing around the figure was tight and simple. Some of these were parts of the body: details of breasts, shoulders, arms or chins. Others were truncated torsos that were set in boxes. Rather than being stage sets suggesting 'real-life' scenes, these hint at something more mysterious and sensual. His series of 1975, which includes *Orange Door* and *Gray Door*, was wall hung; each work shows a partially open door cropped top and bottom, with the torso of a naked woman behind it. In these, the white forms contrast with the wood and coloured doors. In both *Orange Door* and *Gray Door* the naked woman is wrapped in her own thoughts, and, while facing the openings, neither engages with the viewer, nor do they seem aware of the surrounding environment, so the assumption is that they think they are alone. More disturbing is that the relationship of the cast to the model has become stronger, with the accidents of process minimised. The surface articulation of skin is more defined and modulated than in Segal's earlier sculptures, with the underlying anatomy of bones, muscles and veins visible.

Linda Nochlin has argued that the use of the fragmented body in nineteenth-century art was a means of depicting the modern experience. She considers that it expressed a new relationship to the world by fetishising parts of the body and suggesting the fragmentary nature of the new urban reality, in which the spectator was simultaneously intimate and alienated.[78] She particularly refers to the paintings of Degas in which the spectator and dancers are visible, although radically cropped, arguing that our viewpoint on the stage coincides with that of the painted spectator, making strange traditional narratives of human connectedness. Here there are elements akin to display in the gallery, where the audience looks towards a spotlit fragment of constructed life. As Brian O'Doherty said about the perception of the frozen moments in time in Segal's work and that of his contemporary Duane Hanson, there is a conflict between 'sensation conceptualised and concept actualised'.[79] In other words, the occupied tableaux and the distancing of reality, while suggesting the real, are mediated by the gallery. His argument is that distancing and mediating techniques are important in order to understand, and even to create, experiences.

Segal's wall-hung works suggest film stills and the techniques of photography that both Nochlin and O'Doherty promoted as modern ways of experiencing the world, in which cropped framing is integral to the languages of the mediums. However, in Segal's sculptures the door or window also becomes a contemporary interpretation of Alberti's window onto the world, but in some works we are on the inside looking out, and in others we are on the outside looking in, like Socrates' window into the soul.

WINDOWS – SIGHT DENIED

Duchamp's irreverence towards the institutions and traditions of art was profoundly influential, especially, as discussed, with the younger American artists and musicians. His *Fresh Widow* of 1920 was an ironic statement about art being a window onto the world, which joined wordplay with pre-existing knowledge of a full-length French window that could act as a door and window. To make it, Duchamp asked a carpenter in New York to make a miniature French-style window. He then covered each of the panes with black leather, which were to be polished every day like shoes.[80] Through this covering, Duchamp was denying the metaphorical and real ability to see through the window, with its philosophical, literary and artistic traditions.

Roy Lichtenstein also played with this idea in *Stretcher Frame with Cross Bars III* (1968). This painting depicts the back of a canvas, with the crossbars of the stretcher suggesting the window frame. Rather than alluding to traditional painting techniques and the depiction of a world beyond, Lichtenstein used those from advertising and mass media, including Ben-Day dots and simplified graphic forms, but denied that seductive world and instead suggested the links between art and commerce. Like Duchamp's *Fresh Widow*, it was a rejection of the traditions of 'fine-art' painting and the systems underpinning the art market.

He was to make this rebuttal of the traditions of art more complex in *Painting near Window* of 1983. In this work he quoted from a number of his earlier paintings, including one of his Brushstrokes series from the 1960s, which reduced the gestures of the abstract expressionists to comic-book ciphers. Through the window, which is framed by curtains – alluding to references to the theatrical in the work of painters like Vermeer and Gris – is a painting of a palm tree and vista suggesting travel advertisements. In this work the traditions of art, the idea that the eye is the window to the soul and dreams of exotic travel were all uniformly flattened into image.

Jeff Wall made a series titled Blind Windows between 2000 and 2006. Displayed in light boxes, his transparencies are in one sense already windows. However, his images of windows that have been blocked, barred or painted over deny sight. They no longer function as windows. However, the decay, the loss of the idea of an interior life and the DIY adaptations are all rendered beautiful.[81] Like the urban found objects incorporated by Segal and Rauschenberg, these chance findings of worn and disregarded areas are framed and formalised. Unlike the paintings by Matisse, Picasso and Gris, in which the window within the paintings acted as a frame for another world, in these images there is no world beyond – the audience stays within the present image.

The American sculptor James Croak has also engaged with the window motif in a series of sculptural objects dating from 1991 that depict domestic and ecclesiastical windows removed from their contexts. They are simultaneously objects that suggest minimalism and objects that have metaphorical content. Like Segal he uses the casting method and has also made sculptures of figures that convey emotions through their poses, as in the series After Rodin (1997). However, rather than casting from life, his are made, as Rodin made his sculptures, through modelling in clay and then following the traditional casting method.[82]

His windows are of cast dirt, a process involving the mixing of soil with binder. His first use of this material was after he moved to Brooklyn from Los Angeles, and as he has recounted, 'it was neutral and loaded! It was everywhere but never used.'[83] The material is both attractive – it glistens in gallery light and has a variety of subdued colours – and repellent because of what it is. Earth can be about fecundity as well as being a cultural taboo in the wrong context, as shown in Walter de Maria's *Earth Room* (1977). It is at the heart of the difference between the cleanliness and order of the inside of a civilised home and exterior nature, which is repeatedly expunged through cleaning. By forming his windows of this material, Croak alludes to this dividing line.[84]

Croak initially used dirt swept from gutters. While earth is the substance that keeps all life forms on the planet alive, dirt swept from a city is the by-product of economic growth, of overcrowded humans in vast cities, and is a real threat to millions of people through harbouring disease.[85] In the American home the fear of dirt is promoted in advertisements for cleaning products and has become a tool of class and race discrimination. As such, dirt itself has become a social taboo within the home, while being tolerated and ignored outside.[86] Our complex relationship with dirt, combined with an allusion to windows, is expressed in Croak's work *Soiled Widow* (2011; figure 2.1). 'Humans end up dirt, and a painting still has veracity as direct experience irrespective of the evaporated theory.'[87]

Croak's windows relate to many twentieth-century art movements, including, in his own words, 'abstraction, surrealism, earthwork, expressionism, [and] Duchamp's sight gags'.[88] Like Duchamp's *Fresh Widow*, which denies sight, and more recent windows by the Greek artist Jannis Kounellis, in which rocks, construction materials or anthracite completely or partially block real windows and openings, Croak's dirt windows complicate readings. His *Soiled Widow* is a parody of Duchamp's *Fresh Widow*, but many of his others, like the Untitled Window Series of 1993, are of domestic sash windows. They deny sight as either internal or as a mediation between mind and the world, and the isolated, decontextualised objects are simultaneously windows and sculptural objects. Unlike anti-art, he wants his work to have a mysterious presence, and not be just rebellious. 'I want to create beauty.'[89] While *Soiled Widow* is a continuation of Duchamp's irony, Croak believes that one can still have an emotional response to works, even after the original ideas that created particular works of art have been forgotten.[90]

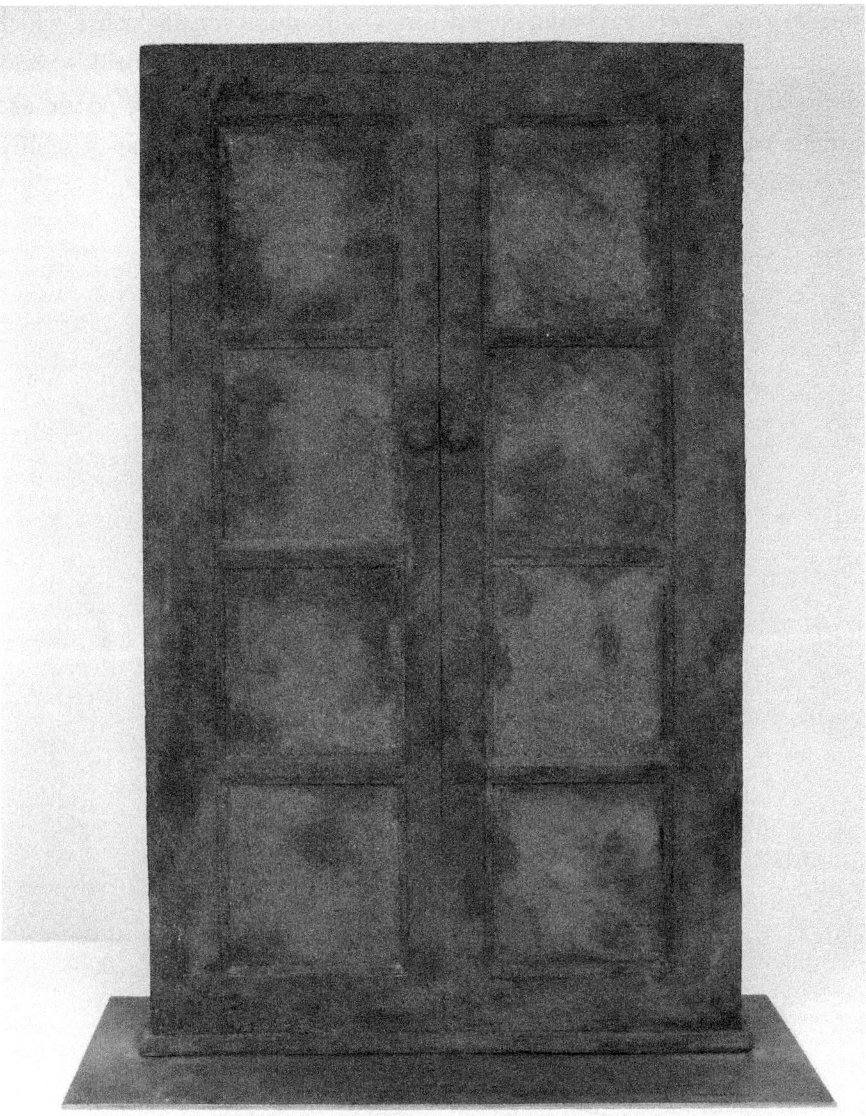

FIGURE 2.1 James Croak, *Soiled Widow* (2011).

This chapter has explored how art has drawn on the traditions of windows and doors as the thresholds between the inside and outside in poetic and formal ways. As well as being the openings in the domestic enclosure, which suggest the interface between interior life and the material world beyond, doors and windows are emblems within a long philosophical, poetic and artistic tradition and have been used to explore different areas of reality, creativity and the relationship between art and life.

3

Female Space

When, in 1863, Charles Baudelaire exhorted artists to paint modern life, he did not mean life in the home, but life on the street, in cafes and places of entertainment. These public areas were where the male *flâneur* could watch and capture the 'transient, the fleeting and the contingent' of everyday life in his art.[1] Although some male nineteenth-century artists, like Pierre Bonnard and Édouard Vuillard, did paint interiors in addition to outside scenes, most female Impressionists painted the life that they had access to, which was contained within the home and selected outside environs.[2] Unlike the male domain of the streets, the perception was that the home was the female space for the middle classes, and that domestic creativity operated outside any accepted notions of 'high' art. It was not until the late 1960s that women artists began to turn around the negative connotations associated with the home and domestic forms of art.

This chapter will concentrate on the art and ideas developed in California in the late 1960s and 1970s, where two important courses laid the foundation for the American feminist-art movement: one at Fresno State University in 1970 and the other at California Institute of the Arts (CalArts) a year later, the latter coming to prominence through the exhibition *Womanhouse* in 1972. It will consider the means by which the artists and art students associated with these courses destabilised the apparently seamless narrative of the development of Western culture. The work they developed was hugely influential and paved the way for much contemporary art, although it is only recently that this has been acknowledged institutionally – through, for instance, the recent exhibitions *Global Feminisms* at the Brooklyn Museum and *WACK! Art and the Feminist Revolution* at the Museum of Contemporary Art, Los Angeles, both from 2007, and also through the opening of the Elizabeth A. Sackler Center for Feminist Art at the Brooklyn Museum in 2002, which houses many of the key early works.[3]

To define a subsection of the art world as 'female' or to discuss the contribution of 'women' artists is now seen as problematic on two accounts: firstly, it assumes that there is a difference between art made by men and art made by women, and secondly it assumes that all women produce the same work, regardless of individual experiences, culture and social background. This has been successfully disputed by many critics, including Griselda Pollock, and in the more recent writing by Linda Nochlin and Marsha Meskimmon.[4] However, in the early 1970s the artists and students needed to create a unified voice in order to be heard. There were no pre-existing frameworks of subject matter, techniques or histories to work within to counter the dominant understanding of what constituted art that had been ratified by the powerful forces of institutions, critics and historians. Through their efforts they reclaimed a hidden history of female artists, developed patterns and themes of making that were relevant to their needs and histories, and paved the way for future developments.

BACKGROUND

The 1970s was an important decade for feminist art and its history in three main ways: the art and ideas of female artists became legitimised; the histories of art were investigated in order to understand why female artists had previously been marginalised and to reinsert them into the meta-narratives; and new paradigms for art and its criticism were created.

The decade followed one of civil unrest, which saw the assassinations of Martin Luther King and President Kennedy, and demonstrations against war, racism and sexism. It was the era when feminism, gay rights and black politics sought to understand their relationships to establishment frameworks, to reclaim their histories and to turn sites and practices that had been perceived as centres of oppression into those of resistance. As a result, a change in understanding about the relationship of the individual to central authority occurred, and identity came to be perceived as formed not only through contemporary relationships and conditions, but through a culmination of particular histories of experience and socially conditioned roles. This new and more complex understanding led to new forms of criticism and a rewriting of histories, in a way that upset the presumptions that had underpinned mainstream narratives.

Three key surveys of art history at the time were Ernst Gombrich's *The Story of Art* (1950), H. W. Janson's *History of Art* (1962) and Kenneth Clark's *Civilisation* (1969). In none of these were the contributions of female artists acknowledged. Kenneth Clark was one of the most respected and influential art historians of his era. In keeping with contemporary ideas, his many books discussed art that conformed to the accepted notions of art's parameters; they covered 'high-art' materials – paint, stone and bronze – and themes that acknowledged traditional genres; overall they represented a form of art history in which a canon of the 'best' examples created a seamless narrative to the present. However, in America it was Janson's book that caused the most upset among college students: having seen and read about feminist art, they started to question the history that assumed that women were represented and objectified, but not the creators.[5]

In 1971 Linda Nochlin published one of the first feminist art-history texts, 'Why have there been no great women artists?', in the journal *ARTNews*. This special issue of January 1971 was entitled *Women's Liberation, Women Artists, and Art History*, and included a history of women artists, personal statements by contemporary artists including Eleanor Antin and Lynda Benglis, and articles by women critics and art historians like Nochlin and Suzi Gablik. Nochlin's argument was not that there had been an overlooked female Michelangelo, but that the structures underpinning the production and criticism of art, and the social and educational constrictions experienced by women, had consistently militated against their becoming professionals.[6]

Through the research undertaken for the article, Nochlin realised that art history had not addressed the changes that were emerging in art and feminist literature. As a result she changed the title of her undergraduate course at Vassar to 'The image of the woman in the nineteenth and twentieth centuries', and set out to develop an entirely new approach that did not follow the existing paradigms.[7] She and her students explored the relevance of feminist issues for art together, which was also a new way to approach learning, being less directed and more collaborative.

When Judy Chicago studied art during the 1960s she was the only female in the sculpture department and there was no expectation that she would go on to become an artist.[8] She quickly learned that if she included imagery about women's experiences, like birth, her tutors became confused, could not take the art seriously and referred to it as 'one of Judy's cunts'.[9] This form of derision and exclusion continued after she left college and moved to Pasadena, when she found it difficult to get galleries and museums to even look at her work.[10]

Marginalisation of art by female artists was endemic. Because they were frequently excluded from exhibitions, women artists were also not included in reviews and articles, and therefore failed to get collected within the major institutions. Women artists accounted for fewer than 5 per cent of the *Whitney Annual* exhibition in 1969, for instance.[11] This lack of representation caused protests, firstly in New York and then in Los Angeles when no female artists were included in the major exhibition *Art and Technology* at the Los Angeles County Museum in 1970.[12]

WOMEN AND CONFINEMENT

World War II was a watershed in America, and marked the beginning of radical political, social and economic changes that affected everyone. The Servicemen's Readjustment Act of 1944 gave returning soldiers access to university study. During the 1950s women also enrolled, and universities were inundated with a much broader range of students than before, many of whom chose to study arts subjects.[13] California also attracted migrants through increased employment prospects.[14] The increase in diverse young, idealistic and educated people in the state stimulated a radical activism during the 1960s and 1970s that paralleled what was happening both in Europe and the rest of America. The fragmentation and real unease in society led to the question of what the role of art was to be. How much should it attempt to comment upon, reflect or critique the situation?

Martha Rosler was one of the first female artists who addressed these issues and, in order to do so, used techniques that had less gendered histories. Using some of the strategies of conceptual art, the return to imagery by the pop artists and the political application of photomontages by the German Dada artist Hannah Höch, Rosler combined disparate illustrations from magazines to critique social manipulation and the disposability of news.[15] The images that she culled from magazines reduced the different genders to their stereotypical roles and circumstances. By juxtaposing them into scenes that fractured the logic of any situation, she found a way of commenting on the framing of the original imagery without resorting to traditional male paradigms.[16]

Rosler's series Bringing the War Home: House Beautiful (1969–72) incorporated selected images from the interior-design magazine *House Beautiful* that promoted attractive middle-class homes cared for by beautiful, well-groomed, middle-class women, and combined them with grim photojournalistic images of the Vietnam War from *Life* magazine. In one work, an immaculate woman is shown using the latest vacuum on her curtains, while outside soldiers are fighting in rocky landscapes. In another, a traumatised Vietnamese woman is depicted carrying her dead baby up the stairs of a beautifully appointed and expensive split-level home.

The idealisation of the home and the promotion of domesticity in magazines like *House Beautiful* hid an issue that Betty Friedan discussed in her 1963 book *The Feminine Mystique.* While working as a journalist she increasingly heard about the despair of American suburban housewives who apparently had everything – a comfortable home, healthy family, education and labour-saving devices.[17] Yet they felt trapped, isolated and bound by an idealised depiction of femininity.[18] Even artists who had a mission outside the home found that they were stretched with the range of commitments expected of them. The sculptor Eva Hesse wrote in her diary in January 1964: 'I cannot be so many things [...] I cannot be something for everyone [...] Woman, beautiful, artist, wife, housekeeper, cook, sales lady [...] I cannot even be myself or know who I am.'[19]

While the promotion of the home as the place for women was a practical political solution to the problem of the return of the troops – which meant that men were able to return to the jobs that during wartime had been done by women – this ideal is one that has been integral to Western thought since Ancient Greek times. Writing in the late 1950s, Hannah Arendt discussed its origin in Ancient Greece and how it came to be adopted within Christian thought. For Aristotle and Plato, the home was for family life, nurture and shelter, whereas public spaces were for reasoned debate, contemplation and political organisation. The home enabled political activity, but because nurture and shelter were linked with mere animal capacities they were inferior to the heroic nature of public life.[20] Therefore, life outside the home represented a completely different order of freedom, one that was not bound by the labour required for biological necessity, and this was the culture of men.[21]

The division between gender roles in different societies and how this affects power relations was explored from the 1960s onwards in feminist texts, and was also an important focus in the studies of anthropology, ethnography and sociology.[22] Claude Lévi-Strauss' archaeological studies of the 1960s were important for their articulation of the asymmetry of gender power in societies where women are kept within the home and isolated from larger social groups.[23] This was further developed in the ground-breaking text *Woman, Culture and Society*, written in the mid-1970s, which argued that the confinement and isolation of women within the home were things that were created by society rather than inevitable biological conditions, and it was this isolation that consistently stopped women from gaining power and having a voice in the public world.[24]

WOMEN ARTISTS AND THEIR EXPERIENCES

In order to overcome some of these structural and perceptual attitudes, women artists in America started to group together in the mid to late 1960s, forming coalitions of similar interests, like the Artists for Black Liberation, Art Workers' Coalition and Women Students. These became important in agitating against the power of museums, for setting up alternative exhibition spaces, for discussing common experiences and for legitimising traditional female domestic creativity as art.

Unlike previous depictions of women within the home, feminist art from the 1960s and 1970s in America revealed the cracks in traditional male cultural narratives. As Lydia Yee wrote in relation to an exhibition that considered 'women's work' in art from the vantage point of 30 years later, this practice 'served to [...] complicate simple binary oppositions [...] [through] [...] the redirection of traditional women's work towards unconventional ends'.[25] These artists challenged the hierarchy of materials and male, Euro-American judgements about 'good' art, and instead used media like textiles, performance and video, which had less cultural baggage, as well as humour and parody, in order to destabilise accepted norms. Through these means and by directing their focus to the margins of perceived culture, these artists drew attention to and rewrote hegemonic histories, making them more complex and diverse.[26]

Eleanor Antin moved to California in the late 1960s from New York, where she found the culture more transient, as people moved there in the hope of a better life. Unlike on the East Coast, shopping was done through catalogues that provided everything from furniture to food.[27] In a series called California Lives (1969), which was to be the forerunner of her later performances, in which she adopted particular identities, she ordered consumer goods from the Sears catalogue and arranged the furniture and other domestic items into 'portraits' of characters that she either knew or made up. *Jeanie* (figure 3.1) was the first of these. The text accompanying the 'stage set' described her as a single, working-class mother who worked nights and did not get much sleep, but who liked to watch the surf. She worried about her daughter, and hoped that her mother in Idaho would send her money, but she never did. Twice a week the lifeguard with a moustache would come over and they would go inside.[28] The installation consisted of spindly-legged, cheap metal furniture, a melamine cup, an unlit cigarette, a plastic hair curler and a matchbook from Bully's Prime Rib, the arrangement of which suggested a

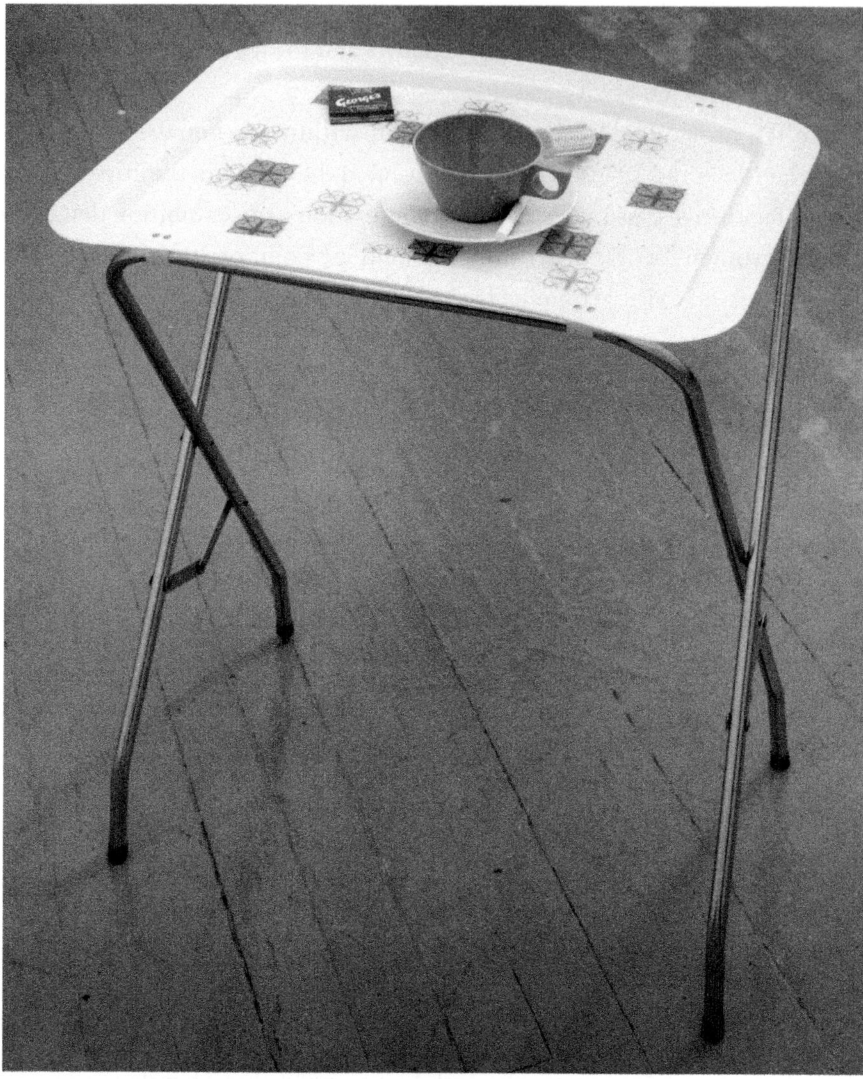

FIGURE 3.1 Eleanor Antin, *Jeanie*, from the series California Lives (1969).

dwelling that had just been vacated.[29] The very banality of the objects, their lack of individuality, and yet their part in locating a type of person who was poor and lacking in roots, came together to create psychological associations.

This installation and others in the series were shown in the first alternative space in New York: Gain Ground, which was run by Robert Newman. In keeping with the Dada influence, rather than the installations becoming collectors' items, after the show people took home any items they wanted.[30] Like the conceptual-art movement of the 1960s that she was drawing on, these works critiqued the modes of production, the systems of display and the commoditisation of art, all of which fed into early feminist art.

Jeanie was part of an overlooked reality, as well as having parallels in downbeat characters in fiction like those in novels by Raymond Chandler and Ross Macdonald. But the idea of objects depicting the status or character of people also has a strong artistic lineage, from humanist portraits like those by Quentin Matsys or Hans Holbein the Younger to the 1911 cubist portraits of art dealers by Picasso. By depicting the characters adjacent to cultural artefacts and within a particular setting, such works set the scene for the characters. This echoes the argument set out by the phenomenologist Mikel Dufrenne, who articulated how background details or stage scenery set the scene for the hero in novels and plays. If this background is consistent and creates a mesh of meaning, then the audience believes in and lives with the character.[31] Antin thought about life as one big theatre. 'It's at the core of my work, and in a sense at the core of my life, which is spent imagining all these roles and these people.'[32]

While practising as an artist in Pasadena, Judy Chicago realised that there was no frame of reference for women artists in which their struggles, experiences or histories were valued. It was 1970 and, as already discussed, feminist journals, art coalitions and art about female experiences were being initiated, and artists were moving from the East Coast to California. During the 1970s there was a great expansion of non-profit exhibition spaces and this, combined with the development of a number of experimental college art courses, meant that the state became a dynamic hotbed of experimental art.[33] Geographically, California is large, so when Chicago chose to set up the Feminist Art Program at the California State University in Fresno, it was partly because it was isolated from the art world, which would leave her with space to experiment with her work. However, it was also a good time as there was already an established 'Experimental College' at Fresno, a kind of unofficial university within the university, which 'offered courses in Marxist politics, anarchist theory and Black, Chicano, Armenian and Women's Studies'.[34]

However, rather than trying to align forces with the rest of the campus, Chicago persuaded those in charge of the university to allow the programme to be held off-site. Understanding the marginalisation of art by women within the larger establishment, she wanted to create a 'safe space' where the women could develop their own voices. Many students worked at this site full-time and therefore did not mix with other students. Although their backgrounds were fairly narrow, with all but one being working class and white, many had already been taking or were teaching on other courses. Faith Wilding and Suzanne Lacy had taught the first women's studies class at Fresno in 1969, called 'The Second Sex', and Wilding also attended meetings of the Women's Caucus of the New University Conference during the same year and was already politically active. Suzanne Lacy was a zoology and chemistry graduate and was likewise politically active. Together they had founded a successful consciousness-raising group prior to enrolling on Judy Chicago's Feminist Art Program.[35]

The works produced by and the influence of both Fresno and the later CalArts Feminist Art Program have been criticised for offering an apparently universal, 'essentialising' view of what it is to be female.[36] However, the collaboration and group identity that was demanded on the programmes was a way of giving strength to the individuals, and in turn gave rise to many subsequent collaborative groups like the Guerrilla Girls and Ant Farm, and the performance-art group subRosa, which was started by one of the alumni of Fresno, Faith Wilding.[37] The rehabilitation of the spaces and the subsequent activities at Fresno were to be a prototype not only for the later installation at CalArts called *Womanhouse*, but also for the Feminist Studio Workshop and the Los Angeles Woman's Building.[38] As Wilding later wrote, the Feminist Art Program at Fresno was based on consciousness-raising, building a female context and environment, having female role models and having 'permission to be ourselves and make art from our own experience as women'.[39]

The course that Chicago initiated at Fresno was the first of its kind and was pivotal in the beginnings of the feminist art movement.[40] Both it and the later programme at CalArts were aimed at women students who wanted to become professionals. The style of teaching was new. One of the techniques involved group discussions in the 'rap' room, where students were required one by one to reveal personal, intimate experiences. Although many found this difficult, it was a way of discovering that their experiences were not unique.[41] The students were also required to undertake research about previous female artists, biographically and artistically, and evaluate their contributions to the history of art.[42] They assembled an archive to be held at CalArts of women artists and their work.[43] This complemented the research Linda Nochlin and her students were undertaking at Vassar. As Marsha Meskimmon has said, these feminists uncovered substantial evidence of the importance of women to the political and cultural life of the past, which 'changed the way in which they understood history and their place within it'.[44]

The media that were used at Fresno were broad and not limited to paint and sculpture. Chicago had known the work of Allan Kaprow during the 1960s and had created and taken part in some temporal, site-specific artworks in Los Angeles.[45] Just as Kaprow emphasised the overlaps between art and life, so the students experimented with making work about their experiences, including household chores, using performance, Super 8 film, photography and installation, as well as paint and sculpture.[46] Feminist performances of the 1970s and 1980s gave the medium new life by being political and by affirming group and individual identity.[47] It was a fast and direct way of engaging with particular issues, and was also linked to the theatricality of occupying buildings and the marching and singing of demonstrations, which were part of the political activism of the time.[48] Film and photography allowed these fleeting performances to be documented and thus to be permanently available for future research.

In 1970 Judy Chicago and her students staged a mock beauty pageant called 'Miss Chicago and the California Girls', in which stereotypes of women were paraded and then photographed. In a photograph of the same year, called *The Cunt Cheerleaders*, four students have donned bright cheerleading clothes emblazoned with letters that when seen together read 'CUNT'. *Cupie Doll*, another image from 1970, showed one of the students, Cheryl Zurilgen, dressed up in scanty attire of ribbons, feathers, wig and pantomime make-up to give a parody of femininity, and woman as desired object.[49] While these images were humorous and crude, they sought to expose and destabilise the frameworks of expectations within society.

Having spent a year at Fresno State, Judy Chicago and the Canadian-born artist Miriam Schapiro spent the summer of 1971 visiting female artists in their studios. Like Chicago and Schapiro, they all had difficulty showing their work, and tours like this were not part of the contemporary art circuit. One of the things that became clear to Chicago was that although these artists were serious about their work, many of them were frequently making art within the home – either because they had children or were seen to be responsible for the household tasks – unlike male artists who often had studios, and therefore there was a porosity between art and life. While they waited for the paint to dry they might do the washing-up. Pets, old postcards and toiletries surrounded them.[50] Consciously or not, they were enacting the feminist stance of the time, where personal experiences had value and 'who you are' could not be separated from 'what you do'.[51]

Antin, Chicago, Wilding, Lacy and Schapiro became friends, and also got to know Pauline Oliveros, Linda Montano and Ida Horowitz. Addressing the recent discoveries about how isolation in the home had kept women marginalised, they formed a women artists' group. While visiting women artists in the San Francisco Bay area, they also met with the members of the three women artists' consciousness-raising groups that were active in the area and that were giving voice to women's experiences and traditional ways of working.[52] It was the beginning of the process of opening up private lives to public and artistic scrutiny.

In 1971 Chicago gained a position at CalArts and argued successfully for a Feminist Art Program to be run by her and Miriam Schapiro with only women students, where the experiences of women could be explored in art.[53] Ten of the 15 students from Fresno followed Chicago there and enrolled on the course.[54] Schapiro was older than Chicago and more established as an artist. Like Chicago, Schapiro's early training had been in minimalism, and her works of the 1960s were hard-edged, abstract paintings. From 1970 she had begun experimenting with paint combined with everyday 'female' materials like textiles, and with using traditional techniques to create works that celebrated and acknowledged the domestic, and that also erased the line between 'high' art and craft.[55] These were techniques that were to be explored by the students, and also became vital in later developments in contemporary art.

Womanhouse

The project that was undertaken by the students and staff at CalArts entitled *Womanhouse* was internationally important at the time, and although no longer in existence has played a crucial part in the development of feminist art in particular and contemporary art in general.[56] By drawing attention to and making more complex the relationship with constructed and biological female identities and roles, *Womanhouse* sought to illuminate and subvert these through installations and performances that were staged within a large, derelict house in Los Angeles.[57] The work gained national attention and, by being reviewed by *Time* and other magazines, had about 10,000 visitors before the exhibition closed and the house was demolished.[58]

The context of *Womanhouse* was the international feminist movement, feminist theory and the voicing of the everyday experiences of women, and it employed a range of activist strategies synthesised from different avant-garde movements.[59] By altering an existing house and showing work within it, *Womanhouse* was consciously operating outside the institutionally accepted spaces of 'high' art, and presenting the 'female space' of the home as a legitimate place of both creation and exhibition. The materials and techniques used in the works were either those that had not been considered appropriate for 'high' art within the classical canon because of their association with domesticity and the home, or those that did not have the cultural history associated with mainstream art. Rather than drawing on existing themes from the male-formed canon, *Womanhouse* gave voice to individual and collective female experiences.

Although Rauschenberg, Segal and other East Coast artists had been experimenting with incorporating textiles and domestic elements into their work since the late 1950s, and pop artists made soft sculptures related to everyday life in the 1960s, mostly these were concerned with the everyday of the street and in making social comments on capitalism. Although the performances at *Womanhouse* had some overlaps with the Happenings staged by Kaprow, Cage and others, the former were voicing women's experiences rather than being broader comments on art and culture. Although Segal's bedroom and genre scenes, discussed in Chapters 2 and 6, were concerned with relationships between people and their lived environment, they drew on particular paradigms within art, and were neither overtly politically motivated nor questioning of the status quo.

The teaching methods used on the Feminist Art Program were unusual for higher education, but developed from the course at Fresno and built upon the ideas being explored in the political feminist movement. Students started projects by sitting in a circle and, having selected a topic, each spoke about it in turn. One of the major issues they confronted was that everyone absorbs socially conditioned roles from infancy onwards, and for females these roles were heavily practised within the home. The consciousness-raising aimed at unpicking the seemingly 'natural' and in creating an understanding of its social inscription.[60]

Womanhouse began in this way, with the students and staff considering the closest associative memories of the home.[61] An art historian called Paula Harper encouraged them to see whether the issues that they were exploring could be applied to a large-scale art project set in an actual house. The students debated how they could create a place in which they could develop their own dreams rather than fulfil their usual role of pleasing others.[62] First they looked for a suitable building, and when they found a large, abandoned mansion in Hollywood – 553 Mariposa Avenue – they contacted the owner, Amanda Psalter, who, after having the project explained to her, donated the house for the duration of the exhibition.[63]

On 8 November 1971, 23 women arrived and spent two months scraping walls, replacing windows, building partitions, making furniture and installing lights. This work not only crossed the gender and sexuality divide, but also class distinctions. Working collaboratively as well as individually, they then created environments in 17 rooms, along the corridors and up the stairs.

There were also sculptural works outside.[64] As well as the student installations, three established artists from Los Angeles were invited to participate and hang their work – Sherry Brody, Carol Edison Mitchell and Wanda Westcoast – and Chicago and Schapiro also contributed.

Womanhouse – DECORATIVE TECHNIQUES AND CRITICAL DEBATES

Each of the rooms was a self-contained installation; there was no implied narrative that led from one room to the next.[65] Some of the rooms referenced women's traditional skills, like Faith Wilding's *Crocheted Environment*, in which she used the domestic technique of crochet to make a shelter that suggested those that her female ancestors had built for themselves.[66] This web-like structure was made up of an informal grid of threads, between which open patterns were crocheted while others extended beyond the squares. It had a crocheted boundary opening through which one could enter into the womb-like space, which was large enough to enclose several seated people. The installation brought together all the female paradigms: enclosure, suggestion of the biological, female techniques and free, decorative patterns.

In 1975, Lucy Lippard listed some of the recurring motifs that she thought represented a female sensibility, which included circles, domes, eggs, a preoccupation with the body and body-like materials. She argued:

> the overwhelming fact remains that a woman's experience in this society – social and biological – is simply not like that of a man. If art comes from the inside, as it must, then the art of men and women must be different too.[67]

However, as Tamar Garb and others have argued, part of what the artists in this project sought to do was to appropriate subjects, invert stereotypes and undermine assumptions.[68] The work by Wilding used female techniques and suggested the womb or shelter, but it was to be read as art.

Domestic, creative techniques were also demonstrated in the quilts that were hung along the upstairs corridor of the house.[69] Like the *Crocheted*

Environment, this display took the medium away from its functional role and presented quilts as art, something that, as Chicago said, was against contemporary perceptions.[70] Traditional quilts had always had both decorative and social significance, with mourning quilts and those made to celebrate births, political and social occasions and nature.[71] Although perceived as important in the history of America, their decorative and functional associations demarcated them as craft, which was marginalised from mainstream art debates at the time. Since before the war, craft had developed its own support networks, with no overlaps with those of art.[72]

In 1969 an exhibition entitled *Wall Hangings* was opened at the Museum of Modern Art, New York, consisting of works that challenged traditional weaving and ways of working with textiles. However, it only received one review, which was by Louise Bourgeois, and that was in the craft journal *Craft Horizons*. Although she made art using sewing and other non-art materials, and referenced the domestic in her work, Bourgeois was scathing, writing that these works were not as demanding for the onlooker as a painting or sculpture.[73] When the eminent critic Harold Rosenberg visited *Wall Hangings*, he was enthusiastic. However, when asked to comment on it, he said that he would not know how.[74] This was a key issue: there was no existing critical language to discuss work that ran counter to accepted norms.

The female artists who contributed to *Womanhouse*, or who worked professionally but whose output did not conform to the 'male' system, faced the same problem of critical exposure. The antagonism to making, decoration and the decorative that had been explicit in so much modernist architecture, and forcibly expressed by modernist art critics like Clement Greenberg in, for instance, a short essay on Milton Avery or his famous article 'The avant-garde and kitsch' from 1939, meant that all that existed outside this paradigm was marginalised.[75] The favouring of an engineered and clean aesthetic over that which was decorative, and of fine art that could be linked back through a canon of 'masterworks' over art for the masses – both of which combined implicit gendering and class distinctions – meant that art made by women using traditional gendered techniques and craft suffered from the same problems of being linked to the domestic, being 'easy' to understand and not being able to carry meaning.

However, it was this kind of art that *Womanhouse* sought to legitimise, and was also the area that Miriam Schapiro explored and encouraged the students to consider in their decorative artworks, which incorporated handkerchiefs, doilies, aprons and other household objects. As Lucy Lippard argued in 1973, the feminist movement gave women the confidence to untie their apron strings – and in some cases keep it on, flaunt it and turn it into art.[76] In a review in the *Los Angeles Times* about *Womanhouse*, William Wilson wrote that it was a 'lair of female creativity', which 'reminds us that the female is our only direct link with the forces of nature and that man's greatest creative acts may be but envious shadowings of such fecundity'.[77]

Womanhouse – FEMALE ROLES

Nurturant Kitchen, by Susan Frazier, Vicki Hodgetts and Robin Weltsch (figure 3.2), could be seen as a depiction of Betty Friedan's female lives, in which women care for others, cook and clean, as well as being attractive sexual partners, all while being contained within a large, well-equipped and apparently enviable environment. The students discussed their experiences of the kitchen, and discovered that for most, far from being a warm place, it was a battleground between them and their mothers as they tried to get an appropriate share of love, because their mothers were locked into a situation about which they felt bitter.[78] Magazines were promoting the modern kitchen as an area of style and fashion rather than the more relaxed room it had been in the prewar era, and these images and advertisements inevitably depicted immaculately groomed, white, middle-class heterosexual women working happily and apparently effortlessly within its walls.

The tools used by the students to critique these experiences were exaggeration and parody – tools they also used in their performances.[79] They painted everything in the kitchen pink and stuck tourist images of faraway places in the drawers.[80] The frilly plastic curtains, which could have come straight from a catalogue, were by Wanda Westcoast, which added another layer of consumerism to the home.[81] The walls and ceiling of the kitchen were covered in egg–breast forms, cut off from their contexts and offered for consumption. Those on the ceiling were closer to egg forms, but as they came down the walls and surrounded the shelves of pre-packaged food and the fridge, they increasingly resembled sagging breasts.[82] Echoing ideas from pop art – although with more irony – the hanging aprons had soft, padded sculptural reliefs of giant lips and breasts surrounded by feminine frills, emphasising the equation between domesticity, sex and the feminine.

The *Dining Room* in *Womanhouse* was designed to be a feast for the senses and, like another of the environments, *Leah's Room*, celebrated not only women's experiences but also their creativity. The ceiling and a frieze were in brilliant colours, with a mural of fruit and flowers inspired by the nineteenth-century American painter of miniatures and still lifes Anna Claypoole Peale, one of the famous Peale family of artists.[83] The table was covered by a tablecloth and spread with bread-dough sculptures of ham, turkey, vegetables and a three-layer chocolate cake, all set onto sewn fabric plates. Unlike the unappetising street food that Claes Oldenburg created in the 1960s, this was a sumptuous feast, a ritual meal designed to bring together the family. Just as in seventeenth-century still-life paintings, some of which depicted humble repasts and others of which were about excess, this overloaded table was about indulgence, time and the nurture of the American family. Magazines like *Good Housekeeping* reinforced the association of good meals with happy families and successful marriages. However, while promoting this, they elided the fact that these meals can also be sites of tension and power.[84]

Two of the performances undertaken by the students during the exhibition were *Ironing* by Sandra Orgel and *Scrubbing* by Chris Rush. For *Ironing*, Orgel silently and laboriously ironed a large plasticised sheet with a cold iron, and then tightly folded it for storage. *Scrubbing* again highlighted the monotony and drudgery of everyday tasks, with a performance of repetitive floor cleaning. These performances had originated in those that Dori Atlantis and Nancy Youdelman had undertaken the previous summer while waiting to start at CalArts. Working at Atlantis' sister's house in Santa Monica, they collaborated on making a series of representations of the housewife persona. In these, a housewife in her curlers did the laundry, mopped the floor, fluffed the bedclothes and finally napped on the bed.[85]

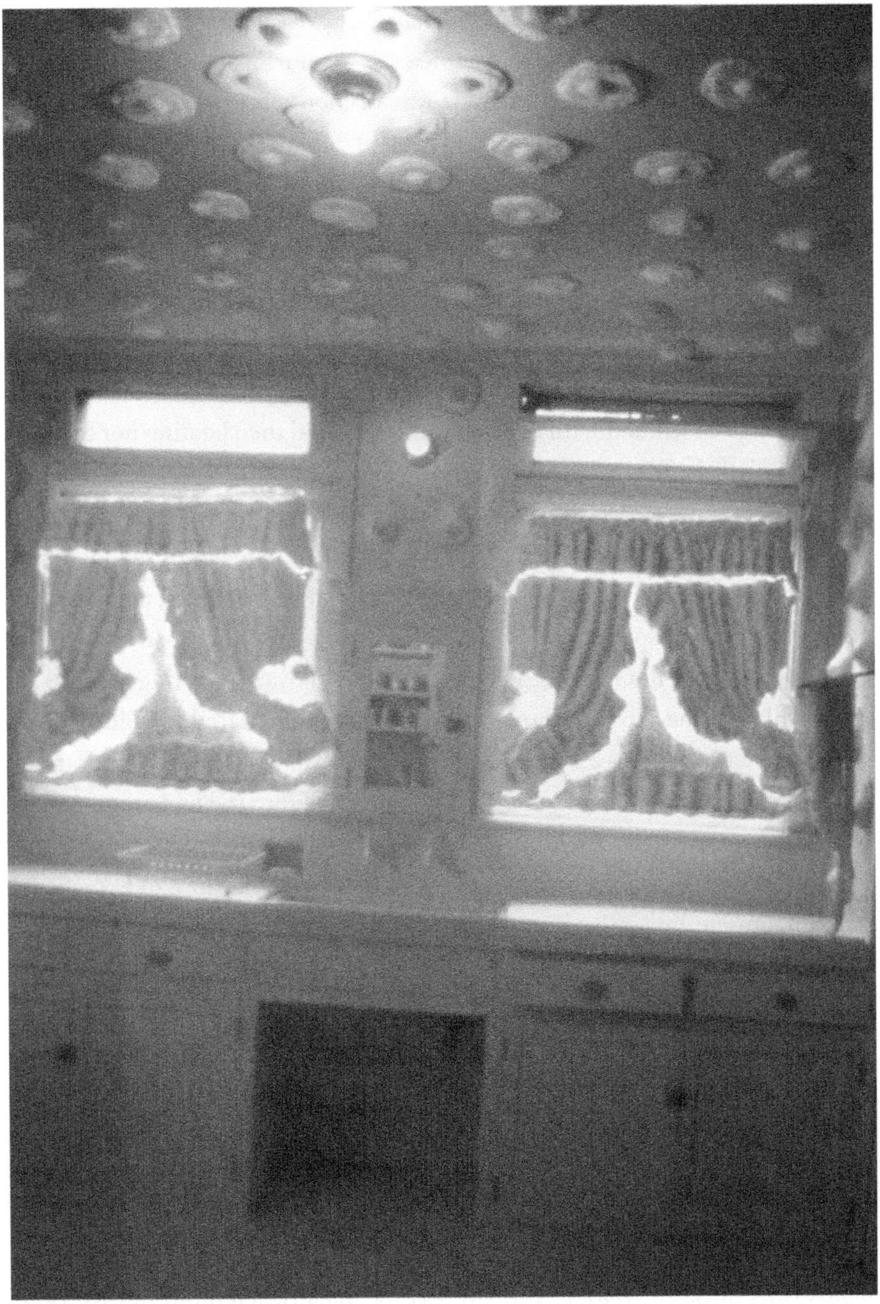

FIGURE 3.2 Susan Frazier, Vicki Hodgetts and Robin Weltsch, *Nurturant Kitchen*, from *Womanhouse* (1972).

Gender roles were explored in the play *Cock and Cunt*, which was regularly performed by Faith Wilding and Janice Lester during the exhibition. The script by Chicago questioned why it was women who did the washing-up, debunking the apparently natural equation of 'female' with 'home' by staging a spurious pseudoscientific argument related to the biology of the different sexes. The two performers had giant genitalia strapped to their bodies to demarcate their genders – and their perceived roles in life. 'She' asked 'He' to help with washing the dishes, but his reply was that having a cock meant that he did not do tasks like that. A cunt is round like a dish, where as a cock is long, hard and straight, which is suitable for firing guns and missiles.[86] The performance continued with He mounting She, and then beating her to death with his phallus. While being a comedy, the link between sex and violence and the asymmetry of power in the home is telling.[87]

Schapiro and Chicago thought that the iconographic use of sexual difference could be used to state the 'truth and beauty of her identity', and although contentious, was also vital.[88] As Broude has argued, the early use of cock and cunt imagery was not meant to be reductive but a way of testing the stereotyped roles of the day, and how these had been inculcated.[89] Wilding later wrote that 'cunt art' was essential at the time to reverse negative connotations, and was also something that could not be absorbed into the male mainstream of art. It countered the apparent passivity of women by suggesting an active, generative role.[90] This combining of the body as site and cause of experience with enactment became a powerful method of self-transformation that was adopted by many women's centres in the 1970s.[91] At the time no one talked about bodily functions or sexual violence, so performances that focused on and opened up these issues were contentious.

Leah's Room (figure 3.3) was both an installation and a performance, and was based on Colette's novel *Chéri* (1920), which told of the ageing courtesan Leah, who needs all her survival skills to retain her younger lover, Chéri. The parallel between the kept status of Colette's fictional character and that of contemporary women who were economically dependent on their husbands runs through *Womanhouse*, but was specifically acted out in this room. The students made the bedroom very elegant, by going to an antique dealer and persuading him to lend them Victorian furniture. It was perfumed and

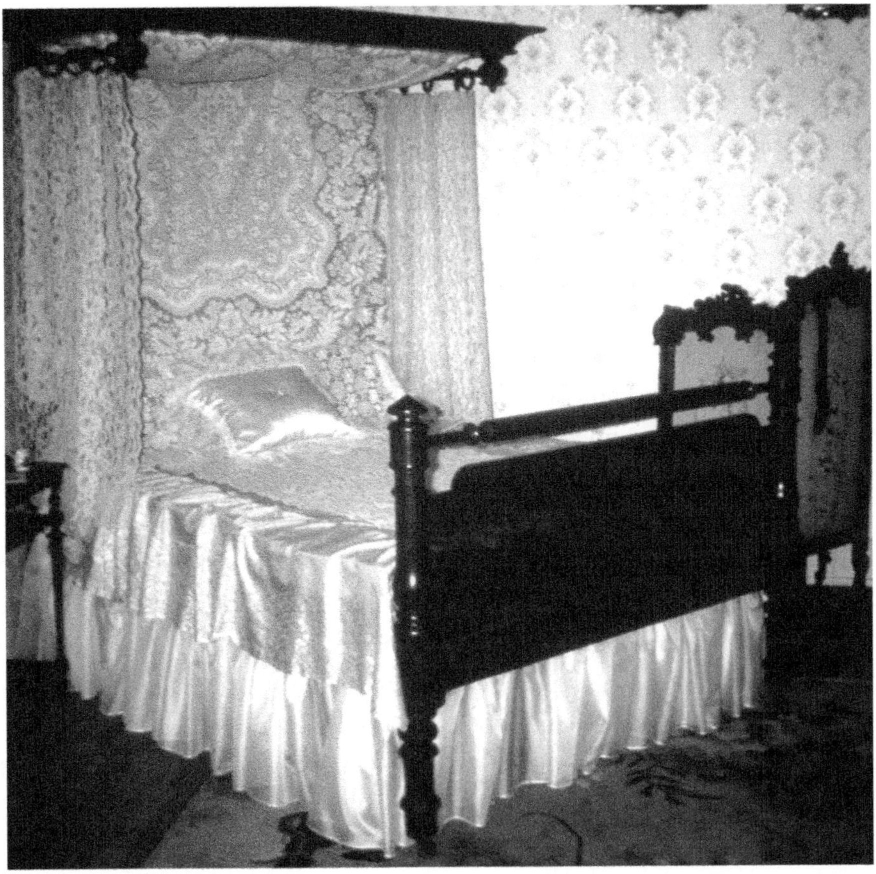

FIGURE 3.3 Karen LeCocq and Nancy Youdelman (performers), *Leah's Room* (based on a story by Colette), from *Womanhouse* (1972).

dense, with silver hairbrushes and lots of lace and satin.[92] In the performance, Leah – alternately performed by Karen LeCocq and Nancy Youdelman – sat in front of the mirror, repeatedly applying and removing make-up, in a way that suggested an almost desperate self-evaluation against a 'norm' of beauty. However, as suggested by some traditional *vanitas* paintings, which place an ageing but immodestly dressed woman in front of a mirror, age cannot be hidden for ever. Biological time weathers features, but in magazines the constant parade of images of the ideal, feminine woman against which real women were measured, was growing. The transformation from the natural to cultural frameworks of femininity were necessary for Leah in the novel, and also for many housewives at the time, as they sought to be nurturers and homemakers whilst remaining attractive.

One of the linchpins of the feminist movement in the late 1960s and 1970s was its condemnation of cosmetics. The perceived importance of make-up and fashion was articulated in certain installations in *Womanhouse*, including *Shoe Closet* by Beth Bachenheimer and *Lipstick Bathroom* by Camille Grey. As underlined in the magazines of the 1960s and 1970s, female beauty was no less artificial than that espoused by Baudelaire in the mid-nineteenth century.[93] Magazines like *Vogue* promoted adornment both through scent and make-up. 'Everything you always wanted to know about perfume but never thought of asking', boasted one *Vogue* article: 'A scentless woman is incomplete, lacking impact, not entirely present.'[94] The magazine *Ms.* countered this pressure with articles like 'Louis Gould faces her face…', which condemned make-up as artificial.[95]

A new approach was developed in feminist articles, whereby rather than being condemned for presenting a construction of femininity that required one to wear make-up and perfume, advertisements were analysed to understand their allure.[96] This was also considered by artists working outside *Womanhouse*, including Audrey Flack in her glossy, seductive, photorealist still-life paintings. *Chanel* (1974) and *Jolie Madame* (1972) were detailed and closely framed paintings of make-up tables, adorned with commodities, cosmetics and jewels, rendered in shiny Technicolor, thereby aping the many advertisements in magazines like *Vogue* and *Harper's Bazaar*.

While the photographs and performances in *Womanhouse* were of the moment, other artists extended this so that their performances lasted years and were very public. For instance, in 1973 Lynn Hershman created a series of manipulated photographs in a work called *Roberta Breitmore's Construction Chart*, which documented the transformation of the artist into a fictitious character called Roberta Breitmore. Her new persona had her own bank account, owned homes and had a driver's licence. Each photograph marking the transformational steps was annotated with bright cosmetic colours that defined and shaped areas of the face, together with dotted contour lines and handwritten notes suggesting improvements, similar to those given in magazines: 'Lighten with Dior eyestick light […] Shape lips with brush'; 'polish!'[97] The results were exaggeratedly strange, but also reflected the manipulation of promotions and advertisements, which, as John Berger said, are designed to make one feel dissatisfied, but hopeful that this will be rectified through consuming the offered products.[98]

John Berger's *Ways of Seeing*, a book based on a BBC television series of the same name broadcast in 1972, was first published in America in 1973, and was profoundly influential. It was radical in that it articulated how individuals and cultures are manipulated by the mass media. Berger argued that judgements about beauty, choices and values are not natural, but informed by a belief system. The second chapter was a photo essay that juxtaposed images of celebrities, mannequins and advertisements for make-up, deodorant and stockings with female nudes culled from the history of art. It made the point that contemporary notions of beauty and sexiness are constructions that build upon a legacy of ideal types.[99]

All of the installations and performances in *Womanhouse* centred on the roles played by women, their experiences and the media pressures on them. Chicago later wrote that male visitors were much less comfortable in the exhibition than women visitors. She argued that men were placed in the unusual position of being outside the cultural and everyday narratives being articulated, which was the normal experience of many women.[100] Schapiro wrote something very similar:

> When we did *Womanhouse*, we were scared to death, because it had never been done before – such a mammoth project, you know, on an idea that had never been set forth before. And the thing I think that impressed me so much [...] was when I saw women walk into that house and just gasp! Some of them crying. [...] There was never a word said; it was always the expression on the face, 'I know this. This is art, but I know what this is about. I know what this is about. I know what this is about.'[101]

AFTER *Womanhouse*

One of the many projects directly derived from and influenced by *Womanhouse* was Womanspace, the first cooperative women's gallery on the West Coast, which in turn led to the Women's Building.[102] After the end of the exhibition, the students published two books: *Anonymous Was a Woman* (1974) and *Art: A Woman's Sensibility* (1975). As is demonstrated by these and many other achievements, *Womanhouse* set an indelible mark in the sand of art made by women about women's experiences, not only in America but also in Europe. Many of the students who had worked on the project went on to become major artists in their own right.

Both Judy Chicago and Miriam Schapiro continued to make feminist work. The most famous of Chicago's works of the decade was the installation *The Dinner Party* (1974–9). Unlike Nochlin's 'Why have there been no great women artists?', which did not try to insert unremembered female artists into the argument, this work reinscribed the names of women who had been pivotal within culture.[103] The triangular arrangement of tables has place settings for 39 famous women, some historical and some mythical, each consisting of a textile, embroidered runner, gold chalices and utensils, and a ceramic plate decorated in ways that were intended to represent the named woman. At the empty centre are a further 999 names of women inscribed in gold. It is not my intention to discuss this work in detail – this has been rehearsed many times.[104] However, for the purposes of this chapter, there are some key elements to be noted. It was a collaborative project that brought together many different artists and overlooked artisans, who painted the ceramic plates and undertook the embroidery. The materials and techniques, especially of sewing and ceramic painting, were those that had been ignored in the histories of art. Rather than conforming to male elitist ideas of 'good' art, it is unabashedly bright and decorative.[105]

In 1972, Miriam Schapiro started to make what she termed 'femmage', in which materials associated with the home and female roles, including aprons and tea towels, and things that had been made using female techniques and creativity, such as hand-crocheted doilies, pulled and hooked work, cutting and appliqué, were combined with paint. These, in effect, rewrote the idea that abstraction was exclusively male – and instead put forward the notion that women had always been involved with this kind of art through collage and textiles. Likewise, the inclusion of everyday items addressed the trivialisation of artistic practice outside the mainstream.[106] Her first group of works, called Explosion Series, set pieces of fabric that revolved around a central axis against a geometric, abstract, painted backdrop, so that two areas of creativity formed a dialogue. They challenged the spatial expectations of modernism, while also referencing the female domain.[107] As Schapiro later wrote: 'I wanted to validate the traditional activities of women, to connect myself to the unknown women artists who had made quilts, who had done the invisible "women's work" of civilisation. I wanted to acknowledge them, to honor them.'[108]

This chapter has considered the initial phase of feminist art in California, which had a profound impact, not only on the art subsequently produced, but also on the way that that art has been received. As Jeremy Strick wrote in the opening of the catalogue to the 2007 exhibition *WACK!*:

> Feminism transformed social relations, personal identities, and institutional structures [...] it is difficult to overstate the movement's impact. The feminist revolution in art was no less radical and transformative [...] The very terms of current practice are made possible in numerous respects by the ground-breaking works produced by feminist artists in the 1960s and 1970s.[109]

4

Alienation

In the previous chapter I discussed how feminist artists in California during the 1970s presented the domestic space as a place of resistance. Rather than showing the positive and nurturing aspects traditionally equated with the home, these artists revealed the constraints and tensions created by the roles assigned to women, using techniques that either had few gender associations or were derived from domestic creativity. Through working together and being politically active they gave strength and legitimacy to the articulation of marginalised practices and subjective experiences.

This chapter will focus on artists whose work also describes alienation within the home. However, this work has different roots and is not only linked to gender. The first part will discuss the influence of Dada and surrealism on postwar art, with particular regard to those movements' articulation of Freud's ideas, as well as their artistic strategies. There will then be a discussion of more recent work that draws on an international and contemporary understanding of the Freudian notion of the *unheimlich*, the 'uncanny' – or, literally, the 'unhomely'.

The prewar movements of Dada and surrealism had a great influence on postwar art in both America and Europe. This was not only because of the migration of some of the key figures, including Marcel Duchamp, to America and the annual surrealist exhibitions at the Julien Levy Gallery in New York between 1932 and 1936, but also because of various postwar exhibitions held in New York, including that at the Sidney Janis Gallery in 1953, as well as important shows in Germany, such as the one at the Kunstverein in Düsseldorf in 1958 and in Paris at the Galerie de L'Institut in 1956.[1] Although this postwar development of Neo-Dada was contentious with many of the original Dada artists – Max Ernst, for instance, considered that Dada was an exploded bomb that did not need to be glued together again – nonetheless the original movement's artistic strategies and interest in non-rational depictions were influential.[2] The manifestation of their influence, including the incorporation of non-art practices and materials, and the blurring of boundaries between different methods of expression and between art and life, were discussed in Chapter 2. Of particular relevance for this chapter is the postwar development of surrealist strategies and ideas, and how Freud's ideas about the uncanny have been altered and revealed. Although the street was the primary focus for the male surrealists and the movements they influenced, including Fluxus, Neo-Dada and pop art, many of the female artists who were associated with the surrealists focused on ideas and roles associated with the home. Not all of the artists whose work is discussed here were surrealists, but what unites the work dealt with in this chapter is an element of psychological unease.

DADA, SURREALISM AND FREUD

The surrealists included artists and writers as diverse as André Breton, Marcel Duchamp, Max Ernst, George Grosz, Georges Bataille and Paul Éluard. Underpinning their ideas were the notions of difference, diversity and estrangement. These were mainly manifested in four ways: in the manner in which objects, images and exhibitions were constructed from diverse elements to suggest alternate realities; in the use of the 'feminine' as a central organising metaphor; in the diversity of means of making art so that the style itself could not suggest a 'school'; and in tapping into a world that was the antithesis to the logic of the machine age that surrounded them: a world of the bizarre, the erotic and the unconscious mind.[3] Rather than trying to depict this world from the outside, the surrealists attempted to work from the point of view of the unconscious and from a position of irrationality. Central was the place of 'woman', whom they thought of as being closer to madness, hysteria and the unconscious, and whom they made into an object of desire *and* a sign for desire. Central also was Sigmund Freud, who wrote about dreams, the unconscious mind and how relationships with the world and society are veiled by customs and accepted ideas of normality.[4] To be a surrealist was to live in an enhanced state of mind and express this in ways that did not give way to the habitual platitudes of artistic languages.[5]

The avowed surrealist antagonism towards family and bourgeois ideals, together with their urban focus, was integral to a broader perception of modernism as primarily a masculine movement. This idea was played out in the writings of critics and philosophers like Theodor Adorno and Martin Heidegger, who argued for a dynamic interpretation of modernity and modernism, discussing them as being about change, rootlessness and loss of stability.[6] This urban-focused reading has also been transferred onto understandings about the home, which, far from being entirely *heimlich*, can also be a site of unease and alienation.[7] For the surrealists, the spaces and structures of the home were a metaphor for the imagination and unconscious mind. Breton's house, 42 rue Fontaine in the Pigalle district of Paris, was his 'alchemist's lair', and was filled with diverse objects collected in markets and from the street. This integration of outside and inside, of the flow of diverse languages between each object and between Breton and the objects, was part of how the poetic life was pushed to the limit.[8]

However, the domestic environment requires the attention of 'female' labour, which, if done well, becomes invisible. For women surrealist artists the home was less a place of flourishing creativity, and more about the alienation created through their differently gendered roles: as muses, models and helpmates. Méret Oppenheim and Louise Bourgeois were two artists who were briefly affiliated with surrealism, and who, while not adhering to the masculine themes, utilised particular surrealist strategies to denaturalise ideologies and conventions.[9] These included the incorporation of found objects, odd juxtapositions, the use of non-art materials and making the familiar strange. Drawing on their subjective experiences and memories, many of their works revolved around female roles within the home, and subverted the apparently natural and effortless order of domestic life.

The surrealists read Freud's texts, including *The Interpretation of Dreams*, from which they gained ideas about the mechanisms of dreaming and how dreams can reveal latent desires, or collage together disparate elements in strange ways. They also read Freud's 1919 essay 'The uncanny', which is one of the few texts in which he relates his psychoanalytical ideas to aesthetics.[10] In this he explores feelings of dread, and how these come about, selecting examples from literature and everyday life. Using the example of E. T. A. Hoffmann's tale 'The Sandman', Freud argues that the uneasy feelings that are aroused during the reading of the story are caused only partly by the uncertainty about whether the mannequin called Olympia is alive or dead. For him the whole narrative, which tells of the Sandman, who steals the eyes of children and feeds them to his own children, something that Freud linked to a fear of castration, is imbued with horror. Another way that the uncanny could be felt was through doubling, either through catching sight of something in a mirror or through finding oneself repeating the same action unawares. This he believes arouses dread because it harks back to an early stage of development when one has not fully realised one's sense of self as separate from the world. But Freud's overriding argument is that people project onto everyday situations their own repressed impulses, and that within the everyday everyone can gain feelings of altered reality. While Freud clearly found this feeling hard to define, the *unheimlich*, to use the German term, represents a short-lived incursion into the normal experiences of everyday life.

Over subsequent decades there have been many rereadings and diverse interpretations of the uncanny, both as a concept, and within critiques of Freud's essay. These include studies of the uncanny within a nineteenth-century context that included Gothic narratives such as the short stories of Edgar Allan Poe and Mary Shelley's *Frankenstein*, more recent interpretations that consider it in relation to contemporary displacement through migration or the post-modern condition, and those that just consider how the familiar can appear strange. Nicholas Royle's book *The Uncanny* (2003) discusses these diverse interpretations.[11] His overarching thesis is that the uncanny involves feelings of uncertainty, in particular those involving one's sense of self and how that is fed through experiences. It is not just a feeling of alienation, but an experience of the unfamiliar within the familiar, such as when something strange appears at the heart of the home.[12] Rather than being something that can be represented in art, the uncanny is experienced through an instability within the self, a loss of a fixed point of reference, so that the imagination fills the gap.[13]

DOMESTIC OBJECTS

An exhibition of surrealist objects was held in May 1936 at the Charles Ratton gallery in Paris. Breton had suggested creating objects in 1924 after having a dream about a book with woollen pages bound with a wooden Assyrian gnome. This bringing together of different realities within an object was taken up by Alberto Giacometti and Salvador Dalí later that decade, with the first show of surrealist objects taking place in 1933.[14] The exhibitions of 1933 and 1936 juxtaposed objects in ways that mirrored the layout of contemporary art journals like *Cahiers d'art*, which frequently had photographs of ancient art and crafts adjacent to avant-garde art, or the book *Art without Epoch* by Ludwig Goldscheider (1937), which showed Ancient Egyptian, indigenous Canadian, Japanese and European art without any logical ordering to the sequences. The idea was that all art, past and present, and from different cultures, was contemporary and relevant.

The 1936 exhibition at the Charles Ratton gallery displayed crystals, tribal art and mathematical instruments, along with ready-mades by Duchamp, sculptures by Giacometti and a mobile by the American sculptor Alexander Calder.[15] These juxtapositions mirrored the collage that surrounds us in everyday life and that we accept as normal. Writing later, Gaston Bachelard discussed the interpenetration of our pasts within the present, considering that everything 'comes alive when contradictions accumulate'.[16] But, more than this, these juxtapositions can also be triggers for the uncanny. While each object might be familiar, or have familiar elements, it is their coming together that encourages the viewer to hover perceptually between a known past that unfolds in the memory and an evolving present.[17]

Half hidden within a glass-fronted cabinet at the exhibition, Méret Oppenheim's *Object: Breakfast in Fur* (1936) was displayed. This store-bought cup, saucer and spoon, which she had covered with Chinese gazelle fur, was purchased by Alfred H. Barr Jr and became an iconic work after being shown at his exhibition *Fantastic Art, Dada, Surrealism* at the Museum of Modern Art in New York later that year.[18] Gazelle fur is attractive in that we wish to touch it, to stroke it, but repellent when thought of in conjunction with the lips. This contradiction of feelings is partially caused by the interplay of two expected narratives. The relationship of touch and vision also encourages a reflexivity that, for the empathetic viewer, can collapse the active and passive aspects of touching and being touched.[19] Oppenheim's manipulation and juxtaposition of materials and objects were akin to surrealist free association, where a clash between the different materials and objects created space for a more layered interpretation.[20] *Object: Breakfast in Fur* has also been interpreted by Renée Riese Hubert as alluding to the feminine: the fur relating to an expensively clothed woman and the hollow round shapes referring to female genitalia.[21]

Oppenheim continued to collect a broad range of materials that she incorporated into her work, which included fashion and jewellery as well as object sculptures. Her materials ranged from the exotic, like fur, to the banal, like plastic or imitation lizard skin, even to garbage picked up from the street. As Breton wrote in the catalogue to the Ratton show, 'Every piece of debris should be considered a precipitate of our desire.'[22]

Oppenheim refused the many requests to make another *Object: Breakfast in Fur*, but instead made *Squirrel* in 1969 – a beer mug with a squirrel tail attached. In being a male counterpart to *Object: Breakfast in Fur*, it was an ironic comment related to traditional still-life representations, and the gendering of objects and materials. Still-life paintings can be seen on one level as depictions of consumption in an increasingly bourgeois Europe. However, the starched tablecloths, cooked meals and cleaned copper pots of traditional still lifes appear ready-made, without the effort and hours of toil being revealed.[23] In these and in traditional genre scenes women were represented as the gatekeepers of domestic order and harmony. *Object: Breakfast in Fur*, with its cup, saucer and teaspoon, suggests the domestic space and its rituals, while subverting polite etiquette and expectations. The body of *Squirrel*, by contrast, is a beer mug, such as would be used by men in bars, and therefore in the public sphere. Both objects expose the mythic quality of gendered roles and traditional representations, and thus destabilise these narratives.

Oppenheim's *Souvenir of Breakfast in Fur* (1970), a kitschy, colourful, two-dimensional framed collage was inspired by souvenirs that the artist saw in Turin.[24] In its use of soft materials and decorative means it also has links with feminist art of the time that drew on domestic creativity, and insisted that the decorative could carry content. In this work the cup, saucer and spoon were made in appliquéd fur, and laid on a damask place mat that was set against an elaborately embroidered pink background with plastic flowers arranged at the bottom. It suggested the home-made pictures – hung on the walls of pioneer houses or shown in films like Buster Keaton's *The Scarecrow* (1920) – that extolled the virtues of 'Home sweet home'.

The docility of place settings could also subverted by including repulsive and unexpected imagery. Lee Miller's photograph from 1929 *Severed Breast from Radical Surgery in a Place Setting (Still Life – Amputated Breast on Plate)*, for instance, was a photograph of a neatly severed 'breast' served on a plate within a formal setting, complete with ironed mat and carefully arranged cutlery. This tactic of suggesting the memory of a fixed and unified reality while giving it different slants creates a fluctuation in the mind between two understandings. It is this uncertain wavering that constitutes one form of the contemporary uncanny.[25]

Another motif that female surrealist artists adopted was the caged woman, unable to escape from her home and role. This was an image used frequently in male surrealist art as an extension of the male idea of the female muse. Giacometti's *The Palace at 4 a.m.* (1932), for instance, was inspired by a fictive woman who transported the artist to a constant state of enchantment and with whom he would construct a fragile palace out of matchsticks every night. It shows a woman drifting alone within a many-roomed cage. In Man Ray's *Mannequin with a Bird Cage over Her Head* (1938–66), the mannequin is shown looking through the open door, but gagged with a flower, and with other flowers under her armpits, and feathers for pubic hair. Jane Graverol, however, parodied this in her painting *The Celestial Prison* (1963), which showed an angel standing on the bar within a birdcage.

LOUISE BOURGEOIS – HOME AND MEMORY

It was Louise Bourgeois' many drawings and sculptures from the 1940s in the Femme Maison series that continued this notion of entrapment and began her lifelong artistic exploration of the woman in the home.[26] Although she denied that she was a surrealist, preferring to be thought of as independent of art movements, she knew many of the artists and was particular friends with Marcel Duchamp.[27] Many of her early drawings and paintings suggest the confined woman, a theme that she was to develop in marble and other sculptural materials.[28] A series of drawings from 1945 show the upper part of the body encased within a roomed house, with small, inadequate arms protruding from the sides and the suggestion of breasts within. The constrained parts are ill formed, whereas the legs and lower body are robust and, although not finished and smooth, cartoons of the 'ideal' sensual body. The disparity of parts suggests the surrealist game of 'exquisite corpse', in which a drawing or poem would be begun at the top of a sheet of paper by one artist, which was then folded over and passed on to the next artist to draw their contribution. This would continue so that at each stage the artist or writer would add to the whole unaware of what had been created before. Only at the end was it unfolded so that the complete picture or poem could be seen. The idea was that through artistic contagion the unconscious personality of the group would be revealed.

Bourgeois was interested in the links between one's physical home and psychological dwelling, and it can be argued that she remained at least partially trapped within the houses of her past, something that was evident in both her writing and art: 'Remember that I have done many works representing myself as the Femme Maison.' Or again, when discussing her ideas and work: 'they are the history of my life. I try to make them come out of the shadows and make them appear under the light of the present.'[29] One of her earliest memories was of being co-opted into helping repair tapestries for the family business by drawing cartoons of lower limbs and weaving them. As Jan Garden Castro has speculated, this concentration on the lower part of the body might have had something to do with her height as a child – could she not reach higher? Her recollection of working on the tapestries may also have been conflated with childhood memories of being under a table looking at her parents' legs.[30]

From the 1960s Bourgeois explored the idea of mental and physical dwelling in a series of works in latex and plaster. Many pieces from this period lose their obvious figurative allusions and move away from a directly gendered exploration, suggesting instead the animal need for shelter and comfort. These amorphous shapes appear to have none of the aesthetic and cultural overtones of the home. *Lair* or *Winter Refuge* (1963), made of latex and on a scale normally associated with domestic sculpture, perplexed critics when first shown at the Stable Gallery in 1964. Michael Fried, for instance, considered this and the other works in the solo exhibition to be failures, both because the materials made him unable to think of the work as 'finished', and because he felt that the forms resembled entrails.[31]

Bourgeois' works are linked to her own traumas, and she acknowledged that the physical aspects of both making the work and the end result were about exorcising and repairing the damage inflicted by life.[32] She said that she needed her memories, and surveyed and incorporated them into her sculptures.[33] However, this was not an example of Proust's madeleine, whereby a particular action or sensation acts like a trigger, transporting one back through time to relive memories from one's past. For Bourgeois her work was a balance between the past and the future, with memories crystallising into shapes, images and metaphors.[34] Unlike the earlier works, the Cells series, which began in 1986 with *Articulated Lair* and continued until the artist's death in 2010, consisted of room-like structures that incorporated a variety of materials, and juxtaposed made and found objects to create an atmosphere of unease. Like the surrealists she did not want to dictate their interpretations: 'The work has to speak for itself. The work may be subject to many interpretations, but only one in the mind of the artist.'[35]

The name 'cell' alludes to something biological and regenerative, and also to prisons and confinement, and the works frequently play with this paradox. The incorporation of mirrors, broken windows, worn metal mesh or containing door–walls that allow only partial views through slits, places the viewer in the uncomfortable position of being a voyeur, of intruding into a private space, of glimpsing a reflected interior while being kept outside. *Articulated*

Lair played with the idea of a transient and flexible place of safety, which Bourgeois linked to her earlier notion of a nest or animal's retreat.[36] She felt comfortable in the installation, and photographs show her sitting on a stool surrounded by the tall, hinged and concertinaed panels. Attached to these were matt-black, rubber, organic objects hung on black steel bands, which resembled nothing, yet instigate a free association of ideas. As Bourgeois has said, she never incorporated things that could be read literally, but she used 'analogy and interpretation and leaps of all kinds'.[37]

Red Rooms (1994) is a pair of installations made up of a mother and father's bedroom and a child's room, each containing disparate objects. Both are surrounded by a spiral of found doors that have been hinged together. Able to see through the cracks but unable to access the rooms, the viewer once again becomes a voyeur, especially in the case of the parents' room, whose interior can only be viewed as a reflection in a long mirror. This suggests some of the strategies of Duchamp, as in *Étant donnés* (1946–66), in which the viewer is confronted with a door with two peepholes, through which part of a dead, naked, female body, with legs spread, lying within a landscape, is visible. While Duchamp's work is a layered set of ironic comments about the nude in art, Bourgeois' work is related both to the sexuality in art that was overt within surrealism, and also to postwar American installation practices in which the personal and cultural were entwined.

As in all of Bourgeois' works, and like those of Rauschenberg and Segal, the found objects and furniture incorporated into *Red Rooms* have a history of usage revealed in their obvious wear. These become laden with metaphorical and symbolic associations that flow between the two installations, and reflect both the artist's memories and those that are more universal.

Red Room (Child) (figure 4.1) is a chaotic space that has overtones of violence. It is not simply a child's room, but contains the shadow of adult control, such as the bobbins of red thread, which indicate both Bourgeois' family history of textile renovation and also the three Fates in Greek mythology, who control the thread of life, which they cut once one's apportioned lifespan is over. There are also things that suggest the process and display of sculpture, such as a group of joined cast, waxy hands and arm fragments, which are emotively flexed and arranged together on a circular plinth. Auguste Rodin

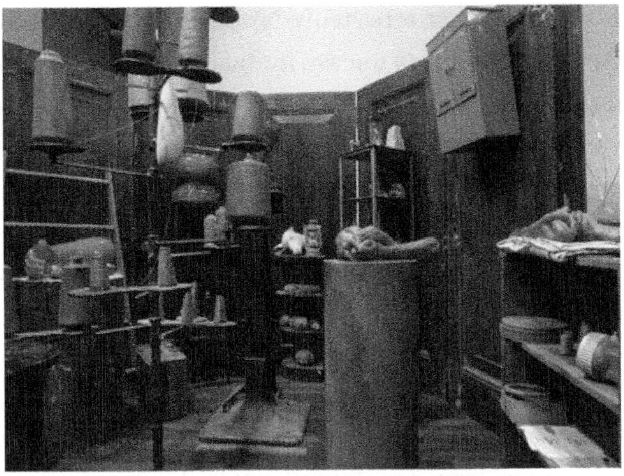

FIGURE 4.1 Louise Bourgeois, *Red Room (Child)* (1994).

and other nineteenth-century sculptors kept plaster fragments of the body, especially hands, for reference, something of which Bourgeois was clearly aware.[38] Like many of the other objects in the cell, these are red, and, in the case of a single, swollen arm and hand on the left, shiny and repulsive. Other elements, like a bookcase, a jar of coins, an old suitcase and some knitted mittens, relate to her childhood, but are part of most people's childhoods. The installation should not be seen as a collection of things as such, but related to Bourgeois' collection of 'spaces and memories'.[39] The conflation of found objects that suggest the 'real' with objects that have mythic overtones and historical precedents, together with those that the imagination has turned into repulsive objects, collapses the stability of meaning and allows the audience to project its own anxieties onto the work.

Like *Red Room (Child)*, *Red Room (Parents)* overlaps childish and adult presences and the two are also linked through colour, texture and mood. The entrance to the parents' room is blocked, and only seen through reflection, which places the viewer on the same footing as the child, who is to be kept out of the private space at particular times. The idea of a child wandering into a parent's bedroom and actually seeing or imagining the parents having intercourse suggests Freud's 'primal space'.[40] Bourgeois continually suggested that her work was an exorcism of her memories, and one of her major childhood traumas was that her father repeatedly brought home his mistresses.[41] The presence of the child within an uneasy, intimate adult space is also suggested in the installations by the shiny red, rubber bedcover in *Red Room (Parents)*, which contrasts with the cushion embroidered with '*je t'aime*' and the child's xylophone and train at the bottom of the bed. The mirror, with its suggestion of doubling, the strange forms that trigger unease and the exclusion and partial revelation all suggest the dread that Freud discussed in 'The uncanny'.

The schism within the artist's family is also suggested in her *Cell (Choisy)* (1990–3), in which a marble model of her family home is shown dwarfed within a high cage, with a large guillotine hanging above it. The actual house has since been destroyed, but in the installation the model exists as a pristine edifice carved from a sculptural material that represents traditional establishment ideals of 'high' art and 'good' taste. While families keep things under wraps, Bourgeois wanted to show the split in the family, the lurking violence.[42] She wrote that her use of enclosures for her Cells was intended to represent a section of her memories that was to be eradicated, but the high metal fence in this work is because she felt imprisoned by those memories.[43]

Bourgeois was acquainted with Freud's ideas, and in an article in 1990 she speculated about the collection of art and artefacts that Freud had in his house.[44] She thought that they were a comfort to him against hearing the contents of the broken minds of others. For her they were not real art – which has absolute value and is reality – but were artefacts isolated from their original function, which had attained cultural and personal symbolic value. These ideas are relevant when considering the Cells series, as many juxtapose found objects that most have in their homes.

Bourgeois retained old clothes and materials, believing that they were the raw material of her art, and that they had the potential to express different feelings.[45] She often included clothes in her works as they both hide and reveal.[46] As many were presents, they also revealed how others saw her.[47] *Cell VII* (1998) included outer garments and sleepwear, which are instantly understood in a tactile and almost instinctively comforting manner. It also included a model of her family house at Choisy, a table, a cupboard and old oddments. The cupboard suggests the idea that both Bachelard and Bourgeois discussed: that of containing secrets. Looking into a cupboard is to be confronted with different roles, smells and social situations, but it is also where one keeps things that are private and away from view.[48] For her these materials and objects were the means of transforming everyday memories into art. But, as she said, often it was only when the work was finished that she understood what it was meant to be.[49]

The appropriation of familiar items and their redefinition within art contexts brings to the fore many arguments about artistic agency, originality and replication. The original use of found objects, their framing within photographs and the odd juxtapositions created in surrealist exhibitions were situated within their era and cultural context, and were intended to subvert establishment norms. By the 1990s appropriation had a history. Dada and surrealism had become institutionally accepted, the conceptual-art movement of the late 1960s had championed art as idea and installation had been absorbed into the mainstream. The idea of a ready-made being the bearer of ideas was firmly established as a trope within art, rather than being a way of destabilising social narratives.

Walter Benjamin described dwelling as repeated activities and habitual behaviours, in which gradually the physical aspects become intermingled with the imagination and the inhabitant and the material dwelling become adapted to each other. Through manipulation and constant small changes, an internal logic of the home is created, so that the personality and habits of those living there are revealed.[50] However, Bourgeois' juxtapositions upset this map of continuous presents and unity of purpose. For the viewer many objects are recognisable from his or her own life and trigger his or her memories. Each object has its own propositional content that then becomes subverted through juxtaposition.

Bourgeois' reflexive defamiliarisation of the real world, something that originated with the surrealists, was also a tool used by Mona Hatoum in her installations from the late 1990s. Like Bourgeois, Hatoum has created installations that combine familiar domestic objects in ways that render them strange. Both artists, consciously or unconsciously, draw on their personal backgrounds, and incorporate and manipulate objects in ways that destabilise the gaze of the viewer and bridge the gap between the material and imaginative worlds.

MONA HATOUM – EXILE AND THE CONTEMPORARY UNCANNY

Like many people living in London, and indeed like Bourgeois, who moved from France to New York, Mona Hatoum is living in a country that is not her place of origin. She was born in Beirut to a Palestinian family, studied at the Slade, and from the mid-1970s used London as her base when it became difficult to return to her country. However, rather than being settled, she considers herself a nomad, travelling the world for exhibitions and residencies.[51]

Travel and dislocation are related but different. Both suggest mobility, in which one enters an alternative state of existence, but dislocation, which I would link to being a nomad, implies a state of being in flux.[52] Hatoum's work references her Middle Eastern background, living in a foreign country and the differences between opposing historical–cultural horizons.[53] A home, for an exile, oscillates between the appearance of a stable present and the reality of an absent past.[54] Like Bourgeois' installations, Hatoum's work is related to her identity, but in her case she draws on personal experiences of displacement and alienation to communicate universal experiences of conflict and migration. This destabilising of identity has been identified as a feature in recent interpretations of the uncanny, in which, through the multi-faceted complexity of post-modern identity and the effects of global migrations, a unified sense of self has given way to a perpetual engagement with difference.[55] For people who have moved, feelings of estrangement and alienation have become normal rather than an unusual state unexpectedly disrupting the everyday flow of ordered existence.[56]

Hatoum has an ambiguous attitude to the ideals of the home and its implications of nurture and safety, and as a result many of her works about the domestic have been given a sharp and uncanny edge.[57] Resistance to the idea of the home as natural and comforting has been a particular focus since 1970s feminism, and has manifested itself in literature, architecture and art. In many of these articulations the uncanny home is the setting that suggests the destabilised self.[58] *Home* (1999) was the first of three large installations in which Hatoum made neutral objects associated with cooking threatening

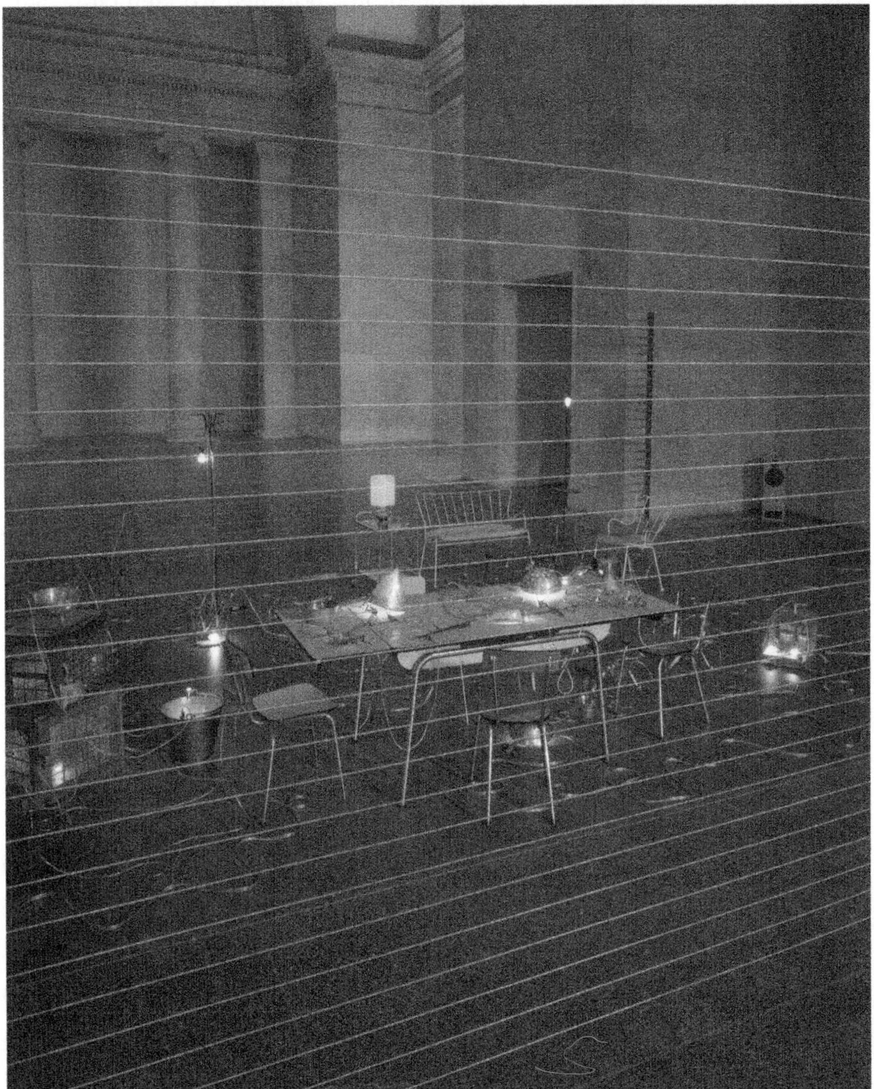

FIGURE 4.2 Mona Hatoum, *Homebound* (2000).

and alien through their staging. The two later works were *Sous Tension* (1999) and *Homebound* (2000; figure 4.2).[59] In *Home* electric cables run through everyday utensils, which have been arranged on a polished wooden table, with a computer program that periodically turns on lights hidden underneath them with greater and lesser intensity, and speakers that amplify the buzz of the undulating electric current. This was staged behind a screen of parallel horizontal wires. The cooking aids are familiar. However, like the tactic used by Méret Oppenheim of suggesting one stable narrative and overlaying it with another, the apparent homely care has been detached from context and rendered uncomfortable.

Home is a development from a body of smaller works in which everyday utensils have been altered to make them aggressive and unusable. *No Way* and *No Way III* of 1996 were a steel ladle and colander respectively, which had bolts sticking from them. Unlike Bourgeois' found objects these were pristine and shiny, with the additions appearing to be integral to them. They acted in a similar fashion to Man Ray's *Cadeau* (1921), which was an iron that confounded expectations and function by having a line of nails sticking out from the smoothing surface. In both Hatoum's work and that of Man Ray, the objects have become edged with an aggression that affects the subject physically and mentally.

In her exhibition in Tate Britain's Duveen Galleries in 2000, Hatoum showed *La grande broyeuse (Mouli-Julienne x 21)* – a larger version of a work from the previous year – and *Homebound*, which was a more complex work than *Home*. As with the earlier works the empathetic body of the viewer was brought into play. *La grande broyeuse (Mouli-Julienne x 21)* stood four metres high, stretching up to the arches of the gallery and dwarfing the viewer. *Homebound* brought together a range of domestic furniture, including an armchair, a clothes stand, a trolley and a standard lamp, and also, as in *Home*, different pieces of cooking equipment, including funnels and graters, which were arranged on a table. Here again Hatoum had amplified the sound of the electric current running through cables connecting all the metal objects, and the whole was set behind a screen of horizontally stretched wire threads. As well as the menace evident in the installation, the title *Homebound* suggests a conflict of emotions: a sense of being on the way home but also being tied to its restraining roles and confining walls. The strangeness within the familiar and the fluctuations set up by the destabilised meanings within both title and installation suggest the uncanny.[60]

All of the elements, like those of *Home*, were hard, functional and suggested 1950s and 1960s furnishings. In this era there was a clear demarcation of materials used within the various rooms of a home, with efficiency, hygiene and standardisation being the fashion for kitchens. The bright-yellow, Formica-topped extendable table, with red Formica seats with chrome legs, used in *Homebound* was typical of the time. Hygiene was promoted in the kitchen through easy-clean surfaces, and cooking was made practical for the housewife through a range of devices, including funnels, sieves and graters. Although not like post-1980s consumer goods, which were designed according to a greater range of socially nuanced desires, these products were part of the new aesthetics of a desirable home. They suggested modernity and nurture, where the wife should be able to cook meals from scratch, which the family would then eat together.

Ursula Panhans-Bühler has argued that Hatoum's repeated use of these kitchen objects represents a resistance to her expected domestic role, as well as the power struggles played out within the private and public spheres.[61] Hatoum grew up in a culture in which the ability to cook was part of one's preparation for marriage, although Hatoum has said that this did not apply in her family.[62] *Homebound*, which references the past in its choice of furnishings, and dislocation through the oddness of its juxtapositions and empathetic fear of the electric currents, suggests the fragmentation inevitable in memory. Objects are displaced in time and context, and by confounding expectations they become simultaneously real and foreign.[63] As well as suggesting an inaccessible past that can be altered in the mind, Hatoum also dramatises the archetypal conflict between two conceptions of human existence: that of the self-contained individual and that of the person as one element within a complex social structure.[64]

Hatoum has described the body as a 'starting point' through which the world is perceived using all the senses, and which gives rise to meaning and associations after the initial physical contact.[65] As well as using hard surfaces, electrification and implied danger, she has also used increased scale to create feelings of unease in the viewer. *La grande broyeuse (Mouli-Julienne x 21)* (2000), *Slicer* (1999) and *Grater Divide* (2002) all reference cooking tools, but their augmented size, measured against that of the viewer, makes them occupy a strange perceptual place between functional and sculptural object. Hatoum is by no means the only artist to play with scale since the 1990s – Ron Mueck and Gavin Turk have done the same thing – but in her work the huge increase in the size of what should be hand-held tools disrupts 'everything, from [...] form and function to [...] interpretation and meaning'.[66] This increase in scale, as opposed to merely size, removes *La grande broyeuse (Mouli-Julienne x 21)* from the everyday and makes it metaphorical.[67] Because humans have constructed the world to conform to the needs and the size of the body, there is an internalised map of comforting expectation. Enlargement in itself creates a sense of alienation, putting us into the strange worlds of *Alice in Wonderland* or *Gulliver's Travels.*

Hatoum wanted to explore the phenomenology of space and materials, so that the audience would experience the works through physical interaction.[68] As Susan Stewart has discussed, the experience of roughness and smoothness takes time, and it is this time taken in touching that becomes empathetically reciprocated through feeling the textures and temperatures of the object being handled.[69] *La grande broyeuse (Mouli-Julienne x 21)* is based on a hand food processor such as might have been found in kitchens before they were filled with electrical gadgets. They were practical and efficient in turning vegetables into uniform, matchstick-sized chunks, and like graters and slicers the blades were very sharp. In contrast, the wooden knob, loosely turning on the metal handle, was formed to fit the hand and was strangely comforting. In its enlarged state this device becomes confrontational, prompting viewers into thinking about the possibility of their own bodies being reduced to neat shavings. As so frequently in her works, it is the vulnerability of the body that is the source of disquiet. The looming sculpture creates its own environment independent of its original space and function.[70]

In 'Domus and the megalopolis', Jean-François Lyotard considers two aspects of existence, one within the private homestead and one within the city.[71] The home, he argues, is a constructed myth and as such is problematic. The simple rhythms of domesticity that control everything and give a feeling of order are being increasingly impinged upon by the alienation and violence of the city. Freud did not explore the space of domesticity as psychologically determined and perceived.[72] He suggested that the familiar and homely could be perceived as unfamiliar and unhomely through the use of narrative devices, creating an atmosphere and exposing childhood dreads. An encounter with Hatoum's works, in which several narratives oscillate in the consciousness of the viewer and refuse closure, suggests the alien within the familiar. These narratives refer both to the haptic knowledge we carry within us and a collective historical consciousness of art and life.[73]

GREGOR SCHNEIDER – UNHOMELY SPACES

Since 1985 Gregor Schneider has been reconfiguring a house, which is owned by the lead mine in which his family worked for generations, in Rheydt, a borough of the German city of Mönchengladbach. It is on the outskirts of the town, and from the outside appears to be normal and suburban. However, over the intervening years he has built walls, created rooms within rooms and made a place where expectations and perceptions are continually thwarted. This project, entitled *Totes Haus ur* (*Dead House ur*), was constructed within an area already becoming a ghost town owing to the poisonous fumes and economic downturn.[74] Schneider is interested in places that become charged through traumatic events, and says that although things might be over, they leave their traces. In the area near the house, stretches have been given over to opencast mining, so that houses and villages have been lost. Nature has started to take over some of the neighbourhood, but, when one walks around, unexpected areas of pavement or domestic trees can be found. 'That is when you get the strongest sense of a time shift.'[75]

On visiting the house, viewers become disorientated as the door shuts behind them and they find themselves within a labyrinth of narrow corridors, crawl spaces and claustrophobic rooms, one of which rotates, and in others the walls or ceiling move. The height of ceilings, size of openings and length of passageways have been altered, and an unexpected draught has been created by a ventilator.[76] The visitors apparently have a choice about which route to take, but some doors are sealed, other spaces are dark and some are filled with objects. Getting deeper into the house there is the realisation that there is no obvious exit, and, even if one has been before, the fact that Schneider is constantly making and remaking means that one's experience and sense of orientation changes. He has lined rooms with sound insulation and lead, so that the outside cannot permeate inside and vice versa, a notion he also explored in his two *Completely Insulated Boxes* (1986), each measuring one cubic metre, in which he imagined someone trapped inside and unable to communicate with the outside world.[77] The lead references both his family history and also that of Germany and the lead-lined death chambers of the Holocaust.[78]

The idea of making sealed rooms, of accessible/inaccessible spaces and of the visitor becoming a performer, has echoes of a project by Bruce Nauman from 1972, in which he conceived of a sealed, buried room that was only visible by television monitor in the house next door.[79] This was one of a number of projects from the late 1960s to 1973 in which the artist reflected on how one can feel disorientated or tense when in spaces that are cramped or enlarged. Some corridors that he built were too narrow to enter; some rooms were too uncomfortable. One, dating from 1968, was a small, domestic-scale room apparently devoid of any objects, but with speakers buried in the walls from which a voice repeatedly intoned: 'Get out of my mind, get out of this room.' The source of this voice was hidden from the visitor, making it more alarming and disorientating.[80] However, most of these works were built within the gallery, so that they were framed within a set of expectations.

The house that Schneider is altering is within the everyday world, so that the visitor sees it in its natural context and expects the normal progression of experiences of real life. Schneider constantly plays with this expectation. One of the techniques he employs is to use artifice to create apparent reality. The few windows that there are do not open to the outside but onto more windows and ultimately a wall.[81] Furthermore, he has fabricated natural light and ventilation that he can adjust at will, so that there is a sense of complete disorientation with regard to actual time.[82] Some of the rooms have the appearance of completion. Some are empty, but others contain furnishings and family mementoes, originally because he was living there, but also as a way to suggest histories and states of being. In this there are echoes of the

Dada artist Kurt Schwitters, who gradually altered his home in Hanover in the 1930s in a work called *Merzbau*. The walls were extended into the lived spaces and housed mementoes of his friends. As he took people around, each object or image buried within the walls was commented on and linked to an anecdote. These tours were long and uneasy.[83]

Some of the rooms in *Totes Haus ur* suggest eroticism, like *Whorehouse*, *The Large Wank* and *Love Nest*, which has a bed, white sheets, glasses, food, a bathtub and a washbasin.[84] They are also reminiscent of Dada and surrealism, like Duchamp's *The Bride Stripped Bare by Her Bachelors, Even (The Large Glass)*, or some of the erotic works by the German surrealist Hans Bellmer. The surrealists did not search for the comfort of bourgeois love, but sought that which was tantalisingly unattainable or verging on the sadistic.

Other influences on Schneider include nineteenth-century literature, such as Edgar Allan Poe's short story 'The Tell-Tale Heart', in which the murderer is haunted by the beating sound of his victim's heart buried below the floorboards, Joris-Karl Huysmans' novel *Against Nature* and Nathaniel Hawthorne's Gothic tale *The House of the Seven Gables*.[85] In all of these stories, particular places became imbued with the legacy of their histories and charged with present desires.

The installation entitled *Die Familie Schneider* (figure 4.3), which Gregor Schneider made in 2004, when he adapted two small adjoining houses in east London, 14 and 16 Walden Street, addressed many similar issues to his adaptations of the house in Germany. It created the doubling and uneasy narratives that, as Freud, Nicholas Royle and Dylan Trigg have suggested, make situations uncanny, subverted expected bodily experiences of space and tactility within the home, and suggested the temporal displacement of a previous era.[86] Visitors received a formal card announcing an 'at-home' at *Die Familie Schneider*, specifying that the visit was by appointment only and giving the main commissioning body – Artangel – as the contact.[87] The houses could only be visited by two people at a time, with only one allowed in each home at a time. The visitors collected the keys from a small nearby office; each would go into one of the houses and after ten minutes would come out and swap keys with the other.[88] They were allowed to roam through the small kitchen and living room, up the stairs to the bedroom and bathroom – both without

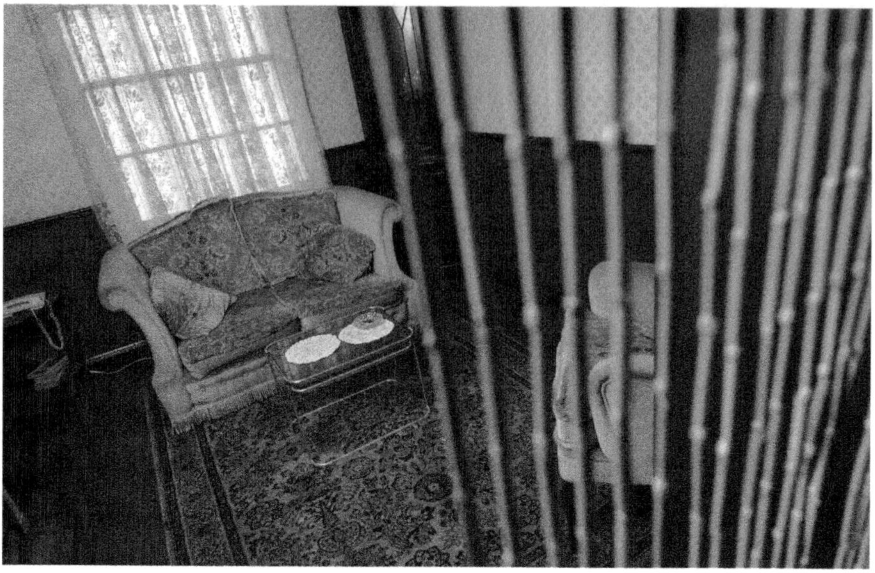

FIGURE 4.3 Gregor Schneider, *Die Familie Schneider* (2004).

windows – and down into the dark cellar. Although the original houses were already small, at the direction of the artist the rooms had been made slightly smaller still, which was sensed by the body and also placed the visitors in closer proximity to the actors.[89] Each house contained a man, a woman and a child, who had identical counterparts, performing identical actions, in the other house, something that echoed Freud's idea of doubling. The women were perpetually washing up, the children hiding under bin liners and the two men hunched under weak showers, masturbating.[90] Particularly unnerving was the fact that these actions carried on as if the visitor were not there, and indeed one appeared to be unseen by those within. Had one intruded into the private lives of others by mistake? More disturbing still was that when one stepped into the second house it was revealed to be an exact double of the first.

This was not the Gothic horror of nineteenth-century literature, but something deeper. Dread suffused the installation, which folded back onto the viewer.[91] The author Andrew O'Hagan described his visit as one that brought to the fore a childhood memory of frequently passing a tenement flat in Glasgow, where an elderly lady had been murdered nearly a century earlier. The sense of awe, the idea that the place might be haunted, that absence might be present, made him frequently stop and peer up at the windows.[92] His vivid memory was triggered by the idea that in some way Schneider's twin houses were haunted, or that perhaps he was the person doing the haunting. Just as Hatoum's works rely on a broad range of senses, so this split installation prompted a broadly sensory and visceral response.

Although according to Freud in 'The uncanny' a feeling of unease is provoked by doubling and the sense of living the same thing repeatedly, it is also aroused in this work by half-forgotten memories of dark hallways, worn brown carpets, dirty flocked wallpaper and overt dysfunctionality, which trigger actual memories of tense films in the mind of the viewer.[93] As explored in the essay by Freud, the uncanny is not actually out there, but felt reflexively within the audience.[94] When one cannot find a resolution to an experience, certainty ruptures and fantasy fills the gaps.[95] This fracture prompts the viewer to consider the incomplete nature of consciousness, something that suggests Jacques Derrida's idea about haunted memories, which he termed 'hauntology'.[96]

In *Die Familie Schneider* the idea of the fragmentation of consciousness as opposed to historical unity was evident in the displacement experienced by the visitor between the outside world and the recently entered house. The living room suggested continuing life, through shopping left under the television, the drinking glasses and photos, and the characters were apparently acting in real time. But the decoration and furnishings of the houses evoked the 1970s home of a lower-middle-class family with limited aspirations. Schneider's 'homes', although complete in themselves, destabilised the expectations of the viewing audience, while simultaneously evoking memories and affirming the disruption and fragmentation of their temporal continuity.[97]

All of the works discussed in this chapter relate to ideas of the uncanny. The surrealists' explorations of different states of consciousness and the non-rational were influential for postwar artists, and were developed and made relevant for later eras. Freud's ideas about the uncanny, which have been reinterpreted over the years as society has changed, were important for creating ideas of displacement and dread. In the gap between the viewer and installations, the known everyday and suggested fictions, that flickering and oscillating uncertainty speaks of the contemporary uncanny.

5
The Unmade House

This chapter will consider how artists since the 1970s in America and Britain have cut into, made casts of and photographed abandoned homes in order to make social and political comments about underlying systems of power, and to illuminate the feelings people have about their personal spaces. Two artists whose work will be featured are Gordon Matta-Clark and Rachel Whiteread, both of whom have altered and destroyed houses. The setting of these works in the real world allowed the artists to articulate the political and social tensions of the areas in which the houses were situated, with the edges of the works bleeding into and having dialogues with their contexts. Making works outside institutions also meant that they had more control over the projects and were not constrained by the funding and expectations of galleries. However, many of the works discussed also have 'souvenirs' and documentation that are seen in the gallery. The different display situations and how they relate to perception will be discussed. The final artist who will be considered is Steffi Klenz, who takes photographs of areas of towns and cities that, while showing no people, suggest presence. Nummianus (2008) is a photographic frieze of a poor area of a city that has been almost abandoned, leaving the houses in a dilapidated state, while traces of previous occupancy remain.

The ruin has been an important emotive and imaginative feature of art since the Renaissance, when the life cycles of buildings were linked to those of humans and cultures. In the art and texts that have expressed these ideas over the centuries and in the contemporary work discussed in this chapter, there is an exploration of the permeable boundaries between art and life, absence and presence, and past and present.

THE ORGANIC HOME AND THE RUIN

One of the major preoccupations of the American artist Robert Gober in 1982–3 was a painting on a board, measuring roughly 28 centimetres by 36, called *Chests*. Over time, the image morphed from one idea to the next as he scraped back the previous work and then built up the next layers of paint and imagery. At frequent intervals he would take a photographic slide, so that when edited down to be shown in an exhibition, the images would track the progress of his ideas. His intention was for it to be a 'memoir of a painting', which would be as much about the process of removal and application as about the imagery that bled from one idea to another.[1] The first few images depict a torso that mutates back and forth from male to part female. Then they become more iconographically complex, and by image 17 a door appears over the sternum, which, over the next few paintings, develops into a room with windows that is enclosed by the chest cavity. This then becomes darker with other outlets, including stairs and doors, leading into a shadowy interior.

This development of ideas relates to the humanist concept of the equivalence between architecture and the organic structure of animals and humans. The Renaissance artist and writer Leon Battista Alberti, for instance, equated the beauty and proportion of buildings to those of the human body. When discussing the columns of ancient buildings he linked them to the bones of animal legs.[2] Alberti lived in Rome, and like his humanist contemporaries was appalled by the continuing plunder and devastation of the city's ancient ruins, partly because he felt that they evoked the past glories and life cycles of civilisations.[3] A constant theme in his architectural treatises was the battle against the destructive powers of nature, which acted on buildings and humans alike. 'The batteries of old age are dangerous and very powerful; the body has no defence against the laws of Nature and must succumb to old age; some think even the heavens mortal, because they are a body.'[4]

Alberti's ideas about the natural decay of buildings and the moral imperative to build appropriate urban developments reflected the biblical *vanitas* theme that spoke of the transience of life and the vanity of earthly accumulation.[5] These ideas were picked up by the Italian architect and artist Giovanni Battista Piranesi, who lived in Rome from 1745 and made many etchings of the ruins. The second half of the eighteenth century saw a proliferation of printed material, and Piranesi's grand and sublime visions in the series of etchings known as Vedute di Roma (Views of Rome) moulded the sensibilities of European culture.[6] These etchings were not just faithful replications of buildings for the Grand Tour market, but brought together the deaths of humans with the deaths of buildings. His *Opere Varie, Fantastic Landscape with a Herm* (1745), for instance, was a medley of fallen masonry and sculpture mingled with bones and skulls. These etchings reflected the eighteenth-century passion for antiquity, not as learned archaeology captured by experts, but as something for the educated elite to engage with imaginatively.[7]

This cultural fascination with the ruin and its perception as part of an organic cycle that paralleled that of humans, combined with the political and economic ramifications of postwar housing, will be at the heart of the discussion in this chapter.

ESTABLISHMENT POWER

One of the most important factors in art's postwar engagement with the urban environment, where in some cases artists literally 'unmade' homes, has been the move away from considering the gallery as the primary artistic venue. In both America and Europe, this has been part of the broader social and political unrest that has questioned those in power and the establishment elite. Specific issues concerned the roles of artists and curators and the impact of the patronage of museums by those with money and power on what was collected and promoted. Museums have frequently been seen to be out of touch and, as one commentator put it, 'scolding curators [...] is one of the easiest (and therefore most popular) activities around.'[8]

Some, like the German–American artist Hans Haacke, have made direct attacks on the patronage systems that support museums and galleries, whereby those with money are courted to sponsor them. All of Haacke's work is concerned with revealing how systems operate, and since the 1960s he has worked on those underpinning the political and natural worlds.[9] The major exhibition that he planned for the Guggenheim in New York in 1971, and which was subsequently cancelled by the museum, had three sections: physical, biological and social systems. It was the last of these that was controversial, as two of the three works in this category attacked the accumulation of housing for profit. One of them was *Shapolsky et al. Manhattan Real Estate Holdings, A Real-time Social System, as of May 1, 1971*, in which Haacke displayed photographs of the property owned by one of New York City's biggest slum landlords, and adjacent to these articulated his business transactions of the previous few decades in short, typed documents. These revealed that instead of the apartments being places where people felt 'at home', the tenants had become the pawns of landlords, as the spaces they occupied were bought, sold and rented for profit.[10] Haacke's work was overtly political, something that Thomas Messer, the director of the museum, said went against the educational and aesthetic objectives of the charter of the gallery.[11]

One of Haacke's defending letters came from his erstwhile dealer, Howard Wise, who wrote that these works were following the tradition of art. Haacke, Wise argued, had photographed the landscape of Manhattan, had created order by emphasising particular aspects over others and had aided the understanding of the viewer by being realistic and 'telling it like it is'.[12] However, although there has been political art for centuries, it would be disingenuous to believe that Haacke was not aware of the implications.[13]

Messer wrote that although 'the exposure of social malfunction is a good thing, it is not the function of the museum.'[14] However, there are tensions that were not being expressed here, as the funding of the museum required money from the wealthy and powerful, and the success of the gallery rested at least partially on the ability to please the trustees.[15] The outcry on the withdrawal of the exhibition was significant. A number of artists refused to exhibit their work there, and the one curator who had supported Haacke and the artistic right of reasonable expression, Edward Fry, was sacked.[16]

The Guggenheim was not the only museum in New York to come under the spotlight. The Action Committee of the Art Workers' Coalition, for instance, invaded a banquet of museum trustees of the Metropolitan Museum of Art and poured a jarful of cockroaches over the table, declaring that 'there is a big gap between art and what you people are about'.[17] This type of dissension was frequently reported. In a published discussion in 1974 between writer and curator Lawrence Alloway and the director of the Museum of Modern Art (MoMA), William Rubin, Alloway suggested that there was a crisis of confidence in New York museums, especially MoMA, in that the institution was seen as being out of touch with the contemporary art scene.[18] Rubin's reply was that museums should not try to cover all contemporary art, and that perhaps not all forms were suitable for the types of spaces that a museum could offer. Clearly both saw the debate about the role of the museum from different standpoints, with Alloway having been an early champion of pop art, and Rubin being an important institutional figure. At the core of the arguments was the power of the establishment in the promotion of particular types of art.

ART OUTSIDE THE SYSTEM

As well as institutional frameworks for exhibiting art that express a particular canon of art practice, there are also hierarchies within cities to do with architecture, planning and lived spaces. The structures underpinning construction, planning, commissions and commerce bind buildings to politics, and in many cases architects are executors of a physical and social order designed by those with political authority.[19] However, there are also cross-currents of power relationships, which are dependent on dialogue and the relationships that people have with their places of living and working. This is another form of politics that cuts across and frequently works outside the normal systems, and actively participates in making things change.[20]

The American optimism of the 1950s was taken over by the social anger, cynicism and violence that first simmered in the early 1960s and then erupted later in the decade. At the centre of this was the declining American city and the rush to the suburbs.[21] While it is not my intention to analyse the complex problem of the American city in the 1960s and 1970s – that would be a book in itself – New York, where Gordon Matta-Clark and others in the Anarchitecture group were living and making art, was in decline: the critic and sociologist Lewis Mumford described the midtown area as 'solidified chaos', and the architect and writer Clarence Stein considered many of the policies that had led to this sorry state 'haphazard, antagonistic whims of many self-centered, ill-advised individuals'.[22] As the Dutch architect Rem Koolhaas said in the late 1970s, 'Manhattan's architecture is a paradigm for the exploitation of congestion.'[23]

A result of the disputes with establishment-run galleries and museums, combined with the number of derelict buildings within the city, was that artists began to make work outside institutions and show it in new spaces. Some were derelict buildings that, unlike traditional commercial galleries, were not made to look 'precious', like 112 Greene Street, the Clocktower, 98 Greene Street and the Kitchen. These spaces gave artists greater control over what their art could be and how it could be shown. Many works were made specifically for and about the spaces. Gordon Matta-Clark, for instance, excavated the site below 112 Greene Street as part of his exhibition.[24]

In 1973, in another exhibition, 34 artists were invited to make art for the loft where Jean Dupuy lived and worked. The chosen artists interrogated and manipulated the architectural spaces. The windows were dirty, so Matta-Clark washed one pane of glass and left the others grubby. Brendan Atkinson sealed off another window by extending a brick wall. Chris Murphy made rubbings of the ceiling textures and placed those onto the floor, so they mirrored each other.[25] As reflected in the reviews in *Artforum*, this engagement with architectural spaces in works that were temporary and which used non-art methods was widespread. Many also brought in domestic elements that became decontextualised from their original function and setting. Alice Aycock, for instance, built a set of wooden stairs for her exhibition at 112 Greene Street in

1973–4, and Les Levine simulated windows by placing enlarged photographs of some onto the walls of the Fischbach Gallery in 1972.[26]

Gordon Matta-Clark was one of a group of artists, musicians and choreographers working fluidly across visual art and performance in downtown Manhattan during the 1970s. Others of the Anarchitecture group included Laurie Anderson and Trisha Brown, and all actively engaged with the immediate urban environment, the social issues that were visible in the abandoned buildings; increasing lawlessness and poverty.[27] Matta-Clark had been trained as an architect, but the works and events that he and the group performed were related to the destabilising effects of gentrification, suburbanisation and economics. Some were community events, like the pig roast that he staged for the homeless and fellow artists in the derelict Lower East Side in 1971, and others related directly to buildings and the systems underpinning real estate.[28]

For the series Reality Properties: Fake Estates (1973) Matta-Clark bought up 15 tiny plots of land in Queens and Staten Island in New York that had reverted to the city's ownership through non-payment of taxes. All were useless and aberrations of the property market, and included kerbstones, a foot-wide slice of land down someone's driveway and a square foot of pavement.[29] Through his documentary photographs, plans and title deeds, he exposed the lack of logic in the system, and also explored the American dream of owning property.[30] The framed documentation of these sites has a visual similarity to the earlier work of Hans Haacke, whom Matta-Clark had known while studying architecture at Cornell University in Ithaca, New York, and for whom Matta-Clark had been one of the signatories on the protest letter about the cancellation of Haacke's Guggenheim exhibition.[31] As Haacke wrote, any work done in a social situation cannot be separated from its cultural and ideological context. Although one's responsibility increases, the exchange of necessarily biased information provides the energy for social relations to develop.[32]

Other works that Matta-Clark made were less obviously political, but were playfully related to urban life at the time. For *Open House* (1972) he divided a large industrial-waste container in a street, using found barriers and domestic doors that could open and close, into small central rooms with a corridor down each side. His friends were filmed improvising in the spaces. It was not just an exploration of inside and outside – the container was open at the top and there were several doors at the ends – but also about bodily relationships with boundaries.[33] In 1972 he extended these ideas into a group of photographs called Bronx Floors: Threshole, which documented the holes created by cuts that he made in the floors of derelict buildings, frequently close to the symbolic zones of doorways. Unlike the deadpan photographs taken for Reality Properties: Fake Estates, these were taken from different angles, with some looking through the floors to the previously lived spaces beneath and some angled upwards, with one framing a female figure in a doorway. There is a drama to these images, as in film stills that isolate and give resonance to emotional events through angles and framing. These photographic records providing evidence of particular projects after they have gone coincide with the ideas of land artists, who also document their art, which is practised outside institutional spaces. Here Matta-Clark was drawing on his previous experience as a post-graduate student at Cornell in 1969, where he helped install an exhibition of international land artists called *Earth Art*, which included Richard Long, Robert Smithson, Jan Dibbets and Dennis Oppenheim. As part of this he photographed and filmed their performances.[34]

Like the land artist Michael Heizer, who removed a line of land in a deep cut, or the minimalist artist Richard Serra, who acted out a range of sculptural techniques, Matta-Clark also used the act of cutting as one of his important methods. As Rosalind Krauss wrote in 1979, from the late 1960s there had been an exploration of the limits of what sculpture could be, and a blurring of the relationship between art, landscape and architecture.[35] The post-modern condition meant that sculpture was no longer determined by actual material or perceptions of that material, but organised around a set of terms that were in opposition within a cultural situation, and which inevitably were linked to both the era and the place.[36]

Sections of walls and floors cut from the apartments in Bronx Floors: Threshole were brought back into the gallery. Although suggesting the geometry of minimalism, these fragments were clearly part of something larger and held traces of human activity in the layers of wallpaper, the worn lino and successive coats of paint.[37] One of Matta-Clark's arguments against modernism concerned its erasure of history. Like the Situationists, with whom he had become acquainted in Paris during the 1960s, he thought that the layers of occupancy, memory and ambience imbued in buildings were important.[38] The sculptural fragments also showed a complete cross-section of walls, floors and ceilings, including the normally hidden structural timbers. They expose alternative insides and outsides, some totally hidden within the walls, and some hidden from those living in adjacent apartments on the alternate sides of the walls. Unlike industrial minimalist shapes, the obvious domesticity of these sections contrasted with the institutional spaces, creating a tension with the hierarchies of art by bringing into the gallery the debris of everyday lives.

GORDON MATTA-CLARK – *Splitting*

In the spring of 1974, Gordon Matta-Clark approached his dealers, Holly and Horace Solomon, and asked whether they knew of a house that he could cut in half. As it happened, they had recently purchased an empty, soon to be demolished house, 322 Humphrey Street in the suburb of Englewood, New Jersey – they were interested in the underlying lot rather than the building itself. As the house was going to be pulled down, the Solomons let Matta-Clark work on it for a few months prior to its destruction.[39] It was an ordinary balloon-framed, two-storey house, with a porch back and front and a base of cinder blocks. It was built during the 1930s when Englewood was expanding due to its proximity to New York City and its separation from the decay and lawlessness of the inner city. However, with the postwar economic downturn there had been a decrease in the number of households.[40] The house at 322 Humphrey Street would have been only one of a number of empty lots, and, like the apartment buildings that Matta-Clark had appropriated, was part of the larger system of profit and loss.

Having enlisted the knowledge and help of the German-born artist Manfred Hecht, Matta-Clark jacked up one end of the frame, including one of the porches, removed a layer of cinder blocks, and cut through the entire side of the building – inside and out – with a chainsaw. Gradually he lowered the back of the building onto the remaining blocks, leaving a gap in the cut of about two-thirds of a metre at the top that tapered to a slit at the base.[41] He called this work *Splitting*, and part of the filmed record features Matta-Clark stripped to the waist, at different times pulling hard on the jacks, up a ladder directing the saw and manipulating the cuts; he appears to be as engrossed in his work as Jackson Pollock in the films that show him dripping paint onto canvas, or indeed Trisha Brown in films of dance performances in which she scales buildings and creates improvised urban encounters. All show the artists' physical and mental engagement with their work and are performances of a type. When writing about *Splitting*, Matta-Clark also gave the house its performative role, saying that having made the cut there was a real moment of suspense about how the house would react, but that it responded 'like a perfect dance partner'.[42] Matta-Clark wrote that the production of the work was not illusionistic, but that it was 'all about a direct physical activity, and not about making associations with anything outside it.'[43]

The importance that Matta-Clark laid on process has overtones of the *Verb List* that Richard Serra compiled in 1967–8, which formed the basis of a series of films and sculptures.[44] These verbs described possible techniques for manipulating material and creating art. They start with 'to roll, to crease, to fold, to store, to bend, to shorten, to twist', and include 'to tear', 'to split', 'to cut', 'to remove', 'to open', 'to support', 'to expand' and 'to light', all of which Matta-Clark performed in the creation of *Splitting*. Serra worked through the list without design or intention, but as a way of involving himself

> in a process of making so that [he] could understand the physical potential of what it was to do something in relation to material without having to get into a hierarchy of judgement or evaluation about its definition as art or sculpture.[45]

Although Matta-Clark's *Splitting* was not as open-ended as Serra's experiments, nonetheless the physical acts involved in making the work, and how these fed into the result, expanded ideas about the edges of sculptural practice and what it could be. Even though the house itself was being unmade, the work represented a brief change of state executed with care and precision, which gave it a new life that was documented in film and photographs, before the final destruction.

The split, and the later cutting away of the upper corners, meant that the outside permeated the inside along those edges, but in a fundamentally different way from the liminal zones of windows or doors. As the film stated in one of its captions: 'The abandoned home was filled by a sliver of sunlight that passed the day throughout the rooms.' Unlike the cuts made for Bronx Floors: Threshole, the gap was not made to cut across a symbolic area, but served to make the abandonment more obvious. The house was no longer a home, and no longer had the debris of habitation – these had been removed. In parallel with the ideas underpinning Cornelia Parker's *Thirty Pieces of Silver*, which is discussed in Chapter 7, the emotional bond between owner and dwelling place had been severed, and the house was no longer invested with the American suburban dream.

Matta-Clark understood the psychic power of buildings over people. In one notebook from 1976, he wrote that he wanted to 'convert a place into a state of mind'.[46] This bond between home and occupant was articulated in the correspondence that Matta-Clark received after *Splitting* was opened for viewing. A number of letters complained about what he had done, saying that he had violated the sanctity and dignity of abandoned buildings; one even likened it to rape.[47]

Matta-Clark felt, like the Situationists, that this dream had been used as a political tool by the ruling classes through the provision of convenience and dwellings, in order to contain and control the masses.[48] It was also integral to the return to family values in America after the war, which were promoted in television programmes, films and magazines. While the home was seen as private, the family was also encouraged to be part of a network of neighbourhood relationships, where conformity was important, but these relationships were 'sold' as intrinsic to the 'good life'.[49] Matta-Clark questioned the interests involved in developing this dream and then providing for it:

> The very nature of my work with buildings takes issues with the functionalist attitude to the extent that this kind of self-conscious vocational responsibility has failed to question or re-examine the quality of life being served.[50]

Neither the photographs that Matta-Clark took to document the project nor the film set the house within the context of the surrounding neighbourhood. The catalogue that was published by the Greene Street Loft Press showed the house first in its original state, with subsequent images depicting interior and exterior views, including one that depicts half of the house end on, with the floors and walls intact in the remaining portion.[51] The shots from the inside have the split as the formal determinant, with some revealing the real world beyond. The cut creates the edges of the floors, stairs and architectural structures that jut into the enveloping space. However, these photographs are not just documentary evidence but, like the images for Bronx Floors: Threshole vertiginously look up and down into other spaces. Other images related to this project are compositions made up of cut photographs pieced together, with the slit being the organising principle. Again, the eye is directed up, down and around in an almost sensuous manner. As Richard Serra wrote, 'Perception has its own logic [...] The size, scale, and three-dimensional ambiguity of film and photographs is usually accepted as one kind of interpretation of reality.'[52]

A coach full of friends came from New York in the June of 1974 to see the work, and wandered around the house, jumping across the gaps.[53] This was only one set of many visitors who came. The photographs show the floors devoid of covering, so footfall and voices would have echoed around the spaces. Unlike the photographs by Gilbert and George of their home before renovation, here there was no potential for future dwelling. As the review in *Art in America* said, the web of meanings and associations linked to houses had gone, leaving the building freed from the weight of habitual assumptions, and the viewer open to make his or her own links.[54]

All that remain of Matta-Clark's works are the documentation and sections of the building that he brought back into the gallery. However, in spite of the loss of the original, Matta-Clark felt that the audience was crucial.[55] Rather than using architecture as a means of solving housing problems – he had seen first-hand the effects of postwar developments – he worked through architecture to make sculpture, and enacted the cuts of the buildings in his photographs.[56] The performance of making and turning derelict buildings and documentation into performative works was intrinsic to his work, as were the social themes articulated through the audacity of these transformative acts.

'SCULPITECTURE', RACHEL WHITEREAD, THE PERSONAL AND THE POLITICAL

Until the mid-1970s there was a great difference between cities in America and those in Europe. Whereas those in the United States had partially abandoned, derelict centres that housed the poor and ethnic minorities and were surrounded by rich suburbs, in European cities there was an emphasis on preserving the historic and commercial centre, and surrounding this with homes.[57] However, in both places housing was important both for those living in it and making it their own, and as a political and economic tool. This section will consider work made in England after the 1980s.

The huge reforms made by the Thatcher government to housing policy in Britain were only one part of a radical social and economic shake-up. One of the great changes was the promotion of homeownership. On an individual level this encouraged the idea of independence and security, with owning a home becoming a badge of prosperity and success, and at a strategic level housing became a vehicle for business speculation and financial control by the government.[58] The increased availability of mortgages and credit meant that the whole climate of ownership altered dramatically, but also the economic divide between rich and poor became greater.[59] The 1980s was the decade when sleeping rough on the streets of London became accepted as part of modern life, while there were many others making a lot of money.[60]

The British sculptor Rachel Whiteread and a number of other artists including Anthony Caro have made 'sculpitecture' since the late 1980s.[61] As well as being concerned with the physical aspects of the built environment, they have also embraced the political and emotional connection of those spaces to everyday lives. Caro's 'sculpitecture' is often concerned with how people engage with physical spaces. *Child's Tower Room* (1983–4), a wooden structure made of Japanese oak, was one of his first works to consider this question. The viewer was encouraged to enter the confined space, to climb the stairs and look out of one of the windows, just as one would within the home. Some of his related sculptures have spaces one can move around, and others have low entrances, so that one must stoop on entering. These works force the viewer to be aware of his or her body within the surrounding spaces and to move accordingly, triggering related feelings about his or her relationship with the built world.

While also exploring psychological and spatial relationships with places of dwelling, the British sculptor Antony Gormley includes sculptural figures within his works and keeps the viewers on the outside. *Home* (1984) is a lead cast of his body with the head stuck through the front door of a small terracotta house, which has echoes of Louise Bourgeois' sculptures and drawings in the Femme Maison series discussed in Chapter 4. Gormley's *House and Body* (1985) shows dismembered body parts piled next to a house. Just as Matta-Clark and Whiteread consider the overlaps between body, memory and the physical world as part of their explorations, Gormley wrote that his work 'evokes both claustrophobia and dream space, as well as tackling the mind–body divide'.[62] In some of Gormley's later works, like *Site* (1993), there is a performative quality to the cast bodies that scale gallery walls or the outsides of buildings, suggesting Matta-Clark's and Trisha Brown's earlier explorations of the body acting on architecture.

Rachel Whiteread extended her vocabulary from making casts of the spaces below tables and chairs or within wardrobes to making them of, for instance, a room from a derelict house, in a work that became known as *Ghost* (1990), and an entire terraced house, in *House* (1993; figure 5.1), for which she received the Turner Prize. Her use of derelict houses as a vehicle to explore the personal and political can be compared with the projects by Matta-Clark, whose work she had studied through his photographs and drawings.[63] However, rather than altering an existing building and bringing fragments back into the gallery, Whiteread casts the interiors and then removes the surrounding structure.

While studying at Brighton Polytechnic, Whiteread attended tutorials with Phyllida Barlow, Alison Wilding, Edward Allington and, most importantly for her methods, Richard Wilson, who taught her and the class the techniques of casting. However, rather than ending up with a replica of the original, Whiteread stops at an intermediate stage, so that what is revealed is the negative of the object, complete with the internal traces. In both *House* and *Ghost*, these were the unwitting signatures of occupancy: the wear on a windowsill or door, the soot from a fireplace or traces of colour that had been part of the decorative choices. Unlike the sculptures by Matta-Clark, the viewer cannot enter – even vicariously through photographs – her unmade objects, but can only look at the solidified negative of the interior, sharing and absorbing the traces of the private lives that remain.[64]

Although Whiteread made some body casts early on, she wanted to move away from autobiographical or sentimental resonances, so started working with architecture. For her, domestic spaces are measured and marked by our bodies and movements, and, as in the images and ideas of Robert Gober, Giovanni Battista Piranesi and Leon Battista Alberti, not only is the scale of a home measured in relation to the body, but a building is itself a body that breathes, gets sick and has a structure and organs.[65] When making *House*, Whiteread commented that it 'was like exploring the inside of a body, removing its vital organs'.[66]

Completed in 1990, *Ghost* was Whiteread's most ambitious project at the time. She had originally conceived of casting a room in 1988, but the search for funding and the planning of the project took two years.[67] She found a room in what would have been the master bedroom in a derelict house, 486 Archway Road, London, and made a cast of it using plaster nine centimetres thick supported by a steel frame, which was cut into roughly metre-long panels that varied in size according to the overall composition.[68] She likened this cast, which was built up inch by inch with scrim, to covering a broken leg.[69]

When looking for a suitable house, Whiteread said that she wanted particular architectural elements in the room: doors, windows, a fireplace, cornicing and skirting boards.[70] *Ghost* was a personal project, in that she grew up in nearby Muswell Hill, and knew the area well. Like contemporary speculative builders, those from the Victorian era used very similar patterns of internal layout across their developments, so the room itself was similar to one that Whiteread had as a child and another she had as a student.[71] The proportions and height of ceilings, as well as the architectural details, help to place the house in its era. These factors take the cast beyond the personal into the universal. Most British people will know houses and rooms like this, and many will have lived in one.

As in all cities, the social groups living in any one area fluctuate greatly over time. When Whiteread made *Ghost* the borders of Highgate were run-down, a product of Thatcher's Britain, when unemployment was over 3 million, yuppies were experiencing a boom and whole areas of London were being erased and redeveloped as private money became increasingly bound up in developments and councils could make decisions about future housing plans.[72] Today it is a wealthy area, so that the status of houses is less to do with the buildings themselves than with the vagaries of the property market.

What the viewer sees when entering the gallery is a stained plaster negative of the internal space – a displaced and manipulated found object. The normally vulnerable threshold points of the windows, doors and fireplaces protrude, reversing the poetic and artistic tradition in which those thresholds represent the interface between one state of reality and another.[73] As Anthony Vidler has said, this filling of space not only suggests the excavation of towns like Pompeii and Herculaneum, in which casts were made of the voids left in the volcanic ash by decomposed bodies, but also hints at the nineteenth-century literary interest in tales of interment by writers like E. T. A. Hoffmann, just as the blank and protruding windows suggest Romantic tropes of blocked vision and mirrors that cease to reflect the self.[74]

There is a perceptual oscillation between the internal and external, mental and physical, as one looks at *Ghost*. There is also a sense that traces of people's lives have been preserved. Whiteread herself discussed her works as being death masks. Jennifer Gross has argued that Whiteread's sculptures are like *vanitas* paintings, or *memento mori*.[75] However, rather than representing the perfect moment, as in most *vanitas* paintings, where every cut flower is shown at its peak, or in Holbein's *The Ambassadors* (1553), in which the two figures are shown in their finest regalia and surrounded by their cultural learning, both *Ghost* and *House* are mummifications of occupancy, in which the viewer becomes in some sense the wall, looking in.

House was made and viewed on site, at 193 Grove Road in Bow, until it was finally demolished after considerable debate. Like the house from which *Ghost*

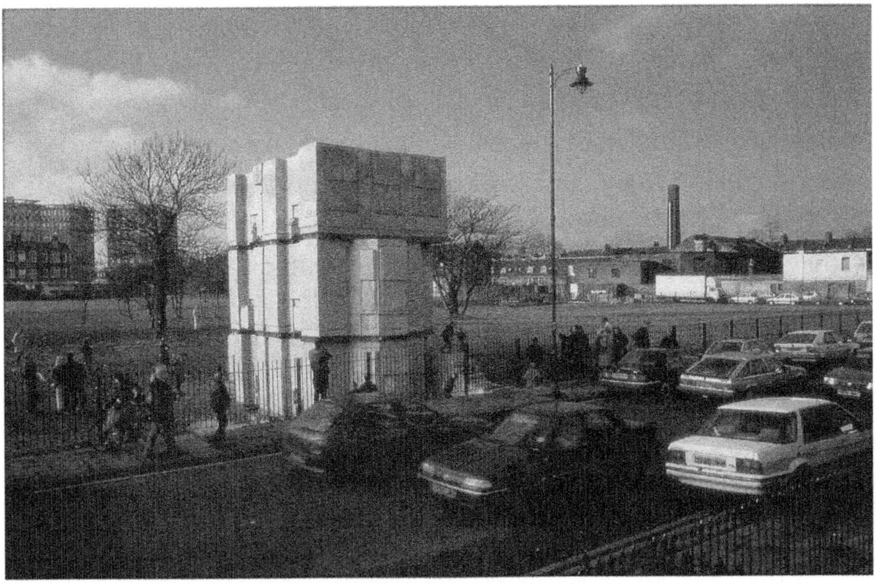

FIGURE 5.1 Rachel Whiteread, *House* (1993).

was cast, it represented many houses in the area that were being demolished at that time. The whole neighbourhood was being razed and this house was the last remnant. Seen from a distance, the cast, alone in a flat expanse of land, looked fragile and insignificant. All that now remains is the documentation and memory of the controversy.

Starting in 1991, Artangel, the commissioning body for *House*, filled a need for creating places for art outside mainstream institutions, and that could be driven by the artists themselves. Being funded by both private and public capital has meant that each project can be unique and contradictory.[76] The location of *House*, as with all the works that Artangel has enabled, was integral to its meaning, so that the edges seep into the surrounding 'real' world, which in turn feeds back into an understanding and interpretation of the work.[77] Photographs of *House* taken from different angles show it in relation to the new banking centre of Canary Wharf, which brought investment into the city, to three churches and to postwar housing. As Lisa Jardine has commented, *House* was equated with Artangel because of the relationship of the work with the real-world context.[78]

House was a cast of one house that could stand for many Victorian homes, with steps leading up to the nonexistent entrance, and a street lamp on the pavement outside, just as there would have been when the street was a busy community. As Doreen Massey said, social spaces are not just physical, but are where people interact with others. On the streets friends and acquaintances meet and greet each other; over back walls people chat with neighbours; but inside the home people become annoyed with the noises from outside invading their private sphere.[79] It was not just the rows of terraces that were destroyed, but a whole way of life, one that extended beyond the front door, and included the setting, the neighbourhood, social spaces and facilities.[80]

As part of her preparation for *House*, Whiteread made a number of drawings, in which she altered photographs of the partially demolished group of houses. By blanking out the house next door using correction fluid on photographs of the front, back and oblique elevations, she gained a sense of an isolated fragment of what had been a community of linked houses, with their architectural rhythms and modest ornamentation. Her use of pencil on the layer of white gives a suggestion of a ghostly presence in the absence.[81]

Demolition is a messy business. *Blight* (1994–6) is one of a number of films that the video artist John Smith made as a result of the forced demolition of many houses in his area of east London, which occurred in spite of a strong and vocal battle with the local population. The film is not a straightforward documentary, but, as discussed in Chapter 1, an emotive montage of still and moving images, containing edited fragments and longer clips of the ex-residents talking about their memories of living in the area, set to a background of orchestral and real sounds. Initially it appears as if one of the houses is self-destructing, with timbers moving as if directed by an internal force. Only later does a wall fall dramatically outwards, creating clouds of dust, to reveal the builders behind.[82] In the documented destruction of *House*, however, scaffolding was used, and the walls and roof were disassembled with care using plastic shoots to direct the bricks and mortar away from the building in a noisy rumble. What was left of 193 Grove Road were three layers of white concrete negative spaces, with the original framework of stairs, interior walls and floors visible.[83] These reveal, like Whiteread's drawings on graph paper and indeed the etchings by Piranesi, the underlying structure of wooden bearers and bricks that is normally hidden. Like Whiteread's casts of floorboards and spaces, these hint at the movements and habits of the occupants. However, unlike in *Blight*, there is no wallpaper left clinging to the walls.[84]

As James Lingwood, the co-director of Artangel, has said, opinions and meanings ascribed to this last remnant of the streets were contradictory, divided and unstable.[85] Normally people's perceptions of both art and the world are filtered through expectations, systems and frameworks that help create a shared language, which in turn helps create stability. *House* was provocative in being opaque and indeterminate.[86] Rather than being nostalgic, this work was concerned with revealing the contemporary world, and forcing the viewer to reflect on his or her relationship with it.[87] London was changing dramatically at the time, and Canary Wharf and the developments along the Thames that were visible from *House* were destroying working-class life through the loss of jobs and destruction of neighbourhoods. Doreen Massey has argued that the memory of an apparently stable identity became focused onto *House*, at a time when the idea of what it is to be British was complex – as it continues to be.[88] However, *House* did not conjure these aspects up for the local population. They did not see it as being located in and about the locality. They disliked it, primarily because of its classification as 'art'.[89] It was also mocked in the press. Kipper Williams' cartoon strip 'The Lady and the Wimp' in *Time Out* showed the arms and legs of squatters bursting from the windows and doors.[90] After a lengthy debate in the media, in the council chambers and among the public, *House* was demolished on 11 January 1994 and the area that it occupied was covered in turf a few months later.[91]

House now exists in people's minds, through the criticism, interpretations and documentary photography. No longer is the encounter unmediated and related to the experience of the thing itself. As Rosalind Krauss wrote in 1971 in relation to the photographic and filmic documentary of art, it creates an extra layer of evidence.[92] 'If the function of photography must be located within the nature of documentary [...] its medium is literal space [...] which is recorded and later produced as evidence.'[93] If one transfers Krauss' discussion of Robert Smithson's earthwork sculpture *Spiral Jetty* (1970) to the creation of meaning in *House*, then the documentary is one layer among many. First there is the house and community and their relationships to life, then the applied forces of the council, then the work of art, then the documentation of that work and then, finally, further writing and interpretation. This is important, not only for Whiteread's use of documentation, but also for that of Matta-Clark. The decontextualised, framed and edited images and films are the remaining evidence of the sculptures, designed to reposition ideas about architecture, politics and social change.

Ghost, however, is shown in galleries. In each installation the experience is different according to the light, surrounding spaces and architectural details. Whiteread has written that the encounter is important to her, and that she wants people to spend time looking, walking around and peering through the cracks.[94] Earlier in her life she worked in Highgate Cemetery in north London, where many of the graves were in a state of disrepair and the tomb lids and doors were ajar. She wanted people to have a similar sense of looking in uneasily to see what was hidden when looking at *Ghost*. She was aware of the suggestion of sarcophagi and of the silence of the room when people are confronted with the large white sculptural block.[95] However, as with the beds, floors, wardrobes and mattresses that she has cast, *Ghost* is about people, everyday lives and recording these things. There is an interrelationship between her political views – she has said that she is a socialist – and her art that provokes discussion about the contemporary situation while also exploring formal questions.[96]

STEFFI KLENZ – NUMMIANUS

The recording of absent lives in abandoned domestic architecture is also pertinent to a photographic project entitled Nummianus (2007–8; figure 5.2) by the German-born artist Steffi Klenz. Like *Ghost* and *House* by Whiteread, this work is both political and about the cyclical nature of decay, destruction and rebirth within cities. However, rather than depicting the poverty of New York in the early 1970s or the immediate results of Thatcherism in London in the early 1990s, in this project Klenz turned her attention to the frequently overlooked housing in a depressed part of north-west England at the turn of the new millennium.

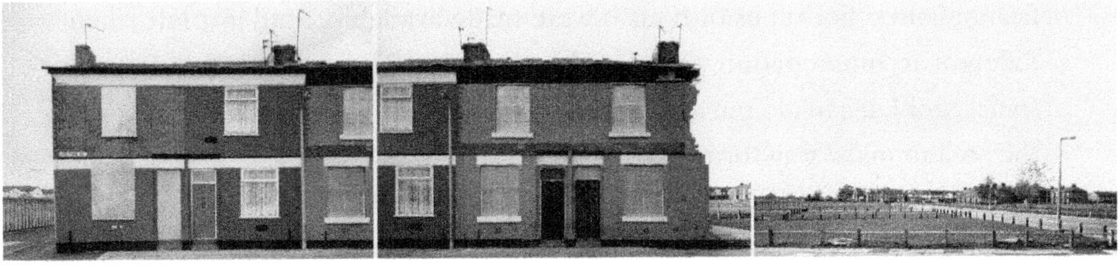

FIGURE 5.2 Steffi Klenz, *Untitled*, from the series Nummianus (2007).

Nummianus is a frieze of over seven metres in length, made up of 56 photographs, taken face on, of derelict and boarded-up terraces in a poor part of Salford, Greater Manchester, where, in a number of parallel streets, nearly all the occupants have moved out. The original housing was built for workers, with doors leading directly from the street into the small front room, one window up and one down, and little architectural ornament. Only a few remain inhabited, with net curtains in place and a few knick-knacks visible. A lone fish-and-chip shop is open. However, as in some of Klenz's other photographic portraits of urban areas, such as the series La Posa (2008), this is a ghost town. There are no people visible, and no hint of the social life, noise, everyday happenings and children's play that once would have bled from the houses into the streets. All that remains of the original occupancy are the few personal details that had been added to the exteriors: a painted wall, some cladding and some concrete rendering. The images have been likened to a cenotaph to other people's lives.[97]

The title Nummianus came from an inscription on the floor of the Siricio house in Pompeii and refers to the name of one of the wealthiest trading companies at the time. The word itself translates as 'coin' or 'money', and in relation to this project is an ironic and critical comment on the debased value of regarding housing as a commodity.[98] Like the town of Pompeii, this area was destroyed – but not by natural forces; the dereliction of these streets instead represents changing economic forces. Unlike the transformation of the area of east London that included Whiteread's *House*, this change was not a direct result of council development decisions or speculative builders, but a consequence of the long-term implications of government policies. First-time buyers deserted these Victorian terraces in the 1980s as they fell from fashion and other types of houses were made available. Students left when different accommodation was offered in the 1990s. Then, negative equity and social problems made the area unattractive. Finally, the council demolished the area to make way for redevelopment.[99]

As with most of Klenz's architectural photographs, there is a silence and absence that one attempts to fill. The artist has likened her work to a tradition going back to the early twentieth century that included photographers like Eugène Atget, who roamed the streets of Paris depicting apparently empty shops and streets.[100] Unlike the work of Whiteread or Matta-Clark, these photographs are not a document of an artistic intervention that had been imposed on the structures, but photographs of the real world, edited to give a particular impression of loss, without even the clutter of clouds in the sky. Drawing on the output of German photographers like Bernd and Hilla Becher, who used a documentary style to photograph industrial buildings, and Andreas Gursky, who made deadpan, frontal photographs of buildings, landscapes and commercial outlets, Klenz's work suggests an objective distance, where the focus is entirely on the thing in hand.[101]

Klenz makes the link with Pompeii when discussing this work, which she feels is 'digging into her unconscious': 'Pompeii is not a silent image; its destruction has an uncanny inversion. It reminds me of the permeability of time, the beauty of decay, the collapse of the future, and of the pitiless inconsequentiality of things.'[102] What punctuates the photographs is the colour red, which many of the previous occupants had applied to the fronts of their houses. In Pompeii this colour would only have been used by the rich, to signify their status, whereas here it is the decoration of the poor.[103]

Like Whiteread, Klenz has discussed her work in relation to the political and social factors that led to the decay, and also to the ideas of the memorial, of inside and outside, and of time and death. Just as in *House* and *Ghost*, the windows of the houses depicted in Nummianus defy the idea of being the meeting point between two worlds: on the empty houses they have been covered with metal sheeting to prevent vandalism. While this was a practical solution to a social necessity, in another photographic project, La Posa, Klenz covered the windows with blackout material, which offered a 'blocked vision', and for her this blindfolding linked to the idea of the 'window as a metaphor for the eye'.[104] In the houses depicted in both La Posa and Nummianus, the covered windows foreshadow their deaths.

All of the works discussed in this chapter emphasise the overlaps between places of dwelling and the occupants, and how that relationship suggests that the building is organic, and therefore finite. However, as well as being personal spaces that bleed out into the community, homes are part of larger systems underpinned by the establishment, and are therefore subject to exploitation, market forces and the need for infrastructure development.

6

Withdrawal

This chapter will consider how artists have engaged with places of withdrawal within the home that separate one from the world and become places in which to dream. Homes are not always sites of emotional comfort, and this chapter covers a range of experiences, from childhood dream spaces to withdrawal for intimacy, excess and sex.

I will begin with a discussion of some of Ilya Kabakov's installations of people's rooms within Soviet blocks. While his concepts of the home and places of withdrawal are drawn from his early years in Russia, the preciousness of a space in which to be alone and have flights of fancy is recognisable to all. His installations also act as a foil for ideas that appear to be natural in the West. I will then consider childhood spaces of withdrawal from the adult world, in which the scale of the found places match those of a small body. In the final two sections I will discuss the adult world of the bed, which can be both a place of intimacy and comfort, and also a place to go when troubled.

ILYA AND EMILIA KABAKOV – FANTASY SPACES

Unlike most artists discussed in this book – who grew up in the West and whose work developed against a backdrop of minimalism and conceptualism – Ilya

Kabakov was born in Ukraine and spent his formative years in Russia. He moved to the West in 1987, and since the late 1980s has collaborated with Emilia Kabakov on particular projects. (They married in 1992.) They now live in America. Initially Ilya was an illustrator of children's books, and his interest in narrative together with the reality of living under the Soviet regime permeates all his installations. I include them here as they offer an interesting alternative voice that comments on the structures and ideas within the West. They are also important in this chapter as the viewer is required to enter into the given fantasies and allow them to work within his or her imagination.

When Ilya Kabakov left Russia he was immediately struck by the differences in the roles of personal possessions and spaces for people. Whereas objects in the West are precious to the owner and designed to help people live and work, Kabakov wrote that in the Soviet Union objects were difficult to acquire and when obtained were broken, old and dirty. Furthermore, unlike the Western idea of surrounding spaces being neutral backdrops for possessions, in Russia these spaces are personal, distinctive and force one to behave in particular ways.[1] These differences have informed Kabakov's installations and the way viewers are meant to engage with them. In contrast to minimalism, where he thought the viewer moves towards a state of equilibrium, Kabakov's installations suggest narratives that the viewer needs to read.[2] Both minimalist sculptures and his installations use the gallery space, but in his work it reminds the viewer of the fictive nature of the situations that Kabakov has constructed.[3] Like all of his works these installations draw on the importance in Russian culture of the soul and sentiment, as well as the country's nineteenth-century literary traditions.[4]

The first installation that Ilya Kabakov made in the West was *Ten Characters* in 1988. It comprised ten rooms off a dimly lit corridor, so that their immediate context was not the white, sterile spaces of the gallery, but an illusion of a Soviet communal apartment block. This helped to create the atmosphere and prepare the viewer for each 'stage set'. Each room belonged to one of the ten characters referred to in the installation's title; each character was a fictional author who was given a biography by Kabakov, and who practised his or her art in uncomfortable isolation in his or her separate room. In common with Kabakov's ideas about 'total installation', the walls and spaces were not just neutral backdrops, but actively set the scene by being painted dark, and through their proportions and scale. The floor – the 'earth' in the artist's terms – suggested the lives of the inhabitants through strewn rubbish, bits of paper and other everyday paraphernalia.[5]

Soviet housing blocks developed after the 1917 Revolution, when the poor, who had occupied the basements, moved into the 12- and 16-room apartments that had previously been occupied by the bourgeoisie. In the continual subsequent housing crises, it became normal for one room to suffice for an individual or family, so that everyone lived in close proximity to those they did not know. In spite of the communal kitchens and bathrooms, people remained isolated while also hearing whispered confidences and the comings and goings of occupants and guests, and smelling their cooking. This meant that there was constant surveillance.[6] In these communal apartments there was no privacy: all were subject to the frequently hostile gaze of the other inhabitants, and the inevitable power struggles meant that it was important to be able to observe others while protecting oneself. In museums, curators frequently align artists in shared contexts, and Kabakov's installation of *Ten Characters*, which represents different artists, can be seen as an equivalent of both of these situations, as Kabakov used the ideas of control and regulation found in Soviet apartments as a metaphor for the Western museum.[7] As Kabakov has said, in both the West and in Russia the individual is burned by society and longs to be 'alone in his small corner with his own constructs of a personal utopia'.[8]

In some of the joint projects by Ilya and Emilia Kabakov the fantasy of improving living conditions takes on an almost childlike logic. *The Palace of Projects* (1995–8) was first shown at the Roundhouse in London, and consisted of a spiral installation in which the viewer walked through 65 projects arranged in 16 rooms. The projects were arranged under three headings: 'How to make yourself better', 'How to make this world better' and 'How to stimulate the appearance of projects'. Ideas included moving a mattress to a wall on which had been tacked favourite childhood book illustrations, and then lying down and regarding them in detail. Another advocated making a small soundproofed room in one's apartment in which one could live without distractions, and another suggested gaining more space by making a large hole into the neighbouring apartment.[9] Other projects suggested ways of gaining solitude within the public realm, such as, in the case of *Closets of Solitude*, small, soundproofed and ventilated rooms placed in busy parts of the city, where people would be able to withdraw in order to alleviate the effects of the surrounding hustle and bustle.

The Kabakovs' series known as 16 Installations (1998), made for the Museum van Hedendaagse Kunst in Antwerp, consisted of 16 autonomous rooms of various shapes and sizes that the visitor could enter and dwell in for a while. One of them, *My Grandfather's Shed*, was an old, semi-decrepit plywood construction, dark inside except for an illuminated area under the stool in the corner, which showed a sentimental country scene. It was a place of withdrawal for the viewer, but it also suggested that the implied character went there to sit and dream of his ideal place. Room number 8, entitled *In the Closet* (figure 6.1), was a built-in cupboard with old and worn doors, placed along a brightly lit corridor in the museum, where it would be least expected. Unlike the rooms suggesting the Soviet apartments or the rest of the installations, this appeared to be a lair subversively constructed within the gallery. The small room had been made comfortable with a bed, a lamp, shelves and hooks, so that living, reading and dreaming could be accommodated. Typically, Ilya Kabakov gave the visitor speculative details about who the inhabitant might have been and what he did there:

> He has fled from that life in which all of us are submerged [...] [and] would like to attain solitude and peace [...] but [...] [this] is doomed, anyone can peer into his life [...] Perhaps he would like to occupy that very position highly desired by all of us – to be near others, to listen to someone else's life, but not to participate in it, all the while preserving himself, his seclusion.[10]

While this installation invites the viewer to peer into someone's private existence, the tenth room of 16 Installations, *Reverse*, invites the viewer to enter a childlike space beneath the skirts of a giant mother figure. The skirt acts like a cuboid tent, with soft fabric for the walls and ceilings. In the room there is a table, on top of which is an illustrated children's book, and a chair, so one can sit and enter into the story in comfort.[11]

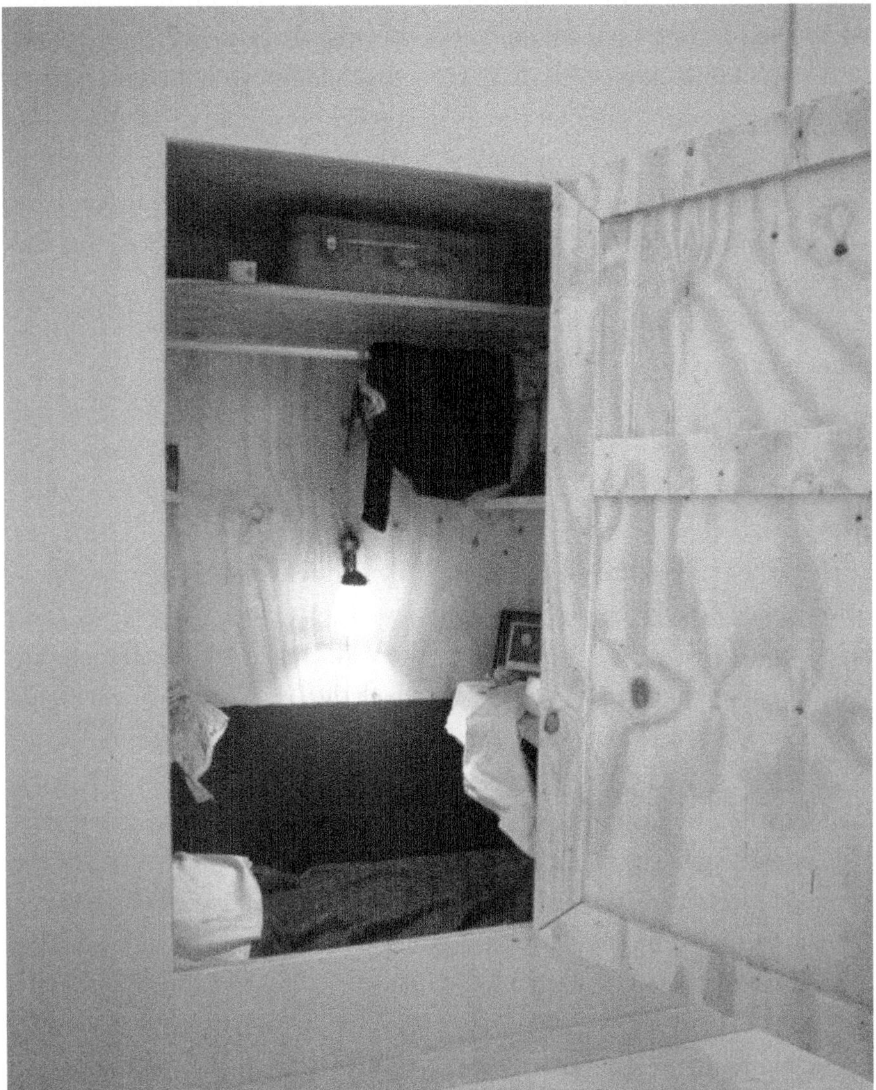

FIGURE 6.1 Ilya and Emilia Kabakov, *In the Closet* (1998).

All of these spaces suggest different aspects of time, and require different imaginings on the part of the audience. When discussing installations and their perception, Ilya Kabakov wrote that the past, present and future should be suggested, but are perceived subjectively by the viewer.[12] Objects perform, so that extraneous things can create a history. The future can be made by presenting familiar things in strange ways. The present is represented by the viewer, 'who is standing in the middle of the installation, in the centre or moving around inside of it'.[13] While all of the objects are everyday and recognisable, it is not just the objects themselves, but the way that they are displayed – their density, juxtaposition, angle and point of view – that provides the narrative. All these the viewer perceives with his or her deep 'internal vision' as he or she contemplates the scene.[14]

CHILDHOOD DREAMS

In this section I want to discuss a particular work by the British conceptual artist Helen Chadwick, *Ego Geometria Sum* (*I Am Geometry*) (1982–4), and a selection of early works by Rachel Whiteread. Unlike the installations and fantasies of Ilya and Emilia Kabakov, in which they suggested types of people and their ways of constructing dreams outside the system, Whiteread and Chadwick drew on personal memories of spaces from their childhoods – typically postwar, English places. As such, their sculptures represent recognisable things that trigger similar memories in the viewer. Whereas Chadwick's plywood forms were geometric representations of objects, each of which had been important at particular times from the artist's birth to her adulthood, Whiteread cast her chosen spaces, maintaining a direct relationship with the original. For both, these sculptures and installations were as much about the actual memories as they were about their formalisation and reconstruction.

The sites chosen by both artists would be immediately recognisable to anyone who grew up in England from the late 1950s to early 1970s. In his book *The Poetics of Space*, Gaston Bachelard wrote about childhood spaces in the home. His was a warm and protective vision, with shadowy spaces where one could curl up and imagine other realities. He described how particular nooks and crannies where one had dreamed are inscribed into our childhood selves, and places to which one can mentally return later in life to relive those memories.[15]

In *Ego Geometria Sum* (figure 6.2), Helen Chadwick charted her childhood and early adulthood through ten schematised, geometrical sculptures with photographic imagery on the surface that represented material objects linked to each stage of her development – from premature birth to the age of 30. Implicit in this condensation was the importance of things for one's development and how one is determined by surroundings. The notebook that Chadwick kept on the project, which is preserved in the archive of

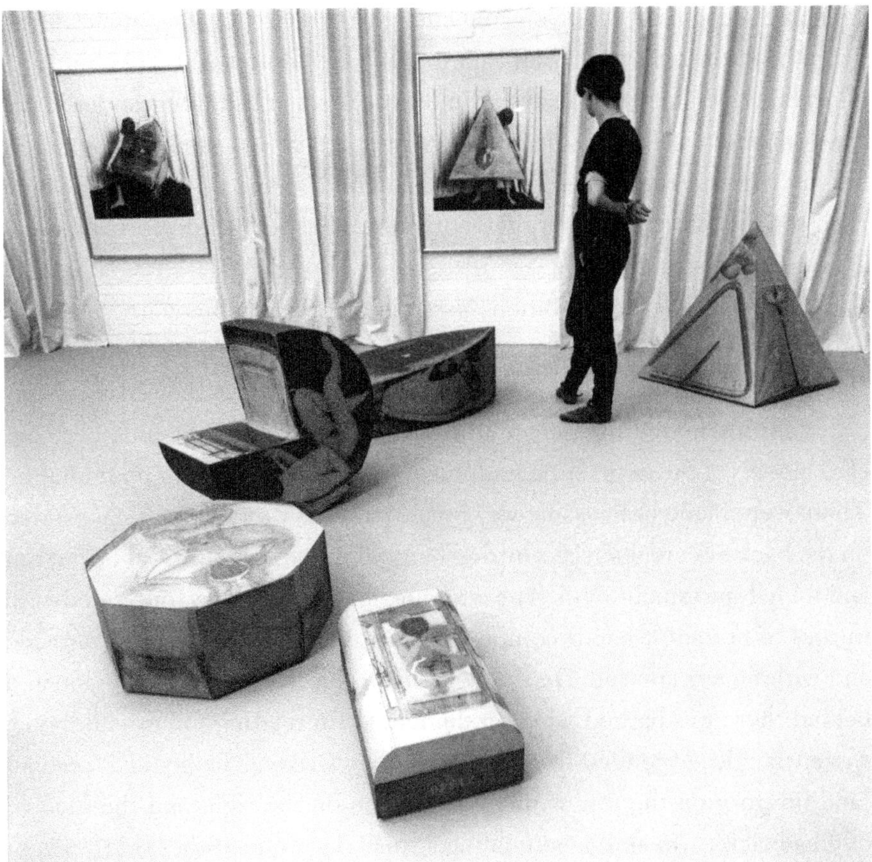

FIGURE 6.2 Helen Chadwick with *Ego Geometria Sum* (1983–4).

the Henry Moore Institute in Leeds, shows her musing on which elements from her past to choose from – a climbing frame or a triangle from infant school, a gym horse or school desk from junior school.[16] Her final choices were an incubator (birth), a baptismal font (3 months), a pram (10 months), a boat (3 years), a wigwam (5 years), a bed (6 3/4 years), an upright piano (9 years), a gym horse (11 years), her high school (13 years) and a statue (15 to 30 years), the last of which combined her upright adult figure with an image of the door to 45 Beck Road – her home and studio in the East End of London. Clearly some of these containing spaces would not have been remembered, but would have surrounded and protected her fragile form. However, a child's wigwam, a common sight in the late 1950s and 1960s, would be recognised by anyone old enough as a space for imagining stories. To go inside and tie the flaps meant to leave the adult world far behind and allow that of fantasy to take over. Similarly the small boat suggests holidays, freedom and making up stories to act out. Then comes the key moment of buying the first full-size bed, which as a child seems so large, but which represents a safe place where the boundaries between childish reality and dream can be stretched.

When shown at the exhibition *Aperto 84* at the Venice Biennale, the installation consisted of these sculptures, a tabletop version called *The Juggler's Table* and ten large framed photographs called *The Labours*, which showed the artist's naked adult self cradling the sculptures. *The Juggler's Table* included cut-out card models of the large-scale sculptures printed with relevant photographs. These were made in the same way image patterns would have been printed on the back of cereal packets during her childhood, which could be cut out and folded into small toys.[17] The wigwam, for instance, was four-sided with images of her adult hands coming through the embroidered flaps, crossed and with fingers splayed. On the right-hand side was an electric pylon and behind there was barbed wire; on the left, again relating to her childhood, was a triangle suspended from a finger with a striker. The boat has sea and sand imagery on the top, with a child's shoe on the right and the shadow of Chadwick's arm and hand holding a small flag on the other side.[18] These fragile and light forms were arranged alongside documentary photographs of the places that were important to the artist's development: the hospital where she was born, the church of her baptism, her childhood homes and grandmother's flat, and her school.

Unlike in the works by the Kabakovs, which draw on general fantasies and systems of living, the articulation of personal memories here has a complex relationship with truth and social context. Memory is not a seamless narrative of the past in which experiences are preserved to be remembered in an unmediated fashion. Inevitably there are choices about what is revealed and what hidden or forgotten.[19] Also, memories are not fixed; rather, as one remembers there is a constantly evolving act of self-discovery and self-creation.[20]

Chadwick took great pains to return to sites that she felt had been important in her past, documented her reactions in her notebooks and photographed each to get the essence. In her notebook she stated that she wanted the photographic record to represent the 'cold hard unsentimentality of camera as truth', but she found that this documentation could only portray the bricks and mortar, as her past life and its memories had evaporated.[21] In a different ink, which suggests a later thought, she noted: 'leave part of yourself behind, caught within the place, a haunting.'[22]

Her notebook also relates how Chadwick tried to recapture those elusive memories. She discusses how the present floats away to allow previous memories to flood in, and later on she suggests that she had taped hypnosis sessions, and experimented with self-hypnosis to help her regress into the past and recover memories.[23] Yet, rather than being an emotive work, her personal museum was to be an 'archaeological presentation of facts'. She noted just below this the idea of lead-lined boxes that preserve things for posterity, and of simple shapes that suggest sarcophagi preserving memorabilia.[24] Chadwick's desire to document, photograph and preserve recalls what the French historian Pierre Nora said regarding memory in contemporary Western society, where there is little collective memory, and personal memory has been 'absorbed by its meticulous reconstruction', and is situated in archives, museums, databanks and other constructed 'scaffoldings' of memory.[25]

However, in Chadwick's work, rather than being simply reconstructed memories, the objects were also invested with ideas the artist gained from reading about mathematics and metaphysics. Her notebook contains comments about the Hungarian–British author Arthur Koestler's book on cosmology and astronomy *The Sleepwalkers*, in which he discusses the Pythagorean idea of creating order out of chaos through mathematical forms. Another major inspiration came from the theories of divine geometry promoted by the seventeenth-century mathematician Johannes Kepler, from whom Chadwick discovered that, in her words, the 'mathematical harmony' of geometrical solids could 'sublimate the discord of past passion and desire in a recomposed neutrality of being'.[26] The forms that Chadwick used in her installation were simplified versions of the objects they represented, but made to conform to mathematical proportions of cubes, octagons, circles and triangles. Some of these coincided with the symbolism of particular forms in Christianity, so that the triangle upon which she based the wigwam, for instance, was related to the Holy Trinity. Although taking ideas from different sources, underpinning all of these was Chadwick's belief that all life is energy and interrelated, so that the geometry of her sculptures relates to the structures of thought and memory and in a larger sense to the structures underpinning the universe.[27] As well as the importance of the forms, she observed that the gym horse, desks and other things at her junior school were formal and the beginning of 'training', which was based less on love and more on order.[28]

Upon these plywood forms she applied ghostly photographic images of her adult self, as well as other images relating to her age represented by the object. To suggest how 'the present [was] caught in the past' she had herself photographed in poses that conformed to the sculptural shapes.[29] These were then reduced to the appropriate scale and transferred onto the sculptures, so that the objects that had been places of withdrawal still contained her.

Chadwick also had images of her adult hands: resting on the incubator, playing the piano keyboard and coming from within the wigwam. She records in her notebook the idea of the 'laying on of hands' as a healing mechanism, as well as of hands 'recovering' and 'repossessing' the past through touch.[30] This idea of touch runs through all of Chadwick's sculptural works. Not only do the adult hands 'touch' the shell of the past, but, as a result of her body's being photographed so that it fits the physical dimensions of the sculptures, her body and the sculptures, performance and stasis, and past and present, become one. By being made and through the memory of making, the works have become 'animate organisms'.[31]

What Chadwick's notebooks also reveal are her thoughts about how she wanted to translate the everyday world into the gallery space. She had many ideas: for a performance to personalise her memories, of conducting tours around the exhibit, of whispered sounds coming from the sculptures and of a video.[32] But her overriding idea was expressed in the notebook as follows: 'the gallery becomes the memory / [the gallery] is the brain / a metaphor for the memory / Walk in space = getting inside artist's head.'[33] In her notebook she frequently questions the relationships between outer surface and hidden lives, between the containing space and different forms that act upon the psyche, and between the tangible and the intangible. She wanted the objects to suggest memories and trigger intuitive and contemplative thought in the audience.[34]

Just as many of Helen Chadwick's objects related to her childhood, many of Rachel Whiteread's early sculptures suggested places where the artist had withdrawn to dream. Her first work was *Closet* (1988), in which she filled a wardrobe with plaster and then dismantled the outer casing, revealing the solidified space within. This she covered in black felt. It was a piece of post-war furniture similar to one that her parents had owned, in which she hid as a child. In an interview with Lynn Barber she discussed how she had a very clear image of herself 'sitting at the bottom of [her] parents' wardrobe, hiding among the shoes and clothes, and the smell and the blackness and the little chinks of light'.[35] However, while for Whiteread the wardrobe was a place of escape, for adults it is also a place of privacy, only to be opened by those who are allowed to do so. It is a private space that in everyday life helps create order, and in artistic and poetic worlds is intimate and deep, with clothes and memories going back over time.[36] But it has also been used in children's literature as a place where extraordinary things can happen, as in C. S. Lewis' *The Lion, the Witch and the Wardrobe*, which even in the title links the mundane with the imaginary.

Bachelard wrote that in the real world children know pain inflicted by others. However, in places of solitude they can relax and give way to flights of fancy, which can be boundless in their creation of worlds outside history, reason or adult understanding.[37] Houses are scaled to the needs of an adult, with door handles too high, seats too large and objects too heavy for children.

As a number of writers have commented, it is scale that matters rather than just size. Children are small, but as they grow their experience and perception of the scale of their immediate world change accordingly.[38] For a child a wardrobe is a room within a room; another layer of skin between itself and the world.

Whiteread developed a range of works that cast small spaces of the type that a child might crawl into and under when wanting to be alone, including *Untitled (Black Bed)* (1991), which is a cast of the underside of a fold-up bed, or *Yellow Leaf* (1989), which is cast from the underside of a Formica-topped kitchen table similar to one owned by Whiteread's grandmother, of the type that could be extended for large family meals. The items that Whiteread used were not the originals, but were found in junk shops and salvage yards and stood in for furniture that had contained her, around which family rituals had been played out, and where her imagination and sense of self were framed and formed.[39]

Like Chadwick, Whiteread was abstracting her own recollections and emotive feelings from earlier years. Her casts are of 'happy places', where she went to dream, mutilate dolls and be in her own world. But childhood is also invested with anxieties and fears, and the artist has acknowledged that these works have sinister aspects, and speculated that she might have been investigating her own fears.[40] Bachelard has written how as adults we revisit our childhood imaginings by descending into ourselves.[41] For the viewer, the sculptural blocks taken from beneath and within domestic spaces, while resembling the geometric shapes used by minimalist artists, show the wear of human activity. By making these spaces unfamiliar, Whiteread hoped that the viewer would consider his or her spatial relationships in the world.[42] Furthermore, they provide a means for the viewer to consider his or her own childhood places of escape and dreams. 'By dreaming on childhood, we return to the lair of reveries.'[43]

ADULT WITHDRAWAL – THE BED

In a home, certain rooms are more private than others, or are open at certain times to certain groups of invited people. The bedroom is one of these. Here guests rarely venture. It is a place of intimacy, of comfort and where one goes when ill or sad.

Bedrooms were depicted from the mid-nineteenth century by the Impressionists and post-Impressionists, who frequently painted prostitutes and brothel scenes as representations of modern life. When looking at such images, the viewer's gaze is often that of a voyeur. However, unlike paintings, installations are able to include the visitor's memories of the sensations of the materials used, and can therefore allow him or her to enter into and engage with the situation.

In 1955 Robert Rauschenberg made *Bed*. A fellow student from Black Mountain College, Dorothea Rockburne, gave him an old quilt that had been used to cover a station wagon and was no longer needed. Not having any canvas one day, Rauschenberg started to paint on it, trying to use the patchwork as an abstract background. Finding that it still remained a quilt, he added a pillow, part of a sheet and painted some more. He said of this work that it was 'one of the friendliest pictures I've ever painted [...] My fear has always been that someone would want to crawl into it.'[44]

Rauschenberg, like Jasper Johns, with whom he was living and who also combined painting with found or recreated objects, wanted to make art that related to life, but that acted 'in the gap between the two'.[45] Rauschenberg liked to incorporate things that surrounded him and were worn by their relationships with humans.[46] Unlike the feminist artists discussed in Chapter 3, he was not trying to reclaim the quilt or gendered techniques for political reasons. It was a found object that carried an echo of its original function, but, due to the addition of gestural paint marks akin to the work of the abstract expressionists, the viewer not only had the visceral memories of the soft warmth of quilts but simultaneously an object containing the codes of art framed within the gallery. *Bed* was related to Rauschenberg's life, and, as Jasper Johns wrote: 'We have ties, we coexist with certain people and certain objects, with which we become a single body, a single family.'[47]

Rauschenberg's *Bed* was hung on the gallery wall and viewed from behind a barrier. The Greek-born American artist Lucas Samaras' *Bedroom* (1964) was, by contrast, an installation that recreated his living quarters and studio, and in which the bed occupied most of the space. The gallery visitor could walk into the room, look at the books and music, and lie down. This idea of allowing the audience to linger on beds and daydream was also used by Ilya and Emilia Kabakov in *The House of Dreams* at London's Serpentine Gallery in 2005, in which visitors were invited to fall asleep on beds that had been arranged in the galleries, and enter a dreamscape.[48] As in many of the Kabakovs' projects, the artists were suggesting answers to everyday problems, in this case: 'How can we fall asleep like we did in childhood, in a way that brings us rest and tranquillity?'[49] This brings into play the utopian ideas we carry about childhood – was it really that tranquil? The Kabakovs offered three solutions to this dilemma, one of pomp and ritual, another inside a dimly lit room and a third consisting of isolated beds overlooking natural gardens.[50]

Arranged in radial fashion under the Serpentine Gallery's cupola were six monuments, which had stairs going up the sides leading to beds on top. Here one was surrounded by light and the suggestion of a mausoleum. On the ground level doors led into small rooms, inside each of which was a tent of material on which brightly coloured, fairy-tale characters were projected. One could close the door, be quiet and retreat into childhood memories. The West Gallery had a series of beds set in a row, each surrounded on three sides by white gauze curtains, with the beds tilted to look out of the large window into the parkland of Kensington Gardens.[51] The installation was bright, and images from the exhibition show visitors lying down, alone in their private worlds.

Rather than setting up an installation in which the viewer becomes a participant, George Segal created tableaux that included plaster figures on real beds, so that the viewer's engagement is through sight, which triggers memory. Unlike the immersive installations of the Kabakovs, or the distancing used by Whiteread and Chadwick, Segal's use of lifelike figures makes the viewer a trespasser in those intimate and quiet moments.[52] The polychrome, fibreglass figures by Segal's contemporary Duane Hanson, of clothed Americans, posed as if in a frozen moment, are more 'realistic' than those constructed by Segal. Moreover, the latter's use of plaster, with its uniform colour and uneven surface, acts as a distancing mechanism. Nevertheless, Segal's bedroom tableaux are intimate views of people living outside the consumerist dream, one of alienation and resignation. Like Hanson, he wanted to show the world as he saw it, but his figures are more poignant as he aimed to reveal overlooked people, having grown up in the Bronx surrounded by those who were pinched, hurt and angry.[53]

Segal's early works include *Lovers on a Bed* (1962) and *Couple on Bed* (1965). The positions of the figures in the latter work suggest the beginnings of tensions, although the former shows the figures in each other's arms. In *Couple on Bed* the woman is lying naked on her back and the man, wearing trousers, is sitting on the edge of the bed, facing away from her. *Lovers on a Bed II* (1970) is more tender, the figures lying relaxed against each other with the appearance of completed, mutually satisfying love-making. The choreography of the bodies, the shapes made by the bent legs and arms and the natural curves are echoed in the curved lines of the bed's iron frame. The real bed contrasts with the rough, white surfaces of the plaster bodies and textiles, on which the wrapped bandages and abstracted features suggest simultaneously an echo of the real and fabrication.

Segal wrote that these bedroom scenes were part of his exploration of the everyday, but in the bedroom he 'had to face some kind of truth about myself, my own body and the bodies of just a few people I have known very well. I couldn't avoid [...] these kinds of absolutely infinitely complex relationships.'[54] He developed his tableaux first by thinking about the emotional impact that he wanted to create. Then he thought about the air around the figures and shapes, which is important for their expressiveness. He wanted the viewer to encounter them at many different levels.[55]

Segal has been linked with the work and ideas of Edward Hopper.[56] Certainly, he painted everyday and introspective moments of ordinary people in their everyday surroundings, including *Woman on a Bed* (1963), in which a woman is dressing while sitting on the edge of the bed, or *Woman Listening to Music* (1965), in which a woman lies down in a foetal position, wrapped in her own world. Hopper, like Segal, also repeatedly played with internal and external worlds, using the window as a motif. His painting *Morning in a City* (1944) links to other bedroom scenes such as *Summer in the City* (1950) and *Excursion into Philosophy* (1959): in all of these works the window is the key aspect in the room, and the sitter – most often female – is preoccupied with private thoughts. Hopper liked to carry around with him in his wallet a quote from Goethe, which stated that all literary activity 'is the reproduction of the world that surrounds me by means of the world that is in me'.[57]

Gregory Minissale has placed the frames of art into a phenomenological perspective by discussing Edmund Husserl's connection between consciousness and the real world, and how these are layered and interdependent. He argues that the viewer sees everyday events in art and cross-references them against memories and observations, with the frames around the paintings acting as frames to his or her perception of episodes.[58] When considering the tableaux of Segal, the framing within the gallery and the distancing of the real allow the installations to cooperate with the memories and consciousness of the viewer.

SHOCK

These frozen moments in time, framed by the gallery and read by the audience as simultaneously part of life and part of art, have also been considered in the work of the British artists Tracey Emin and Sarah Lucas. However, both work in a different era and social context. Emin and Lucas were part of the 'Young British Artists' (YBAs) phenomenon of the 1990s, which was brash, assertive, urban and commercially savvy in ways that had been equalled only by Andy Warhol and Jeff Koons a few decades earlier. Their relationship with American art is ambiguous, and their work has been considered as a post-colonial response to American domination.[59] However, I would argue that this relationship is more complex, and that, as well as being very British, the YBAs drew on a range of literary and artistic ideas, including American feminist works. I would also argue that, like Grayson Perry, who is discussed in Chapter 7, they belong to a tradition of social and political satire that includes the late-eighteenth-century cartoonist James Gillray, *Punch* magazine and the television series *Spitting Image*, and that has taken a variety of forms, including crude verses, the lambasting of authority in music halls and the intelligent subverting of pretentious arguments and theories.

Lucas, like many of the YBAs, including Damian Hirst and Sam Taylor-Wood, studied under Michael Craig-Martin at Goldsmiths' College in south-east London during the 1980s, where they learned much about self-promotion, marketing and business sponsorship at a time when art, in contrast to literature and music, was viewed with extreme scepticism.[60] Emin graduated from the Royal College of Art (RCA) in 1989 as a painter, but destroyed much of her student work, deciding instead to make herself the subject of her art. Whereas Emin's works suggest autobiographical accounts, Lucas looked to the media and street culture, and incorporated found objects to reflect society and her place within its structures.

In London there was a new cultural vortex in the late 1980s that considered anything outside the capital not worth looking at.[61] British 'yoof' proclaimed the reality of the present and not the sentimentality of the future or sacrosanct past. By spoofing the aggression and humour of the Vorticist magazine *Blast*, an article in *Artforum* from 1992 attacked whole areas of contemporary British culture, including the Turner Prize, the radio programme *Desert Island Discs*, Dering Street, 'the horrors of Hackney (more artists per square metre than any other locale in the Western World)' and 'flabby art collectors and financial backers whose vision of art goes no further than the secondary market'.[62] While humorous, it quoted many of the tensions that had been articulated by others, including the social emptiness, helplessness and apathy of post-Thatcher Britain. Contrasted with this were the violent and aggressive street styles that British youth culture had adopted from the 1950s onwards, personified by mods, rockers and punks, all of which were linked to pop music, and would later be institutionalised in a V&A exhibition of 1994–5: *Streetstyle*.[63]

As noted above, on leaving the RCA, Emin decided to change what her art was about and also the methods. 'I realised that I was much better than anything I ever made [...] I was my work.'[64] By focusing on her experiences and including images of her own body or the apparent detritus left by her, Emin's work has continued to question the relationships between representation, everyday life and the construction of the self in art.[65]

When Emin made *Everyone I Have Ever Slept with 1963–1995* in 1995, it created controversy because the media assumed that it meant her sexual encounters. The work consisted of a tent with flaps held to either side; the artist had embroidered and appliquéd the inside walls and floor with the names of her sleeping partners, including family, friends, lovers and two aborted foetuses. This soft, interior space, which one could only fully view by stooping and peering in, or, if one was bold enough, by going inside, apparently revealed the 'truth' about her life, and also placed the viewer in a situation that suggested both intimacy and intrusion. *Everyone I Have Ever Slept with 1963–1995* echoed confessional talk shows of the time such as *Kilroy*, where individuals revealed to the studio audience their intimate secrets. However, both the television series and the isolated cloth letters that formed names and phrases in Emin's work, together with the stitched framed cloth texts, were carefully choreographed.[66] The womb-like enclosed space can be a metaphor for withdrawal into memories, as well as for the sexual act. Emin denies that she had thought of the sexual interpretation. She chose the type of tent as it was, in her words, 'nice', 'cosy' and 'very feminine'.[67]

This work came just two years after her first exhibition, held at Jay Jopling's White Cube gallery in London in November 1993, entitled *Tracey Emin: My Major Retrospective, 1963–1993*, where, along with her first sewn blanket, *Hotel International* (1993), memorabilia from her past, which had littered her small London flat, was framed and displayed. Unlike the works by Rachel Whiteread that used distancing mechanisms, most of the objects shown were real things in their raw state. Echoing the autobiographical combines of Rauschenberg and Chadwick's *The Juggler's Table*, this exhibition included letters and photographs, a newspaper account of the car crash in which her favourite uncle died, teenage diaries, a phial of bloodstained tissue from an abortion, pills and a hospital wristband.[68] This immersive environment contained the outward manifestations of the life that Emin carried within herself.

Emin has turned her life into a spectacle. As discussed earlier, autobiography requires editing and choices about what to reveal and what to conceal. As we saw in Chapter 3, the combining of personal experiences with female creative techniques was an early American feminist strategy, one that was also adopted in Britain in the 1970s and 1980s. By the 1990s, this had become more complex. Whereas feminist artists had used this strategy to assert a collective voice that would counter dominant male frameworks, Emin's assertion of self is not politically subversive. While the personal remains the political, Rosemary Betterton has written that with the growth of mass consumerism, artistic identities have shifted in line with an increased fascination with celebrities.[69] The result of the personal has been to create a personality.

Emin's use of textiles also links to her past. As well as completing sewing projects early in her life, including an appliquéd elephant when she was seven that was shown in her first exhibition, she also once started a fashion course, where she was required to make and cut out patterns, as well as sew garments.[70] Although finding it hard and time-consuming, Emin has stated that she likes sewing.[71] At the time, making the tent interested her: 'It was about the way I made it in my flat, the moment, the history of it all.'[72] She would have been aware of the political use of textiles through the ages, not least from her art education, but also because of books like Rozsika Parker's *The Subversive Stitch*, published in 1984, which along with other books of the decade placed sewing at the centre of the historical construction of femininity and made it a political weapon. Like the work of many of the early feminist artists, her sewing is frequently collaborative and situated in the domestic space: 'I had friends who would come around to my little council flat and we'd sit there sewing in the afternoon and I'd make dinner for everyone, or tea.'[73] As with all skills that have become internalised, the phenomenological body takes over so that each repeated stitch becomes less about individual labour and more about reconstructing memories over time.

Emin's blankets form an important part of her textile output, drawing on personal experiences of rape, abortion, promiscuity and depression, as well as the ideas of female labour and the domestic. In many of her blankets, the comments that she has carefully sewn are sexual and about her formative years, during which, while living in her parents' hotel, she was not shielded from the abuse of strangers, nor from witnessing acts of adult intimacy.[74] The appliquéd blanket *Hotel International* of 1993 references her childhood in this Margate hotel, with the ironic comment at the bottom: 'The perfect place to grow'. As well as names of places and the date of her and her twin brother's birth, there is also the sewn fragment of speech 'You're good in bed'. As with another blanket, *Mad Tracey from Margate: Everyone's Been There* (1997), the different colours and backgrounds of the lettering, and the varying size and style of the phrases, suggest different voices and times that have become inscribed in the artist's consciousness. The sexual, 'street' language and the domestic become integrated. Alongside comments like 'Leave him Trace' and 'My best friends in New York' are others like 'Pussy cat' and 'Fuck off back to your week [*sic*] world that you came from'. This idea of discontinuous, aggressive phrases and fragments of narrative is similar to the strategies used by Grayson Perry. Like him, Emin uses a medium and scale that suggests the domestic in order to seduce people into viewing her work reflexively.

My Bed (1998; figure 6.3) was different in that it foregrounded a particular episode by unflinchingly presenting Emin's rumpled bed, complete with soiled sheets, bloodied underwear, empty vodka bottles, used condoms and other paraphernalia associated with a drunken sexual encounter. In an interview with Rebecca Fortnum, Emin discussed *My Bed* in relation to the real and staged.[75] When envisaging it, she mentally took it out of the bedroom into the white-cube space.[76] However, she reinstalls it for each exhibition, something that, as she has to relive the events, is emotionally draining. Exactly what is included changes according to location, so that in the Lehmann Maupin Gallery in New York in 1999, for instance, it contained a rope noose that was not included for the Turner Prize exhibition of the same year.[77] The way that it is seen also changes. In Japan, when it was initially shown and nobody knew it, it could be seen from a distance and looked beautiful. Only as people got nearer did they realise what was there.[78]

The soiling is apparently hers: the name *My Bed* implies the artist's ownership. Other artists, from Piero Manzoni, with his 90 cans of *Artist's Shit* (1961), to Gilbert and George, have used or depicted bodily fluids and excrement in their art – Manzoni's work being a repost to the 'genius' status of male artists. Judy Chicago and Carolee Schneemann included real tampons in their performances and installations during the 1970s in order to reclaim control over representations of women, and therefore Emin's inclusion of soiled sheets is part of a complex lineage. Unlike many traditional self-portraits by artists who have depicted themselves working, this shows Emin as a fallible human. In her own words: 'It's a self-portrait, but not one that people would like to see.'[79]

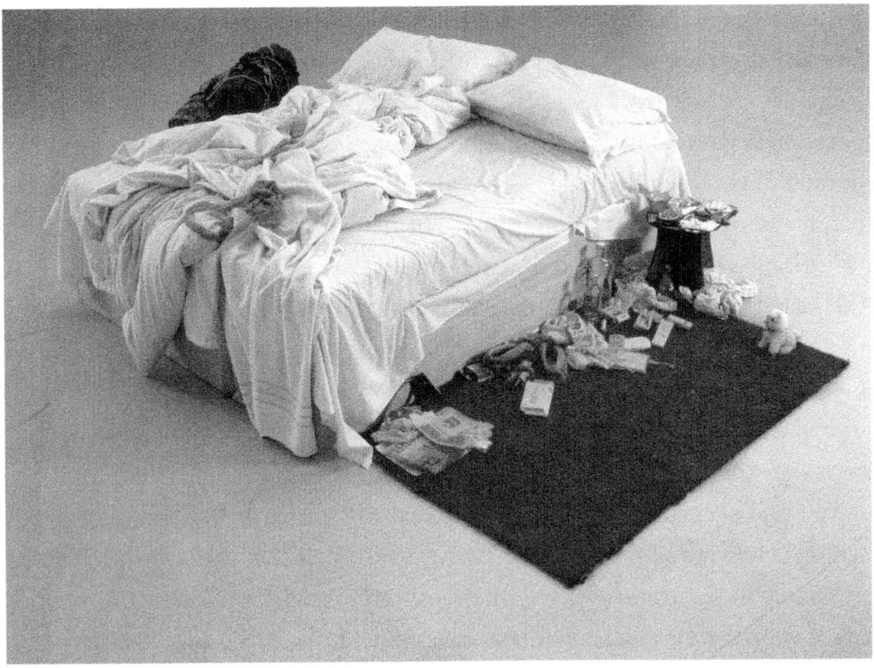

FIGURE 6.3 Tracey Emin, *My Bed* (1998).

Emin is not the first to display emotional pain in art, and links herself with Van Gogh, Edvard Munch, Egon Schiele, René Magritte and the expressionists.[80] Her regard for Munch's *The Scream* is evident from a short film that she made of herself naked, in the same location as Munch's painting, screaming.[81] However, just as Munch's art was created within his Norwegian context, Emin, along with other British artists of the 1990s, used her English, urban background as the emotional context of her art.[82] There is a long poetic and literary tradition of revealing subjective pain. Emin likes Emily Brontë's *Wuthering Heights*, the poetry of Robert Burns and Gustave Flaubert's *Madame Bovary*.[83] While Emin's works are more forceful and irreverent than these literary precedents, they reflect a feature of contemporary media that relishes exposing scandals and violence. Emin argues that she has a right to express her opinions about the world and represent herself in the same way that people from all walks of life now express their emotions.[84]

My Bed was, and remains, controversial. Just as Michael Landy's installation of his parents' home in Tate Britain was taken literally in the press, some critics also conflated art and life with regards to this installation. As part of a debate set up by the *Independent* entitled 'Would you show your bed to the public?' the interior designer Genevieve Hurley said that she thought it represented one's worst nightmare of having just moved and there being no storage space.[85] A related article by the art critic Matthew Collings in the *Observer* questioned whether anyone's bed could be art, and discussed the bedrooms of the artist Gillian Wearing and comedian Arthur Smith. Collings concluded: 'The fact that Wearing is an artist isn't on its own enough to make her bed into art.' He argued that *My Bed* was art as it was part of a series of works about the bedroom and her own experiences that Emin had developed over time. Referring to the real and unreal in Rauschenberg's *Bed*, which is now accepted as being iconic, he argued that Emin's work was not just a pile of things thrown together without thought. Although emotionally 'maximalist', this is the way that her art works.[86]

Her friend and fellow YBA Sarah Lucas has also used street language in her art. But rather than taking an autobiographical approach, often Lucas has situated her work in urban culture and suggested the crudity and sexual nature of the language in the tabloid press that has objectified women, by making installations of stand-in objects that act as humorous metaphors.

Au naturel (1994) is an old and stained double mattress, anthropomorphically propped against the wall; on the left-hand side a bucket lies below two yellow melons that have been placed in two 'pockets'; on the right are two oranges and an erect cucumber. As with so many of Lucas' installations, the construction is informal, spontaneous and made from things readily available. As Lisa Le Feuvre has commented, it is very English. Lucas specifies the types of vegetables and fruit, which are commonplace and until recently the only types of cucumber and melon stocked by British greengrocers. (The curators check the produce daily to make sure that it remains fresh – one of the stains came from a rotting cucumber.) The mattress is an old-fashioned type that had been commonly available in rented accommodation.[87] The bucket, fruit and dirty mattress are uncompromisingly matter-of-fact, preventing the work from epitomising a place of withdrawal into intimacy, dreams and privacy.

Neither is this the carefully posed and idealised female nude on a bed that has been integral to the history of Western art; rather, the male and female have been reduced to their sexual body parts. The soft folds of the slumped mattress suggest those of stomachs, and the pristine fruit that the couple are ready for action. As Amna Malik has said, 'There is no implication of guilt or shame, or even embarrassment.'[88]

However, Lucas says that there is a lot of laughter underneath the apparent darkness in this work.[89] The bawdy humour in *Au naturel* is also very English. Like naughty music hall songs and satirical programmes that subvert authority and bourgeois sensibilities, the humour is inscribed both through the means used and on the work. The mattress label says 'BEKA, Maxim Sanitized', and has a small picture of three kittens in bed, leaning against cushions.[90] The choice of soiled mattress with this small image of implied purity and innocence, together with the pert fruit and vegetables, echoes a well-known photographic gag by Linda Nochlin from 1972. The first of a pair of photographs, *Achetez des pommes*, is an anonymous nineteenth-century image of a woman in stockings and boots offering a tray of apples – and breasts – to the viewer. The second, *Achetez des bananes*, taken by Nochlin, is of a man, naked except for socks and shoes, leaning forward and offering bananas on a tray. While this joke plays with the traditional use of fruit as sexual metaphor in art – apples and breasts are frequently aligned in paintings of female nudes by Matisse and Picasso, for instance – Lucas would also have been aware of the ways in which feminist artists of the 1970s reclaimed the female body in their performances and sculptures. While not being a directly targeted, subversive message, Lucas was playing with previous rhetorical strategies in art. They are not about 'her' as such, but about transformation in the broadest sense.[91]

Unlike the casts of mattresses that Rachel Whiteread made in 1991 – *Untitled (Amber Double Bed)* and *Untitled (Amber Bed)* (of a single mattress) – Lucas' *Au naturel* and subsequent similar works imply human presence and sexual encounters. In Whiteread's sculptures, although the mattresses are slumped against the wall like their counterpart in *Au naturel*, rather than suggesting semi-supine humans they appear abandoned, like mattresses dumped in an alleyway. The familiarity of touch associated with all mattresses has also been subverted by Whiteread's use of rubber and high-density foam, as well as by the colour, which is suggestive of bodily fluids.

Lucas' *Beyond the Pleasure Principle* (2000) uses similar imagery to *Au naturel* to suggest male and female genitals in relation to a futon mattress. Again there is the use of the bucket for the female, but the male is suggested by a fluorescent light thrust through the mattress with two hanging bulbs. In *Fuck Destiny* of the same year, she incorporated found objects and furniture scrounged from markets and stores in and around Barcelona to make 13 sculptures for her exhibition at Tecla Sala called *Self-portraits and More Sex*. Here strip lights penetrate soft sofas, eggs signify breasts and fruit bursts out of T-shirts. These are not highly finished works, but suggest improvisation.

As well as making links with the language of the tabloids and street, Lucas has been influenced by the important feminist text by Andrea Dworkin, *Intercourse*, which was originally published in 1987.[92] This book discusses the complexity of sexual encounters and the asymmetry of power relations, through literary precedents. The opening chapter, for instance, considers the relationship of Tolstoy with his wife through the former's semi-autobiographical novella *The Kreutzer Sonata*. The story describes a man who, like Tolstoy, is completely cold and indifferent towards his wife, except during intercourse. In the end he kills her, and only then does he see her as a human being. Tolstoy locates the hatred of the husband–killer not in the particular woman, but in the sexual act itself and in the power of the man's addiction to sex.[93] In another story that Dworkin analysed, the play *A Streetcar Named Desire* by Tennessee Williams, it is the animal intensity of sex enjoyed by both male and female that is discussed. Stanley Kowalski is a heartless male without an interior life, but in spite of being beaten by him, his wife Stella defends him: 'there are things that happen between a man and a woman in the dark – that sort of make everything else seem – unimportant.'[94] They continue to live an apparently ordinary life similar to that of those around them, even after Stanley rapes Stella's sister, Blanche.

While literature has often discussed unhealthy relationships and sexual encounters, albeit using language to aestheticise the situations, contemporary tabloid newspapers also thrive on that which is illicit, and incorporate sexualised and objectified imagery. Lucas has appropriated this into her works, like *Sod You Gits* (1991), which was one of a series of enlarged double-page spreads from tabloids, in this case the *Sunday Sport*, that showed women in ways that dehumanised them. This article was about a woman named Sharon, described as a 'midget', who was apparently the most popular kissogram in Britain.[95] As Lucas has said: 'I'm dipping into the culture, pointing a finger: directing attention to what's there.'[96]

What becomes evident from all of the work discussed in this chapter is the complexity of the relationship between art and life. While the works by Emin are overtly personal, Whiteread's and Chadwick's, although also about personal memories, employ distancing strategies. Ilya and Emilia Kabakov suggest imaginative fantasy in their installations that encourages gallery visitors to withdraw. Segal and Lucas reflect what they see around them, but blur the boundaries between found things and artistic ideas. However, all represent developments of traditions existing within art and use the gallery space to frame their works. There, viewers encounter installations that invite them to enter into and reflect upon childhood and adult places of withdrawal.

7

Objects, Sentiment and Memory

The turning of a house into a home plays an important part in creating a place where one's identity can be developed and one can be comfortable. Many homes are structurally similar to one another, but the chosen objects that fill the spaces act, and are acted upon, in ways that are intimately linked with our individual psyches. Memories of rituals, both everyday and celebratory, together with the repeated actions of cleaning and holding, bind us to our possessions. Some have special perceived values projected onto them and are displayed and brought out for special occasions. Others are mundane, inexpensive and functional, but nonetheless, through frequent use, form an important part of the landscape of being.

This chapter is divided into four sections: 'Objects and Identity', 'The Commonplace', 'Display' and 'Vessels'. While these themes are integral to the perception of objects in the home, what I discuss are the ideas and strategies used by artists to negotiate the move from the everyday world into that of a gallery, from the personal to the collective, and from the overlooked or cherished to the displaced and formally displayed.

OBJECTS AND IDENTITY

Judy Attfield has discussed the different types of objects that we own. Some are everyday tools that make living easier, which she calls 'lower-case things'. These include kitchen implements, mugs and plastic bottles, which do not draw attention to themselves but are nonetheless important for everyday function. In contrast are 'things with attitude', which are designed, or indeed overdesigned, to become style statements.[1] Clearly there are complexities here. While some things remain anonymous, people hold tactile memories of their usage. Most domestic objects are mass- or batch-produced, even those that are expensive, so that thousands of identical copies exist of the same things. However, by becoming the focuses of meanings and memories accreted onto them by individual owners, apparently identical objects can be viewed in distinct ways. These memories may be associated with everyday habits, or may relate to family or activities and trophies won in the public world. In each of these instances, the material and mental worlds become entwined.

Materials are fundamental both to the values given to objects, and to the roles that those objects perform in the home. Plastic is functional, universal and yet, in the minds of many, invisible. It carries little ritual significance. But in the industrialised world it has taken over from clay as the container of things, and the varied properties of the different forms of plastic make it ideal for many everyday functions. Clay is fundamental to human existence. It is of the earth, yet through the action of fire it is transformed into permanent receptacles for food and drink. In different forms ceramics provide comfort – objects formed of this material are part of personal and family rituals – and status, in the shape of cherished objects of display. Unglazed, ceramic objects traditionally have had little value, but, the addition of glazes to create a coloured skin over the burned earth, as well as decorative features applied onto and into the surface, adds to the perceived value of the material. Different metals have different statuses, but only some are used regularly in relation to food, drink or domestic tasks. Silver is perceived as a celebratory material, frequently used for trophies, for special occasions and for demonstrating status. However, with the invention of mass-production techniques, what had been materials out of the reach of most of the population became inexpensive, so finely decorated ceramics and the appearance of silver have become ubiquitous.

Some objects stay with us throughout our lives, others become less relevant as we change and grow older. In a mobile society – Americans on average move 14 times in their lives and the British eight times – objects become the ballast that people bring with them to provide a sense of continuity between the past and future.[2] The projection of ideas and feelings onto these objects, their forms and functions, and their pervasiveness have proved to be a rich field of exploration for artists. In their reframed existence within the art world, these objects can stand in for a range of memories and sentiments, and can appear domestic and 'safe' while enabling comment on particular social and political issues.

The importance of domestic objects to people has been demonstrated by the anthropologist Daniel Miller, who studied 30 people from a single street in south London over a period of 17 months, focusing on their objects and how they were chosen, placed, ordered and spaced out.[3] The interviewees represented a broad sweep of people from different nationalities, who spoke different languages, had different expectations and had been living on the street for varying lengths of time. As the geographer Doreen Massey discussed in the early 1990s, the space/time compression in the post-modern era has led to a fragmentation of local cultures and a loss of a sense of place outside the home. She and other researchers have discovered that to counter the general sense of disorientation there has been a compensatory drive to create a centred and stable identity by developing one's own place.[4] This was clearly the case for the subjects in Miller's study, which found that although neighbours are no longer really important, people's relationships are key to their contentment in life, and that central to this are possessions, which bind people to their own ethnic and social backgrounds. It is through giving and receiving, rituals, making objects, and social and material routines that order and meaning are created in people's lives.[5]

Three examples that Miller cited are important to our discussion. His first chapter discussed someone whose flat was totally devoid of any form of decoration that went beyond a desire for a clean, minimal space. 'There is a violence to such emptiness. Faced with nothing, one's gaze is not returned, attention not circumscribed [...] There is no sense of the person as the other, who defines one's own boundary and extent.'[6] This was revealed to be a mirror of the interviewee, who had led a severely circumscribed life and was unable to take responsibility for himself. What is also interesting is that this blankness also undermined the self-confidence of the researcher, as he no longer had boundaries and markers against which to identify himself.

Another of the participants was a foster mother who was always particularly concerned when a foster child arrived with nothing of his or her own. Although she had her own children, she wanted those passing through her care to feel integrated and part of that general warmth. She had a constantly changing range of photographs that included pictures of those in her care. All of the children collected souvenirs and things that mattered, even frayed toys, which although normally stowed away, were constantly reappearing and being reused as appropriate, so that past and present merged and a gradual sense of self and others developed.[7]

The third family of interest for this discussion was an elderly couple who had many friends and relations. Objects in the home and presents that were given and received were used to bridge and bond social relations. The care given to the objects matched that given to people, so that things that had been inherited from previous generations were discussed in the context of the now dead relatives, and the repair of old things that mattered was integral to the craftsmanship of love, care and devotion shown towards people. The objects were anchors both back through time and outwards among the network of current friends and family.[8]

THE COMMONPLACE

This section considers how and why artists from the 1970s in Britain began to incorporate commonplace domestic objects into their sculptural practices. The movement known as New British Sculpture emerged at the end of the 1970s after a decade when the term 'sculpture' had been reformulated to include works that were made outside the gallery system, were performative and did not necessarily project into or take up space. New British Sculpture reacted against that reformulation, and also against the abstraction and formalism of minimalism, and moved towards a more active dialogue with trends emerging in Europe. While each artist had a different agenda, they all created work that was conceptual and concerned with addressing ideas from outside the boundaries of art, including social issues, science, spirituality and archaeology.[9] Those artists who will be discussed here made work related to dwelling for the gallery, and appropriated and changed the idea of the ready-made, using individual elements as a form of sociological collecting.[10]

Many of the artists who were important within this movement, including Tony Cragg, Richard Deacon, Richard Wentworth and Alison Wilding, were trained at the RCA in London between 1966 and 1977. This institution was made up of small independent departmental units, although there was a lot of cross-disciplinary discussion.[11] Others in the movement, including Bill Woodrow and Anish Kapoor, studied at the Chelsea School of Art during the same era. The traditional disciplines of painting and sculpture were in crisis at the time, and the student magazine of the RCA, *Arc*, devoted an issue to questioning their relevance within the spirit of the age, when other media appeared more contemporary.[12] What form sculpture should take was also discussed widely in journals like *Art Monthly*, with some articles promoting traditional materials like stone and bronze, and other articles reflecting or contesting different styles and content.[13] It was also a time when budgets for the arts were tight, when the Arts Council and the gallery system were derided, and the Tate was attacked for not having a coherent strategy for collecting.[14]

However, from the late 1970s, British sculpture underwent a dramatic renewal. This new generation created work that was not formulaic, was more flamboyant and witty and incorporated a wealth of imagery.[15] Not only did their work mark a return to the subject, but they also retained a crucial concern with material and process.[16] Although different in style, these artists have exhibited together since the seminal show at the Institute of Contemporary Arts (ICA) in 1981 titled *Objects and Sculpture*, which introduced some of them and promoted them as having shared characteristics, approaches to making and attitudes towards previous generations of sculptors.[17] Tony Cragg was not included in this exhibition, but exhibited at the Whitechapel Gallery during the same year.[18] Most have been backed by the Lisson Gallery in London.

In 1982 Tony Cragg wrote that his interests were 'man's relationship to his environment and the objects, materials and images in that environment'.[19] He questioned what it meant to live among comparatively new materials like plastics with their industrial qualities and commercial colours, as well as the systems that produced and underpinned the consumption of these objects. He felt this environment had become so poor that it was almost embarrassing to consider its metaphysical, poetic and mythological aspects.[20]

From 1978 Cragg moved from constructing montage stacks of diverse, discarded materials into making work out of salvaged plastic that he found washed up on the shore. He chose the objects for their colour, so that they could play their part in his chromatic installations.[21] He hoped that these would 'offer themselves as complex symbols for new experiences, insights and freedoms'.[22] His chosen fragments and objects represented the material waste of capitalist society, each one having been bought originally for its utility, used and then discarded. Although sculpture is not part of the utilitarian system, Cragg believes that it can sow the seeds for change by suggesting some human significance, life and meaning.[23] 'Sculpture is only a method of dealing with the big world [...] of formulating questions about the world we live in, about reality.'[24]

Cragg incorporated many different materials into his work from the late 1970s to the 1990s. He was not interested in romantic materials, but ones that were typical of an urban environment. Although he knew the work of the conceptualists, minimalists, land artists, the Italian Arte Povera movement and the German artist Joseph Beuys, he wanted to challenge the aestheticised purity and geometry of much art of the time, and not to make work that was primarily gestural and conceptual.[25] Whereas British land artists like Richard Long and Andy Goldsworthy might arrange or manipulate natural materials in the landscape and then bring either photographs or 'souvenirs' back into the cultural domain of the gallery, Cragg's work of this era addressed environmental concerns through displaying the debris of industrial production. In contrast to minimalist artists, who used geometry and repetition to suggest industrialisation and the loss of the original, Cragg brought together fragments and stacked, arranged or heaped them into geometric forms. *New Stones, Newton's Tones* (1978) humorously references both land art and minimalism in the plastic fragments arranged across the gallery floor in an open formation, within a rectangular shape. Cragg also played with these artistic precedents in *Spectrum* (1985), which consisted of a low, flat-topped, rectangular pile of plastic debris that, like *New Stones, Newton's Tones*, was arranged according to the colour spectrum, from red to blue.

Harold Bloom has written about the way that ideas are inherited and then reconfigured using fresh dialogues. 'A poet antithetically "completes" his precursor, by so reading the parent-poem as to retain its terms but to mean them in another sense.'[26] Although incorporating objects appropriated from life, Cragg did not intend his work to negate the importance of art, its systems and histories. Instead, he played with influences while using sculpture to promote reflection on art and life. As Peter Schjeldahl has written, Cragg met the cultural crisis of the early 1980s – 'a reign of radically uncentered, fragmented, heady sensibility', which lacked any 'widely shared lexicon of the "body language" essential to sculpture' – head on with his profusion of theatrical, decorative mosaics that spoke of the era and remained 'loyal to a sense of sculpture's prerogative in history'.[27]

Some of his mosaics of plastic debris were arranged on the wall to illustrate everyday situations and objects. *Green, Yellow, Red, Orange and Blue Bottles II* (1982), for instance, traced the image of coloured bottles across the gallery wall. *Real Plastic Love* (1984) was an image of a couple embracing. The title of the latter work suggests the fictions in magazines and film. In both of these sculptures, image, object fragment and material combine for the viewer in an open shape that allows the wall behind to breathe through. Each object acts within the whole, adding weight, colour and accent, but refers back to its origin within the world.

The point about these found objects is that they are ubiquitous in the home, but have also been broken and thrown out to be replaced by cheap replicas.[28] While being integral to many functions, negotiations and gestures of life and the mere sight of different plastics triggers haptic memories, plastic tends not to be a material associated with sentiment. Cragg's use of titles increases the references and layers of interpretation in his works, adding a conceptual underpinning that combines with the formal art references and the incorporation of everyday materials and contexts.[29]

Like Cragg, Richard Wentworth has, since the late 1970s, used rearranged and reconfigured found objects: the residue left by, in the words of Michael Bracewell, the 'relentless momentum of commodity culture'.[30] He too has found inspiration in postwar art from the Continent, including Arte Povera, with its use of transient and provisional assemblages of things, and also the work of the Swedish-born sculptor Claes Oldenburg.[31] Many of Wentworth's objects have been culled from the world of the home and remain complete, so they contain touch and gesture memory related to the routines of life. It is these relationships with things that help build and express identity.[32] He has also captured these informal gestures in his photographs that record people's 'making-do' actions, like using a child's shoe to prop open a window, or a wellington boot to wedge open a door.[33] Although those who have performed these actions have gone, these found images are echoes of their lives.

The objects that Wentworth incorporates into his sculptures frequently carry the names of their materials: a glass, a rubber, a tin. He puts them into odd relationships that, like his photographs, suggest chance encounters and making-do gestures. Like Cragg, his titles add to their combined meanings. *Early Hours* (1982) consists of two pillows: one with a torch on it, the other with a metal DIY tool. *Dry Crying* of the same year is of a light bulb wrapped in a napkin, hanging over the edge of an empty galvanised bucket. While the constant reference is to people, and their movements and rituals aided by objects, the juxtaposition of things suggests linguistic games or meanings beyond the ensemble.[34]

From 1980 Bill Woodrow has also appropriated discarded objects from everyday life, but in his works he has skilfully modified them in order to create a third element. For instance, by cutting through the outer membrane of a Hotpoint washing machine in *Twin Tub with Guitar* (1981), and from these cuts forming a guitar, he created a clash of realities – the guitar being a pop icon and the washing machine being a domestic item. Together the images destabilise the traditional associations of each.[35] Like the works of Cragg, these works could be seen as a positive recuperation of the mass of objects created for the consumer culture of Thatcher's Britain. However, his sculptures are also playful and reminiscent of childhood games, such as cutting around a card again and again to make a loop large enough to walk through, or folding paper into a concertina and cutting shapes from the whole to make a long Christmas decoration of figures holding hands. *Electric Fire with Yellow Fish* (1981) consists of a small domestic fire made of metal, with a fish shape cut from the back; this shape has then been painted yellow and put back behind the grille of the fire. Woodrow said that he liked the formal qualities of the different appliances that he incorporated into his sculptures.[36] The cubic white shapes of his spin dryers and washing machines suggest the blocks of stone used by traditional sculptors, and his cutting is a witty echo of their carving – echoing the playfulness of Duchamp.[37]

Like Cragg, Woodrow also wanted sculpture to make the audience contemplate the everyday environment. In another work from 1981, *Car Door, Armchair and Incident*, he suggested a violent episode from the television programme *The Sweeney*. A car door hangs on the wall, with a sawn-off shotgun on the edge of an old armchair, which has had the back shot away and its stuffing splattered on the wall behind, similar to the cartoon explosion in Roy Lichtenstein's *Whaam!* (1963). As Waldemar Januszczak has suggested, these objects are clever articulations about Britain in the 1980s. In transforming junk that he has found in skips into this and similar situations, Woodrow is not only commenting upon the failed promises of capitalism, but recreating the violent and uneasy world of riots, bombs and dumped goods that overflowed across pavements and out of skips during that era.[38]

All these works by Cragg, Wentworth and Woodrow recuperate the magma of everyday domestic life and reposition it in another context. These are things that people had bought to aid their lives, tools to make things happen quicker or to aid bodily comfort, rather than things with sentimental value. Unlike the found objects used by Rauschenberg and Allan Kaprow that were discussed in Chapter 2, they do not just connote everyday life, but are sensuous and immediate images that are designed to subvert our ingrained cultural responses.[39] As Tomás Maldonado has said, the idea of comfort and hygiene being available for all is a modern concept, created since industrialisation.[40] However, along with these affordable consumer objects came new cultural expectations about the home and people's roles and activities within it; these expectations, Maldonado has argued, are themselves a way of controlling the masses in a capitalist society.[41]

DISPLAY

As well as objects that are part of the stuff of life, most people also create a private set of references by singling out particular objects that give order to their experiences and aspirations.[42] While in the past religious icons would have played their part in creating order through rituals, regular touch and being visible within the home as part of a broader shared culture, in the contemporary secular Western world, domestic religious display is less prevalent. Instead, particular objects become precious in the mind of the owner for a variety of reasons: because they have been won, because they express aspirations or because they remind the owner of others. Often not valuable in themselves, they nonetheless have symbolic and associative resonance.[43] By being singled out, separated from the flow of everyday life and displayed prominently in the home, these things become objects for contemplation, and also suggest the constructed narratives of the owner.[44]

This idea of some objects being special and on display is referenced in the 12 pairs of before-and-after photographs that Cornelia Parker showed as part of her exhibition at the Ikon Gallery, Birmingham, in 1988–9, *Thirty Pieces of Silver*.[45] This was the first of her works in which an act of destruction is the pivotal point between the original existence of an object or group of objects, with their functions, meanings and contexts, and their translation into works of art to be displayed in a gallery. In this case, she arranged a 'path' of 1,000 pieces of domestic silverware that she had collected from garage sales, markets and skips, on a Hertfordshire road, in a witty dialogue with both the land art of Richard Long and Cragg's *New Stones, Newton's Tones*, and arranged for a steamroller to flatten them. Alongside the exhibited 30 pools of suspended, flattened silver objects, the photographs showed particular objects within the home, the first of the pair showing an object looking pristine and cared for, and the second depicting the same object squashed and rejected. In the 'before' images, six shiny silver cups are displayed on a high shelf, a polished wire fruit basket contains pristine fruit on a shiny wooden table, and knives and forks are placed in readiness for a family meal, the light glancing across their ornate handles. In the 'after' photographs, the flattened cups have been discarded under a shelf outside the house in a grass-clipping hod, the wire basket is abandoned outside in a dirty doorway and the knives and forks are stuck in the gap between a brick wall and a peeling outside pipe. The relationship with the owner has been severed, and they have become overlooked and forgotten.[46]

Tom Leddy has argued that in early childhood our first aesthetic experience is about cleanliness and tidiness.[47] We absorb this, and strive to keep special things looking as though they are cared for, arranging them to suit our notions of taste and order. Silver naturally tarnishes, but in our efforts to keep nature at bay and suggest the home as a civilised place this tarnish is repeatedly removed, along with all traces of inappropriate dirt.[48] Each object plays its part in creating the mesh of meaning for the owner that he or she develops over time in the making of the home. This is our part of the world, which, as Bachelard – a philosopher whom Parker admires – Husserl and Merleau-Ponty have argued, is carried around within us, and is understood through bodily interaction, memories and imagination.[49]

Cornelia Parker has made many installations using silver; she says it is a commemorative material and that objects made of silver represent landmarks in people's lives.[50] In the original exhibition of *Thirty Pieces of Silver*, alongside the photographs, the flattened silverware hung in 30 circular 'pools' and a large photograph of the steamroller in action was hung on the wall (see figure 7.1). The title refers to the biblical betrayal by Judas of Christ, and like the titles and wit of the works by Cragg and Wilson makes connections beyond the gallery. As with all of Parker's works, it is less about the objects themselves and more about revealing the investment that humans make in things.[51]

Most of the objects Parker collected were of silver plate, on which a thin layer of silver sandwiched a nickel alloy, so they did not have great monetary value. Although she was planning on transforming these objects through a ritual violent 'death', there had already been violence in their formation, albeit tempered with delicacy so that they could be made with minimal material.[52] The drop-forging, spinning and stamping would have been hot, noisy and unrelenting. Some were so inexpensively produced that they were reduced to powder under the force of the steamroller.[53] Norman Bryson has pointed out that in pre-industrial still-life paintings, a display of

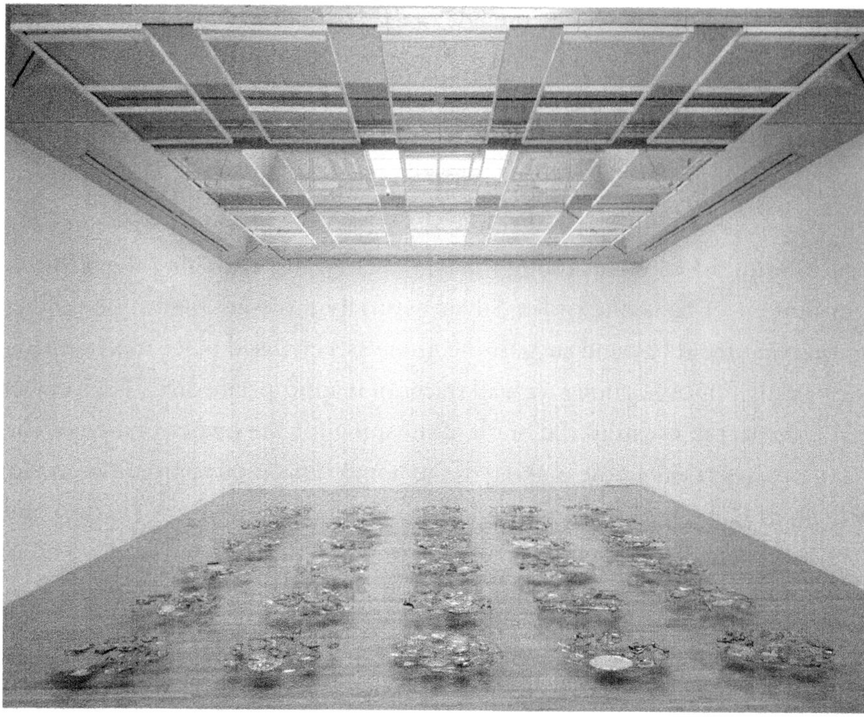

FIGURE 7.1 Cornelia Parker, *Thirty Pieces of Silver* (1988–9).

silver suggested prodigality and waste. However, surplus wealth in today's society is not confined to the very rich. Industrialisation has meant that the appearance of silver has become available to many, although it has retained its associative overtones of 'making special'.[54]

The aspirational qualities of silver plate are a manifestation of the desire for bourgeois respectability, something that was recounted by Alan Bennett in his monologue for radio *An Ideal Home*, in which he explored his childhood recollections of his family home in Leeds in the 1940s. Parker has discussed how she wanted to squash the bourgeois pretensions out of the objects, describing the 'killing' of them by steamroller as being similar to Tom and Jerry cartoons, in which characters are flattened by unlikely – and frequently exaggerated – means, after which they spring back to life.[55]

In the original Ikon exhibition the pools of objects were hung from a grid structure in an overall formation of five by six squares, with a metre between each pool.[56] This meant that the visitor could walk through it and experience the changing perceptual perspectives that he or she has when moving in the home. It also allowed for changing relationships between the body and the sculptural elements, and between each pool and the whole. As one meanders between the suspended groups, the air currents make them waft, causing a light metallic tapping as the individual pieces jostle with each other. These tinkling, shining, moving 'lily pads' of things reflect back to the viewer memories of his or her past life and become a catalyst for stories and personal associations.[57] The light flickers off the surfaces and the silver threads, reflecting the physical fact of being suspended, but also suggesting the idea of being in suspension.[58]

Each deflated object has its place within its pool, and each time they are hung the pattern is followed. Although suggesting the domestic in that every object has its place and is kept at its peak, the display negates the relationship with the real. The order of the pools changes at each exhibition according to circumstances, but the ones with the most interesting objects are distributed evenly.[59] Like the works using plastic debris by Cragg that reference both art and life, in *Thirty Pieces of Silver* the former lives of the individual objects are legible, but the display strategy references the strategies used in art. In the introduction to *The Poetics of Space*, Bachelard wrote about the power of the imagination, where the function of the real and that of the unreal need to cooperate in order to receive the psychic benefit of poetry. Just as Parker has said that she likes the idea of the indefinable, of the space between absence and presence, and to glance at the world from different angles, Bachelard wrote that poetry takes place on the margin, where it can charm and disturb.[60]

Silver tarnishes quickly. Over the duration of an exhibition, the action of oxygen on metal transforms the surface from an optimum state to one where the surface reflects less well. Parker has discussed this constant change through the action of natural forces as being a metaphor for the cycles of life.[61] But the Tate cares for and preserves all of its works of art. After each exhibition they are polished and stored, and at every hanging there is a last-minute polish. Parker has commented on the irony that having been destroyed, the objects are now kept in a plastisote-lined tray with a red tarnish-proof cloth spread over the top, and have teams of people caring for them.[62]

In some of her works Parker has explored the meaning of tarnish. Tarnish has no value and people find it ugly. When Parker acquired two wedding goblets that she was to include in *Thirty Pieces of Silver*, they were so tarnished that she thought that the neglect of the objects could be used as a metaphor for a marriage, so that they became a work in their own right, *Twenty Years of Tarnish (Wedding Presents)* (1996).[63] In her major retrospective in 1998 at the Serpentine Gallery in London, she also displayed cloths with the tarnish that had been taken from particular objects while cleaning them, including a Communion lamp and Charles Dickens' knife. Like her other works these contain a narrative element that illuminates the way that humans accrete values onto objects.

Installations can be a way of engaging with sidelong glances at everyday life. Unlike photographs and films, where the viewer's experience is controlled by, respectively, the camera's viewpoint or the running time, an installation is material, with the substance made from the everyday, around which the viewer moves. There is a spiritual displacement in the viewer so that what was everyday is now perceived in a different way.[64] The installation, which is of life, yet separate from it, serves as a springboard for the imagination of each person.

Tony Cragg has also considered how objects in the home acquire new meanings in the gallery. As well as the broken objects that were discussed earlier, from the early 1980s he has also made installations from containers arranged in ways suggesting domestic display. *Five Bottles on a Shelf* (1982; figure 7.2) consists of five plastic bottles that would have contained useful, household products shown on a shelf as if they were special. They are arranged according to the colour spectrum, with their formal qualities balanced with all the love and care shown in the paintings and etchings of common objects by Giorgio Morandi. This unexpected focus forces the audience to look anew at these containers made from precious resources. Writing about a subsection of still-life painting called rhopography, Norman Bryson has discussed how the representation of things lacking importance is resistant to the human impulse towards singularity and greatness. Rather than suggesting importance, the depiction of food and everyday things suggests a baseline to life which all, however privileged, must adhere.[65] In the display of *Five Bottles on a Shelf*, Cragg has played with the idea of mundanity by suggesting that

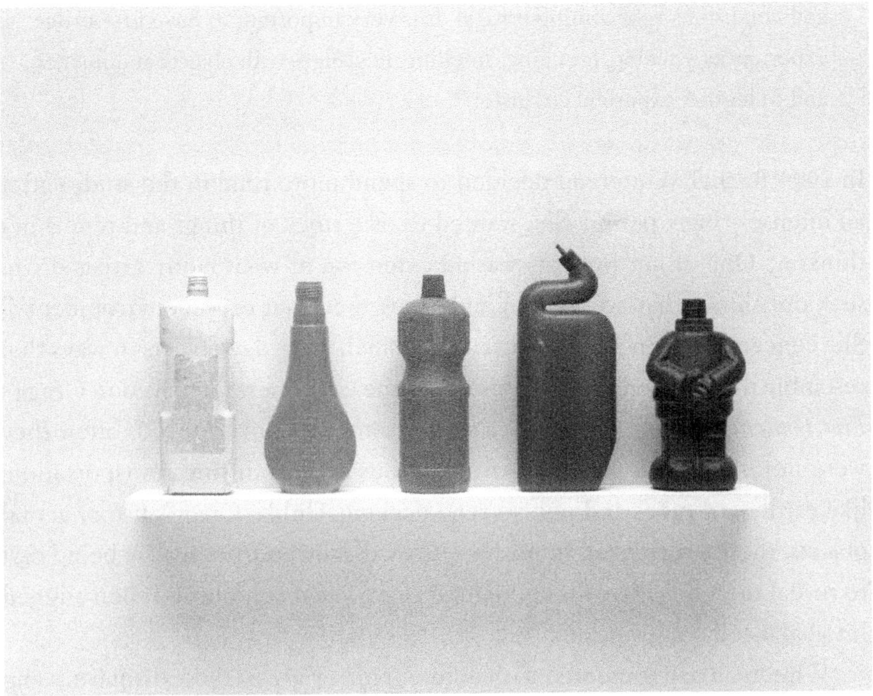

FIGURE 7.2 Tony Cragg, *Five Bottles on a Shelf* (1982).

these possessions would have been items that reflected well on the owner. In using this strategy, he wanted viewers to push their understanding of everyday things and go beyond the utilitarian.[66]

In other displays, the objects themselves have been altered to give distinction. *Cumulus* (1998), for instance, is a multi-storey block made up of glass bottles arranged on glass shelves. Their surfaces have been eroded so that they glimmer rather than shine, and this combined with their complex formal arrangement turns these everyday items into ones worthy of contemplation. As such they have a double reality – there is an echo, an essential qualitative reminder of their mundane life, but they also have a new authority as 'sculpture'. The use of the privileged space of the gallery, combined with the alteration of the objects, has reversed the usual human hierarchies.[67] As Cragg wrote:

> The need to know objectively and subjectively more about the subtle, fragile relationships between us, objects, images and essential natural processes

> and conditions is becoming critical. It is very important to have first-order experiences – seeing, touching, smelling, hearing – with objects and images and to let that experience register.[68]

In 2004 Rachel Whiteread decided to spend more time in the studio after an intensely busy period. She wanted to take stock of things and renew her thinking. One of her projects was an extension of what many artists do: to seek out things that are hidden and 'draw them out of the environment'.[69] She concentrated on assembling casts of small everyday objects in ways that resemble displays within the home. Like the containers displayed in Cragg's *Five Bottles on a Shelf*, these objects represented the overlooked; often they were items made to protect more precious objects during transportation, like cardboard tubes and polystyrene packing. Unlike Cragg's use of actual objects, these overlooked items have been distanced from life by being cast to reveal their negative, functional interiors, given colours and then aligned into balanced compositions.

Whiteread experimented with different materials for these displays, using bio-resin, synthetic resin and plaster for casting, and steel and wood as contrasting materials. In 2004 she stated that she had just started experimenting with new material samples in her studio, and was enjoying the accidents and chance happenings.[70] *Line Up* (2007–8) is made up of 18 casts taken from what appear to be pieces of cardboard tubing, lined up against each other on a shelf. Made of plaster, pigment, resin, wood and metal, the individual objects are coloured yellow, ochre, grape and red. *Focus* (2008) consists of a pale upright cuboid, a bright-yellow vessel resembling an upside-down Florence flask, and a cube cast from a small box, arranged on a shelf. *Scatter* (2008) has 15 elements set on a shelf, each with different colours, textures and densities, but all small and domestic in scale. They include the cast of a wooden box, which reveals the folds and flaws of usage, casts of chunks and nuggets of expanded polystyrene packing, and cast of conical shapes, each now of different materials, in yellow, black and sage green. In placing the casts alongside forms made from natural and manufactured materials, they move to a perceptual state between original utility and acquired uselessness.[71]

Because of the material properties of plaster, resin, wood and metal, the surface textures are varied and the colours are taken up with different densities and qualities. Rather than displaying them because they have personal resonance or to suggest function, Whiteread arranged, stacked and rearranged each element to create formal relationships.[72] As in the work of the modernist sculptor Constantin Brâncuşi, different materials and finishes are combined together. However, in Brâncuşi's works there is frequently a hierarchy from the organic to the man-made, with rough-cut wood juxtaposed with stone and highly polished metals, and occasional incursions of plaster and concrete.[73] In the works of Whiteread the nuances of finish and hierarchies of materials are less clearly defined.

We all are used to handling cardboard, polystyrene and other 'lower-case' objects, many of which are used to surround and protect special objects during transportation, or to store small things like screws and nuts. The packaging is something cheap and 'throwaway' that gets battered. But the temperature of the material and its surface tactility are part of learned bodily understanding that we all carry with us. The eye perceives that residue of usage, the echo of people and actions, but the original function of the objects is gone. The casting of these objects, and the formation of geometric shapes out of materials with potential for use, including resin, metal and wood, provides a levelling of perceptual values. Like the objects in Parker's *Thirty Pieces of Silver*, or Cragg's *Five Bottles on a Shelf*, the careful arrangement, the 'making special', has upended normal social hierarchies, with all the 'things' being given a shared fate.

VESSELS

One of the most important forms of object within the home is the vessel. It has been fundamental to human survival and therefore goes back to earliest man, but over the millennia it has also become integral to the performances of ritual, prestige and celebration. Not only is it functionally and culturally resonant, but as a manipulated shape that wraps air, whose inside and outside are contiguous and can counter expectations of the space within, whose surface texture and appearance are important to our understanding of it, and whose form can be hugely altered before it stops being functional, the vessel form allows for rich exploration.[74]

In the real world vessels have been employed for utility and domestic display, and the surfaces have been used to express political and social issues. Surface embellishment has always been used for higher-status ceramics, with glaze and decoration adding to the perceived value. Through touch and use, mugs, plates and other ceramic vessels gain personal resonance and become part of those in-between areas of life that matter. Their ubiquity means that the form has been fundamental across craft, design and fine-art practices, and has been a particularly important vehicle for expression in recent decades.

The changes in art-school education during the 1970s meant that art schools, including the RCA, began accepting ceramicists, who were taught art and design histories as part of the new Bachelor of Arts degree, and came into contact with a broader range of ideas.[75] In this new environment, it was almost impossible for the students to maintain the concept of 'good, honest potting' and most reacted against the tradition epitomised by the work of the British potter Bernard Leach, reaching out to have dialogues with related practices like sculpture, and to engage critically with the history of ceramics.[76] They also moved away from 'well-made' objects that could be industrially produced, and instead experimented with form and material. As the ceramicist Alison Britton was later to write, there was no need to make finely finished, hand-made, functional ceramics. Instead they needed to be relevant for the era.[77]

Among the first ceramic graduates from the RCA were Glenys Barton, Elizabeth Fritsch and Alison Britton. In keeping with their craft roots, these practitioners and other ceramicists of their generation continued to make work that was domestic in scale, and explored the vessel form in non-functional and frequently abstract works. Britton's ceramic jugs, for instance, are not thrown, symmetric or easy, but built of pieces of clay of differing thicknesses, with textured surfaces overlaid with glazes and patterns. Rather than conforming to the traditional notion of the 'rightness' of particular shapes that have developed over the millennia, each of her vessels develops in an organic fashion, with each step emerging in reaction to previous decisions.[78] *Big White Jug* (1987), for instance has the expected handle and spout, but it is asymmetrical and could not be used. Instead, it is an aesthetic object *about* 'vessel-ness'. In the words of John Houston, the ceramicists of this generation were using forms that were 'unfamiliar', in that they had their own sense of internal dynamics.[79]

A number of exhibitions in the 1980s and 1990s brought together sculpture and ceramics. Anthony Stokes curated an exhibition at the Serpentine Gallery in London on the theme of the vessel in 1987, which included the ceramics of Lucie Rie and Alison Britton with sculptures by Richard Wentworth, Bill Woodrow and Tony Cragg.[80] The exhibition at Bristol's Arnolfini called *The Raw and the Cooked: New Work in Clay in Britain* in 1993 again brought together the two disciplines. Martina Margetts argued in her catalogue essay that the developments in art and ceramics over the previous decade and a half meant that the role of ceramics could be more open to interpretation and connection, and that these changes had led to greater affinities between sculpture and ceramics, especially within the vessel form.[81]

Tony Cragg's *Laibe* from 1991 was an early exploration that the artist made of the material of clay, and consists of solid, thrown vessel forms in unglazed clay, arranged into still lifes. Each form has been sliced vertically into a number of thin strips, and, through the visible pull of the knife together with the outward sag of the slices, the consistency and malleability of the material is evident. Rather than being made with the varied and gritty clays of studio potters, these works are formed of fine, industrial clay. Most of the *Laibe* sculptures are pale; some are brown and, as a result of being fired at a low temperature, retain their visual links to the earth. The cutting and material qualities suggest industrial bread, while the potter's spiralling fingermarks on the surface of universally shaped vessels have echoes of the millennia of potting.

The word *Laibe* is German for 'loaves'. Cragg lives and works in Germany and the quality of German bread is legendary. Like vessels, bread has metaphorical, cultural and ritual resonances, as well as being vital for sustaining life.[82] The humble colour and texture of *Laibe* places it within the category of still lifes discussed by Norman Bryson: rhopography, the depiction in art of the unassuming base material of everyday life, of the overlooked, in a world that is used to industrial finishes and to plenty.[83]

When *Laibe* was exhibited at Tate Liverpool in 2004 in the exhibition *A Secret History of Clay*, it was seen against a history of ceramics made by an international array of artists who had used clay for various reasons.[84] The works by Lucio Fontana, which included small vessels with slits and holes, represented a parallel practice to the long slashes he made through framed canvases. Fontana's was a different agenda to that of Peter Voulkos, who ripped and rejoined clay in his critique of the medium, revealing the influence of the abstract expressionists. In contrast, *Madame de Pompadour (née Poisson) Soup Tureen and Saucer* (1989–91) by Cindy Sherman was a dinner service based upon the forms of fine porcelain, and used surface and traditional decorative motifs to make the artist's ironic comments. This limited edition was based on a design originally commissioned by Madame de Pompadour in 1756 from Sèvres and, representing a parallel practice to Sherman's photography, had an image of the artist's face in place of that of Madame de Pompadour. The tureens are functional, yet they are also subversive.[85] They echo the domestic, but that of the highest states of luxury.

Grayson Perry has used rather different means to seduce the viewer into looking. Like the reflective surfaces of the objects shown in the photographs for *Thirty Pieces of Silver*, the shininess of the glazes and the attractive colours applied to what appears to be a harmless domestic pot are designed to draw the audience into viewing scenes that question and critique the safety and cosiness of bourgeois life. It is a stealth tactic to bring the viewer closer so that he or she can read the imagery.[86] As well as its usefully non-porous surface, majolica has decorative possibilities, which since the Renaissance have frequently been used to comment on everyday life, evoking love, war and myths. Many decorative chargers were given as precious gifts and displayed. Unlike the pots of Bernard Leach or *Laibe* by Cragg, and in keeping with the tradition of majolica, Perry hides the material and covers the surface of his pots with imagery that reflects social concerns.[87] He wants the aesthetic and the idea to come together and create a frisson, believing that the handmade object broadens linguistic possibilities.[88] It is this that, in Perry's words, 'speaks the language of the body, and if we only engage with our heads then we are denying a huge part of the vocabulary.'[89]

Perry's pots are the size and type that would normally be displayed individually and with pride, on a sideboard or on a special shelf. However, the imagery used on their surfaces is frequently reminiscent of that used in the tabloid media, on television news and on the internet, all of which are brought into the home and then emotionally discarded. The prevalence of all these forms of media creates a porosity between the outside world and the private sphere. Charles Baudelaire warned against wallowing in the misfortunes and vices of others, and Perry suggests that the voyeurism of the internet and newspapers allows these images to appear impersonal, fleeting and distanced.[90] However, the pots by Perry are permanent. Like the war images by Roy Lichtenstein, or the shocking images taken from newspapers by Andy Warhol and later Sarah Lucas, the owner is forced to reassess his or her own reactions.

In *We've Found the Body of Your Child* (2000), Perry has used the imagery of a news story, shown in the sensationalist sound bites of the media. The image of the mother giving way to grief at the sight of her dead baby while being restrained by a group of men, is juxtaposed with images of city life and inscribed with frequently heard phrases. 'You'll spoil him' refers to the Victorian notion of 'spare the rod and spoil the child'. 'Ungrateful little sod', 'Never have kids' and 'You fucking little shit' are part of the aural wallpaper that surrounds some children. As Perry discovered, 95 per cent of child murders are committed by a parent of the victim. He wanted people to consider their own actions and the words they habitually use and how these can be the first steps towards violence and abuse.[91]

The imagery in *Strangely Familiar* (2000) depicts the consenting and non-consenting violence that goes on behind the netted windows of some apparently respectable, suburban homes. The suburbs were built as places where respectable people could withdraw after work, be with their family and enjoy nature. In Perry's hands such homes are closer to the eighteenth-century model, in which, unlike city centres, the suburban shanty towns were populated by the disreputable and poor, who apparently led dangerous and licentious lives. The scale of the pot, however, implies intimacy and underplays the message.

Perry's pots satirise his Essex upbringing, the art world, the seedy underbelly of the bourgeois home and fashion victims.[92] They are meant to be socially and politically subversive, and if seen in the light of the British satirical tradition, from Hogarth and the music hall to *Spitting Image*, they are less strange. *Boring Cool People* (1999) is a pot covered by a blue glaze, depicting fashionable people surrounded by desirable consumer items but looking unhappy – a theme that was also picked up in other vessels, including *Posh Bastard's House* (1999). These works critique the world that is built around appearances, and those who aspire to loft living, and try to make their lifestyles fit with those that they see in celebrity magazines and on television programmes.[93] These are lives that underpin Perry's alter ego 'Claire', who appears on some of the vessels and who around the 2000s was a parody of a certain type of woman, who lives in a Barratt home, eats chilled foods and lives a vicarious and superficial life.[94] Perry says that the type of people who own his pots are those who like shocking things, and who watch *Reservoir Dogs*.[95] It is ironic that many who would collect his work are also the butt of his satirical gaze.

All of the works discussed in this chapter are concerned with the relationship of people to their lived environment. As Daniel Miller's research demonstrated, homes are a reflection of their owners, and most important are the material things that make up their everyday worlds. Some are special, some mundane and overlooked, but all are bound to people's lives through memories, sentiment, touch and ritual. In the case of Perry's imagery, as well as in the collections of objects by Cragg and Woodrow, a light is focused on the effects of the capitalist system. However, in all of the works discussed, the emphasis is on memory, the building of a sense of self and what it means to be human.

NOTES

INTRODUCTION

1 Greg Hilty, 'Seeing and breathing', in Ann Jones, ed., *Recent British Sculpture* (London: Arts Council, 1993), pp. 9–10.
2 Alex Potts, 'Installation and sculpture', *Oxford Art Journal* xxiv/2 (2001) [special issue on installation], p. 19.
3 Ibid.
4 Hilty, 'Seeing and breathing', p. 12.
5 Peter Schjeldahl, 'Cragg's big bang', in Tony Cragg *et al.*, *Tony Cragg: Signs of Life* (Düsseldorf: Richter Verlag, 2003), p. 87.
6 David C. Thorns, *The Transformation of Cities: Urban Theory and Urban Life* (Basingstoke and New York, NY: Palgrave Macmillan, 2002), pp. 100–4.
7 Alison Ravetz with Richard Turkington, *The Place of Home: The English Domestic Environment 1914–2000* (London: E. & F. N. Spon, 1995), pp. 205–6; Alison Blunt and Robyn Dowling, *Home* (London and New York, NY: Routledge, 2006), pp. 92–3.
8 Toby Israel, *Some Place like Home: Using Design Psychology to Create Ideal Places* (Chichester: John Wiley, 2003), p. 113.
9 Amos Rapoport, 'A critical look at the concept "home"', in David N. Benjamin, ed., *The Home: Words, Interpretations, Meanings and Environments* (Aldershot: Avebury, 1995), p. 35.
10 Thorns, *The Transformation of Cities*, pp. 103–4.
11 Discussed in Hilde Heynen, 'Modernity and domesticity: Tensions and contradictions', in Hilde Heynen and Gülsüm Baydar, eds, *Negotiating Domesticity: Spatial Productions of Gender in Modern Architecture* (London and New York, NY: Routledge, 2005), p. 21.

12 Judy Attfield, *Wild Things: The Material Culture of Everyday Life* (Oxford and New York, NY: Berg, 2000), pp. 76–7.

13 Andrew Ballantyne, 'The nest and the pillar of fire', in Andrew Ballantyne, ed., *What Is Architecture?* (London: Routledge, 2002), p. 31.

14 Blunt and Dowling, *Home*, p. 21.

15 Ibid.

16 Doreen Massey, 'A place called home?', *New Formations* 17 (1992), p. 3.

17 See for instance Gill Perry, 'Introduction: Visibility, difference and excess', *Art History* xxvi/3 (June 2003), p. 322.

1. ENCLOSURE

1 Walter Benjamin, 'A Berlin chronicle', in Walter Benjamin, *One Way Street*, trans. Edmund Jephcott and Kingsley Shorter (London and New York, NY: Verso, 2000), p. 301.

2 Ibid., p. 314.

3 Charles Baudelaire, 'The painter of modern life', in Charles Baudelaire, *Selected Writings on Art and Artists*, trans. P. E. Charvet (Cambridge: Cambridge University Press, 1972), p. 397.

4 Ibid., p. 400.

5 Please see Chapter 3 for further discussion. See also Hilde Heynen, 'Modernity and domesticity: Tensions and contradictions', in Hilde Heynen and Gülsüm Baydar, eds, *Negotiating Domesticity: Spatial Productions of Gender in Modern Architecture* (London and New York, NY: Routledge, 2005), pp. 1–29.

6 Griselda Pollock, 'Modernity and the spaces of femininity', in Griselda Pollock, *Vision and Difference: Femininity, Feminism and the Histories of Art* (London and New York, NY: Routledge, 1988), pp. 50–90.

7 Amos Rapoport, 'A critical look at the concept "home"', in David N. Benjamin, ed., *The Home: Words, Interpretations, Meanings and Environments* (Aldershot: Avebury, 1995), p. 36.

8 Amanda Vickery, *Behind Closed Doors: At Home in Georgian England* (New Haven, CT, and London: Yale University Press, 2009), p. 24.

9 Ibid., p. 7.

10 Benjamin, 'A Berlin chronicle', pp. 328–9, 340.

11 Ibid., pp. 328–9.

12 See '*Leading Light* (1975)', *John Smith* [website]. Available at http://johnsmithfilms.com/selected-works/leading-light/ (accessed 7 August 2014).

13 See '*Home Suite* (1993–94)', *John Smith* [website]. Available at http://johnsmithfilms.com/selected-works/home-suite/ (accessed 7 August 2014).

14 See 'Jerwood Artists Platform', *Mary Maclean* [website]. Available at http://www.marymaclean.org.uk/?page_id=786 (accessed 7 August 2014).

15 Martin Heidegger, 'Building, dwelling, thinking', in Martin Heidegger, *Poetry, Language, Thought*, trans. Albert Hofstadter (New York, NY: Harper & Row, 1971), pp. 149, 157.

16 Maurice Merleau-Ponty, *Phenomenology of Perception* (London and New York, NY: Routledge, 2002), p. xi.

17 Ibid., p. 24.

18 Juhani Pallasmaa, 'Identity, intimacy and domicile: Notes on the phenomenology of home', in David N. Benjamin, ed., *The Home: Words, Interpretations, Meanings and Environments* (Aldershot: Avebury, 1995), p. 139.

19 For an excellent discussion about this from a phenomenological perspective, see Mikel Dufrenne, 'The world of the aesthetic object', in Clive Cazeaux, ed., *The Continental Aesthetics Reader* (London: Routledge, 2000), pp. 129–50.

20 Catherine Driscoll, 'The moving ground: Locating everyday life', in Ian Buchanan, ed., *Michel de Certeau: In the Plural* [*South Atlantic Quarterly* c/2 (spring 2001)], p. 394. I am grateful for Margaret Garlake's comments that the idea of the home as a sanctuary from the outside world is fairly universal across all different cultures, but also that privacy and safety do not always work out, as demonstrated by domestic abuse.

21 See for instance: Merleau-Ponty, *Phenomenology of Perception*, pp. xiv–xvi; Gregory Minissale, *Framing Consciousness in Art: Transcultural Perspectives* (Amsterdam and New York, NY: Rodopi, 2009), pp. 70–1.

22 Mark Prince, 'Waiting game', *Art Monthly* 355 (April 2012), pp. 1–4.

23 Quoted in Belinda Thomson, *Vuillard* [exh. cat.] (London: South Bank Centre, 1991), p. 18.

24 See 'Richard Billingham', *Saatchi Gallery* [website]. Available at http://www.saatchi-gallery.co.uk/artists/richard_billingham.htm (accessed 7 August 2014).

25 Pallasmaa, 'Identity, intimacy and domicile', p. 131.

26 For an example of Greenberg's perspective, see Clement Greenberg, 'Modernist painting', in Charles Harrison and Paul Wood, eds, *Art in Theory, 1900–2000: An Anthology of Changing Ideas* (Oxford: Blackwell, 2003), pp. 773–9.

27 Donald Judd, 'Specific objects', in Charles Harrison and Paul Wood, eds, *Art in Theory, 1900–2000: An Anthology of Changing Ideas* (Oxford: Blackwell, 2003), pp. 826–7.

28 See for instance Robert Morris, 'Notes on sculpture, part 2', in Robert Morris, *Continuous Project Altered Daily: The Writings of Robert Morris* (Cambridge, MA: October Books, MIT Press, 1995), p. 13.

29 Michael Fried, 'Art and objecthood', in Charles Harrison and Paul Wood, eds, *Art in Theory, 1900–2000: An Anthology of Changing Ideas* (Oxford: Blackwell, 2003), pp. 838–9.

30 See Robert Morris, 'Notes on sculpture, part 1' and 'Notes on sculpture, part 2', in Morris, *Continuous Project Altered Daily*, pp. 1–10, 11–22. For an excellent discussion of this and other contemporary writings, see Alex Potts, *The Sculptural Imagination: Figurative, Modernist, Minimalist* (New Haven, CT: Yale University Press, 2000), ch. 7.

31 Robert Morris, 'Notes on sculpture', discussed in Potts, *The Sculptural Imagination*, p. 239.

32 Eva Meyer-Hermann, *Carl Andre Sculptor, 1996: Krefeld at Home, Wolfsburg at Large* (Stuttgart: Oktagon, 1996), pp. 36–7.

33 See Harold Bloom, *The Anxiety of Influence: A Theory of Poetry* (London: Oxford University Press, 1997), p. 30, quoted in Hyla Robicsek, '"You give us this and we give you that": The British response to the legacy of American minimalism in the 1990s', MA dissertation, Courtauld Institute of Art, 2003, p. 15. This provides an interesting discussing of the transatlantic discussions and tensions.

34 Minissale, *Framing Consciousness in Art*, pp. 66–8.

35 Edmund Husserl, *Ideas: General Introduction to Pure Phenomenology*, trans. W. R. Boyce Gibson (London: Allen & Unwin; New York, NY: Humanities Press, 1931), pp. 101–3.

36 Gaston Bachelard, *The Poetics of Space* [1958], trans. Maria Jolas (1964; Boston, MA: Beacon Press, 1994), p. 4.

37 Ibid., p. 6.

38 Mary McAllester Jones, *Gaston Bachelard, Subversive Humanist: Texts and Readings* (Madison, WI: University of Wisconsin Press, 1991), pp. 9–11.

39 Jane Alison, ed., *The Surreal House* [exh. cat.] (New Haven, CT, and London: Barbican Art Gallery and Yale University Press, 2010), p. 302.

40 'Donald Rodney in conversation with Carol Chapman' [BBC radio, 26 October 1997]. Available at http://www.iniva.org/autoicon/DR/index.htm (accessed 7 August 2014). The title *Nine Nights* refers to the nine nights of vigil that are held in Caribbean countries after the death of a person – in this case, the artist's father.

41 The image is available at http://www.southlondongallery.org/page/collection?surname=R (accessed 7 August 2014).

42 Tanya Barson, 'Donald Rodney: *In the House of My Father* 1996–7: Summary', *Tate* [website]. Available at http://www.tate.org.uk/art/artworks/rodney-in-the-house-of-my-father-p78529/text-summary (accessed 7 August 2014).

43 Eddie Chambers, 'Donald Gladstone Rodney, 1961–1998', *Art Monthly* (April 1998), p. 21.

44 See images at 'Gilbert & George major exhibition: Room guide, room 4', *Tate* [website]. Available at http://www.tate.org.uk/whats-on/tate-modern/exhibition/gilbert-george/gilbert-george-major-exhibition-room-guide/gilbert-2 (accessed 7 August 2014).

45 Gilbert and George, 'Interview with Mark Francis' [1981], in Robert Violette and Hans-Ulrich Obrist, eds, *The Words of Gilbert and George: With Portraits of the Artists from 1968 to 1997* (London: Thames & Hudson in association with Violette Editions, 1997), p. 116.

46 Gilbert and George, 'The fabric of their world: From interviews with Carter Ratcliff' [1986], in Robert Violette and Hans-Ulrich Obrist, eds, *The Words of Gilbert and George: With Portraits of the Artists from 1968 to 1997* (London: Thames & Hudson in association with Violette Editions, 1997), pp. 153, 159.

47 For an excellent discussion about this, see Minissale, *Framing Consciousness in Art*, pp. 68–71.

48 Eckhard Schneider, 'Constructing the ephemeral', in Eckhard Schneider, ed., *Rachel Whiteread: Walls, Doors, Floors and Stairs* (Cologne: Walther König, 2005), p. 7.

49 See image at 'Rachel Whiteread, *Walls, Doors, Floors and Stairs*', *Kunsthaus Bregenz* [website]. Available at http://www.kunsthaus-bregenz.at/ehtml/ewelcome00.htm?aus_whiteread.htm (accessed 7 August 2014).

50 Waldemar Januszczak, 'Room for reflection', *Sunday Times* (21 May 1995).

51 Lisa G. Corrin, 'A conversation with Rachel Whiteread, March 2001', in Lisa G. Corrin, Patrick Elliott and Andrea Schlieker, *Rachel Whiteread* [exh. cat.] (Edinburgh: Scottish National Gallery of Modern Art; London: Serpentine Gallery, 2001), p. 18.

52 Film extract available at http://www.luxonline.org.uk/artists/john_smith/blight.html (accessed 7 August 2014).

53 Image available at http://www.luxonline.org.uk/gallery_viewer/ark_gv/image/880703/index.html (accessed 7 August 2014).

54 See 'Blight (1994–96)', *John Smith* [website]. Available at http://johnsmithfilms.com/selected-works/blight/ (accessed 7 August 2014).

55 Gill Saunders, 'How wallpaper left home and made an exhibition of itself', in Gill Saunders, *Walls Are Talking: Wallpaper, Art and Culture* [exh. cat.] (Manchester: Whitworth Art Gallery, 2010), p. 28.

56 Christine Woods, 'Introduction: It's the background that explains the foreground', in Gill Saunders, *Walls Are Talking: Wallpaper, Art and Culture* [exh. cat.] (Manchester: Whitworth Art Gallery, 2010), p. 18.

57 Saunders, 'How wallpaper left home', p. 28.

58 Pamela Young, 'Off the wall', *Applied Arts* xxv/1 (February/March 2010), pp. 20–22.

59 Kristy Krivitsky, 'Apocalyptic wallpaper', *Art Papers* xxi/6 (1997), p. 60.

60 See 'Wallpaper showroom', *The Studio of Deborah Bowness* [website]. Available at http://www.deborahbowness.com/wallpaper.html (accessed 7 August 2014).

61 See *Showroom Dummies* [website]. Available at http://www.abigaillane.co.uk/SHOWROOMDUMMIES-WEBSITE/index.html (accessed 7 August 2014).

62 'London Toile', *Timorous Beasties* [website]. Available at http://www.timorousbeasties.com/shop/wallcoverings/85/london-toile/ (accessed 7 August 2014).

63 Robert Gober, 'Interview with Richard Flood', in Judith Nesbitt, ed., *Robert Gober* [exh. cat.] (London: Serpentine Gallery, 1993), p. 8. The wallpapers were available for purchase as a limited edition.

64 Martin Herbert, 'It never starts from meaning', *Art Review* 12 (June 2007), pp. 56–63.

65 Ibid., p. 56.

66 Quoted in Hal Foster, 'An art of missing parts', *October* 92 (spring 2000), pp. 128–56.

67 Robert Gober, 'Interview with Richard Flood', in Judith Nesbitt, ed., *Robert Gober* [exh. cat.] (London: Serpentine Gallery, 1993), p. 9.

68 Lynne Cooke, 'Disputed terrain', in Judith Nesbitt, ed., *Robert Gober* [exh. cat.] (London: Serpentine Gallery, 1993), p. 17.

69 Saunders, 'How wallpaper left home', p. 53.

70 Ibid., p. 75.

71 I am grateful to Thomas Dane for allowing me to view the three films associated with *Semi-detached.* I would also like to thank the librarians at the Tate Library and Archive for organising and releasing the correspondence relating to this work.

72 Tate commissioned this work as part of its annual series of installations in the Duveen Galleries, in which artists are asked to respond to the Tate collection. The exhibition ran from 18 May to 12 December 2004, after which the installation was dismantled. Only the films remain. For a more detailed discussion of this installation, see Imogen Racz, 'Michael Landy's *Semi-detached* and the art of making', *Journal of Visual Art Practice* x/3 (2011), pp. 231–43.

73 John Burnett, *A Social History of Housing, 1815–1985* (1978; 2nd edn, Newton Abbot: David & Charles, 1986), pp. 189, 191.

74 Gordon Burn, 'Outdoors indoors', *Guardian* (19 May 2004).

75 Merleau-Ponty, *Phenomenology of Perception*, p. xxii.

76 John Slyce, 'Temporary monumental: Visibility, labour, value and procedure in the projects of Michael Landy', in Judith Nesbitt and John Slyce, *Michael Landy: Semi-detached* [exh. cat.] (London: Tate, 2004), p. 59. The three films were titled *No. 62, Shelf Life* and *Four Walls.*

77 See for instance: Nigel Reynolds, 'Essex man's home truths put on show', *Daily Telegraph* (18 May 2004); Zoe Griffin, 'Neighbours baffled by the fuss over no. 62', *Daily Telegraph* (18 May 2004).

78 'Michael Landy: Judith Nesbitt discusses the artist in relation to his work *Semi-detached*, 15/10/04', Tate Archive audio-visual collection, Tate Britain [tape TAV 2865A].

79 Ibid.

80 Email from Carolyn Kerr to Judith Nesbitt and Lizzie Carey-Thomas, 12 September 2003, Tate Archive, Tate Britain [EX 121.0, A13841].

81 Slyce, 'Temporary monumental', p. 59.

82 Email from Carolyn Kerr to Judith Nesbitt and Lizzie Carey-Thomas, 12 September 2003.

83 Helen Powell, 'Time, television, and the decline of DIY', *Home Cultures* vi/1 (March 2009), pp. 91–2.

84 Daisy Garnett, 'House Master', *Vogue* (June 2004), p. 54.

85 Email from Carolyn Kerr to Judith Nesbitt and Lizzie Carey-Thomas, 12 September 2003.

86 Minissale, *Framing Consciousness in Art*, p. 66.

87 Roni Brown, 'Identity and narrativity in homes made by amateurs', *Home Cultures* iv/3 (2007), p. 262.

88 McAllester Jones, *Gaston Bachelard, Subversive Humanist*, p. 7.

89 Bachelard, *Poetics of Space*, p. xxxv.

2. DOORS AND WINDOWS

1 R. D. Dripps, *The First House: Myth, Paradigm and the Task of Architecture* (Cambridge, MA, and London: MIT Press, 1997), p. 52.

2 Lutz Koepnick, *Framing Attention: Windows on Modern German Culture* (Baltimore, MD: John Hopkins University Press, 2007), p. 1.

3 Amanda Vickery, *Behind Closed Doors: At Home in Georgian England* (New Haven, CT, and London: Yale University Press, 2009), p. 29.

4 Dripps, *The First House*, p. 54.

5 Koepnick, *Framing Attention*, p. 3.

6 Edmond Duranty, *La nouvelle peinture* (1876), quoted in Michael Fried, 'Caillebotte's impressionism', in Norma Broude, ed., *Gustave Caillebotte and the Fashioning of Identity in Impressionist Paris* (New Brunswick: Rutgers University Press, 2002), p. 68.

7 Koepnick, *Framing Attention*, p. 5.

8 Jan Białostocki, 'The eye and the window: Realism and symbolism of light reflections in the art of Albrecht Dürer and his predecessors', in Jan Białostocki, *The Message of Images: Studies in the History of Art* (Vienna: Irsa Verlag, 1988), p. 92.

9 Robert C. Lodge, *Plato's Theory of Art* (London: Routledge & Kegan Paul, 1953), p. 96.

10 Leon Battista Alberti, *On Painting and On Sculpture*, trans. Cecil Grayson (London: Phaidon, 1972), p. 55.

11 Virginia Spate, *Orphism: The Evolution of Non-figurative Painting in Paris 1910–1914* (New York, NY: Oxford University Press, 1979), p. 176. For an excellent discussion, see Shirley Neilsen Blum, 'The open window: A Renaissance view', in Suzanne Delehanty, ed., *The Window in Twentieth-century Art* [exh. cat.] (New York, NY: Neuberger Museum, 1986), pp. 9–16. For the mystical links between the divine and light, see Białostocki, 'The eye and the window', pp. 89–91.

12 Anne Goodchild, *Without from Within* [exh. cat.] (Nottingham: Djanogly Art Gallery, 2010), p. 6.

13 Stéphane Mallarmé, 'The clown chastised', in Stéphane Mallarmé, *Selected Poetry and Prose*, ed. and trans. Mary Ann Caws (New York, NY: New Directions, 1982), p. 5.

14 Robert Cohn, 'Mallarmé's windows', *Yale French Studies* 54 (1977), p. 29.

15 Charles Baudelaire, *Prose and Poetry*, trans. Arthur Symons (New York, NY: Albert and Charles Boni, 1926), p. 63, quoted in Koepnick, *Framing Attention*, p. 2.

16 The group of artists and poets known as the Puteaux Group or the Section d'Or, which included Delaunay, Gris and Apollinaire, met frequently to exchange ideas. They also frequently met with Braque and Picasso and visiting artists and writers at the Café de Dome in Montparnasse.

17 Spate, *Orphism*, p. 188. See Robert Delaunay, *The New Art of Color* (New York, NY: Viking Press, 1978).

18 Guillaume Apollinaire's poem 'Les fenêtres' was printed in the catalogue for Robert Delaunay's exhibition of his Les Fenêtres series in Berlin, 1913.

19 See discussion in Imogen Racz, 'Juan Gris: The uncompromising cubist', MA thesis, University of Central England, 1993, ch. 1. See also Christopher Green, *Juan Gris* [exh. cat.] (London: Whitechapel Art Gallery, 1992), pp. 81–3.

20 Gregory Minissale, *Framing Consciousness in Art: Transcultural Perspectives* (Amsterdam and New York, NY: Rodopi, 2009), pp. 65–71.

21 Letter from Juan Gris to Amédée Ozenfant, 25 March 1921, in Juan Gris, *The Letters of Juan Gris 1913–1927*, ed. and trans. Douglas Cooper (London: privately published, 1956), no. cxxiv.

22 See 'John Cage about silence' [video]. Available at http://www.youtube.com/watch?v=pcHnL7aS64Y (accessed 7 August 2014).

23 John Cage, 'Rhythm etc.', in Gyorgy Kepes, ed., *Module, Proportion, Symmetry, Rhythm* (New York, NY: George Braziller, 1966), pp. 194–203; John Cage, 'The future of music: Credo', in John Cage, *Silence: Lectures and Writings* (London: Marion Boyars, 1978), p. 4.

24 James Pritchett, *The Music of John Cage* (Cambridge: Cambridge University Press, 1993), p. 22. This was dance music for Syvilla Fort to be performed at the Cornish School of Allied Arts in Seattle.

25 See score for John Cage, *A Room: For Piano (with or without Preparations) Solo* (New York, NY: Henmar Press, 1968), p. c.

26 Branden W. Joseph, 'John Cage and the architecture of silence', *October* (summer 1997), pp. 81–104. Available at http://beauty.gmu.edu/AVT307/AVT307-001/Branden%20W.%20Joseph%20john%20cage%20and%20the%20architecture%20of%20silence.pdf (accessed 7 August 2014). See esp. n. 17.

27 Ibid.

28 John Cage, 'Experimental music', in John Cage, *Silence: Lectures and Writings* (London: Marion Boyars, 1978), p. 8 [my emphasis].

29 Ibid.

30 *Not Seen and/or Less Seen of/by Marcel Duchamp/Rrose Sélavy (1904–64)* [exh. cat.] (New York, NY: Cordier & Ekstrom, 1964). I am indebted to the exhibition at the Barbican Art Gallery titled *The Bride and the Bachelors: Duchamp with Cage, Cunningham, Rauschenberg and Johns*, 14 February–9 June 2013.

31 Sabine Eckmann, 'Seeing and performing', in Sabine Eckmann and Lutz Koepnick, eds, *Window/Interface* (St Louis, MO: Mildred Lane Kemper Art Museum, 2006), pp. 68–9.

32 Walter Hopps, *Robert Rauschenberg: The Early 1950s* (Houston, TX: Fine Art Press, 1991), p. 62.

33 Barbara Rose, 'Robert Rauschenberg', *Art and Antiquities* xxx/6 (June 2007), p. 111.

34 Martin Gayford, 'Starting at zero: Black Mountain College 1933–1957: Kettle's Yard', *Modern Painters* (March 2006), p. 123. Subjects covered included dance, music, pottery, photography, poetry and abstract painting.

35 John Cage, 'Foreword', in John Cage, *Silence: Lectures and Writings* (London: Marion Boyars, 1978), p. x.

36 Quoted in Nicholas Cullinan, 'To exist in passing time', in Susan Davidson and David White, eds, *Robert Rauschenberg: Photographs, 1949–1962* (London: Thames & Hudson, 2011), p. 13.

37 See image in Susan Davidson and David White, eds, *Robert Rauschenberg: Photographs, 1949–1962* (London: Thames & Hudson, 2011), p. 40. James Boaden has made the same

point in relation to Rauschenberg's *Untitled Black Painting* (1952). See James Boaden, '*Black Painting* (with *Asheville Citizen*)', *Art History* xxxi/1 (February 2011), p. 175.

38 See images in Davidson and White, eds, *Robert Rauschenberg: Photographs*, plates 24, 27, 32, 39.

39 James Boaden, '*Black Painting* (with *Asheville Citizen*)', *Art History* xxxi/1 (February 2011), p. 174.

40 Charles Stuckey, 'Minutiae and Rauschenberg's combine mode', in Paul Schimmel, ed., *Robert Rauschenberg: Combines* [exh. cat.] (New York, NY: MoMA, 2005), p. 203.

41 'Oral history interview with Robert Rauschenberg, 1965 Dec. 21', *Archives of American Art* [website]. Available at http://www.aaa.si.edu/collections/interviews/oral-history-interview-robert-rauschenberg-12870 (accessed 7 August 2014).

42 Paul Schimmel discusses the way that the increased use of material suggests a personal significance in these works. See Paul Schimmel, 'Autobiography and self-portraiture in Rauschenberg's *Combines*', in Paul Schimmel, ed., *Robert Rauschenberg: Combines* [exh. cat.] (New York, NY: MoMA, 2005), p. 212.

43 See Paul Schimmel, ed., *Robert Rauschenberg: Combines* [exh. cat.] (New York, NY: MoMA, 2005), plate 11.

44 Schimmel, 'Autobiography and self-portraiture', pp. 212–14.

45 Saul Ostrow, 'Foreword: Duchamp, Cage, Roth, and Katz: Accumulative effect', in Moira Roth, ed., *Difference/Indifference: Musings on Postmodernism, Marcel Duchamp and John Cage* (Amsterdam: OPA, 1998), p. xi.

46 Alex Potts, 'Robert Rauschenberg and David Smith: Compelling contiguities', *Art Bulletin* lxxxix/1 (March 2007), p. 149.

47 For an excellent discussion about these works, see Schimmel, 'Autobiography and self-portraiture', pp. 211–28.

48 See Alan Solomon, 'The new art' [1963], in Carol Anne Mahsun, ed., *Pop Art: The Critical Dialogue* (Ann Arbor, MI: UMI Research Press, 1989), pp. 49–60.

49 See Rosalind Krauss, 'Rauschenberg and the materialized image' [1974], in Branden W. Joseph, ed., *Robert Rauschenberg* (Cambridge, MA: MIT Press, 2002), pp. 39–55.

50 Germano Celant, 'I love what I'm doing', in Stephen Robert Frankel, ed., *Jim Dine: Walking Memory, 1959–1969* [exh. cat.] (New York, NY: Guggenheim Museum, 1999), p. 19.

51 See image in Marco Livingstone, *Jim Dine: The Alchemy of Images* (New York, NY: Monacelli Press, 1998), p. 126.

52 Celant, 'I love what I'm doing', pp. 14–15.

53 See Daniel Soutif, 'Found and lost: On the object in art', *Artforum* (October 1989), p. 155–8.

54 Livingstone, *Jim Dine: The Alchemy of Images*, p. 105.

55 Karin Rosenberg, ed., *George Segal* [exh. cat.] (Chicago, IL: Museum of Contemporary Art, 1968) [unpaginated].

56 Allan Kaprow, 'The real experiment', in Jeff Kelley, ed., *Allan Kaprow: Essays on the Blurring of Art and Life* (Berkeley, CA: University of California Press, 2003), pp. 201, 203.

57 Allan Kaprow, 'Performing life', in Jeff Kelley, ed., *Allan Kaprow: Essays on the Blurring of Art and Life* (Berkeley, CA: University of California Press, 2003), p. 195.

58 There is a photograph of a Happening on Segal's farm, dated 1963, involving several dozen people, in which Kaprow seems to be organising the event from on top of bales of hay. See Martin Friedman and Graham W. J. Beal, *George Segal: Sculptures* [exh. cat.] (Minneapolis, MN: Walker Art Gallery, 1979), p. 12.

59 Jan van der Marck, *George Segal* (New York, NY: Harry N. Abrams, 1979), p. 19.

60 For a discussion about this and Hofmann's influence on American abstract painters, see Suzanne Delehanty, 'The artist's window', in Suzanne Delehanty, ed., *The Window in Twentieth-century Art* [exh. cat.] (New York, NY: Neuberger Museum, 1986), pp. 21–3.

61 Henry Geldzahler, 'An interview with George Segal', *Artforum* (November 1964), p. 26.

62 Ibid.

63 George Segal, taped conversation with José L. Barrio-Garay in 1972, quoted in José L. Barrio-Garay, *George Segal: Environments* [exh. cat.] (Philadelphia, PA: Institute of Contemporary Arts, 1976) [unpaginated].

64 'Oral history interview with George Segal, 1973 November 26', *Archives of American Art* [website]. Available at http://www.aaa.si.edu/collections/interviews/oral-history-interview-george-segal-12613 (accessed 7 August 2014).

65 Quoted in Barrio-Garay, *George Segal: Environments* [unpaginated].

66 Delehanty, 'The artist's window', p. 25.

67 For an interesting discussion about the quotes used in Wesselmann's work, see Franz Schwarzbauer, 'Intensified perception: Artificial quotation in the work of Tom Wesselmann', in Nicole Fritz and Franz Schwarzbauer, eds, *Tom Wesselmann und die Pop Art* [exh. cat.] (Ravensburg: Städtische Galerie, 2008), pp. 107–13.

68 Quoted in Carl R. Baldwin, 'On the nature of pop', *Artforum* (June 1974), p. 37.

69 Barrio-Garay, *George Segal: Environments* [unpaginated].

70 For an excellent discussion about film and moving image as a window onto the world, see Koepnick, *Framing Attention*, pp. 3–6.

71 Jan van der Marck, 'Introduction', in *George Segal: 12 Human Situations* [exh. cat.] (Chicago, IL: Museum of Contemporary Art, 1968) [unpaginated].

72 Quoted in Martin Friedman, 'George Segal: Proletarian mythmaker', in Martin Friedman and Graham W. J. Beal, *George Segal: Sculptures* [exh. cat.] (Minneapolis, MN: Walker Art Gallery, 1979), p. 18.

73 Van der Marck, *George Segal*, p. 99.

74 George Segal, 'Commentaries on six sculptures', in Martin Friedman and Graham W. J. Beal, *George Segal: Sculptures* [exh. cat.] (Minneapolis, MN: Walker Art Gallery, 1979), p. 55.

75 Henry Geldzahler, 'An interview with George Segal', *Artforum* (November 1964), p. 27.

76 Suzanne Delehanty, 'Forward and acknowledgements', in José L. Barrio-Garay, *George Segal: Environments* [exh. cat.] (Philadelphia, PA: Institute of Contemporary Arts, 1976) [unpaginated].

77 See van der Marck, *George Segal*, p. 16. The phrase 'frozen Happenings' originates with Irving Sandler.

78 Linda Nochlin, *The Body in Pieces: The Fragment as a Metaphor of Modernity* (London: Thames & Hudson, 1994). See esp. pp. 41–7.

79 Brian O'Doherty, 'Inside the white cube, part II: The eye and the spectator', *Artforum* (April 1976), p. 33.

80 Terry Riggs, 'Marcel Duchamp: *Fresh Widow* 1920, replica 1964: Summary', *Tate* [website]. Available at http://www.tate.org.uk/art/artworks/duchamp-fresh-widow-t07282/text-summary (accessed 7 August 2014).

81 Eckmann, 'Seeing and performing', pp. 67–8.

82 Thomas McEvilley, 'The sculpture of James Croak', in Thomas McEvilley, *James Croak* (New York, NY: Harry N. Abrams, 1998), p. 15.

83 Barbara J. Bloemink, 'Interview with the artist', in Thomas McEvilley, *James Croak* (New York, NY: Harry N. Abrams, 1998), p. 104.

84 See James Croak's writing about dirt in James Croak, 'Summer reading: Body and soil', *Artnet* [website]. Available at http://www.artnet.com/magazineus/books/croak/summer-reading-6-18-12.asp (accessed 7 August 2014). I am grateful to the artist for sending me this link.

85 Kate Forde, 'Introduction', in Nadine Monem, ed., *The Filthy Reality of Everyday Life: Dirt* (London: Profile, 2011), p. 1.

86 See Rosie Cox, 'Dishing the dirt: Dirt in the home', in Nadine Monem, ed., *The Filthy Reality of Everyday Life: Dirt* (London: Profile, 2011), pp. 57–62.

87 Email from James Croak to the author, 10 August 2012.

88 Bloemink, 'Interview with the artist', p. 106.

89 Ibid., p. 107.

90 Email from James Croak to the author, 10 August 2012.

3. FEMALE SPACE

1 Charles Baudelaire, 'The painter of modern life', in Charles Baudelaire, *Selected Writings on Art and Artists*, trans. P. E. Charvet (Cambridge: Cambridge University Press, 1972), pp. 390–435.

2 For the seminal writing on this, see Griselda Pollock, 'Modernity and the spaces of femininity', in Griselda Pollock, *Vision and Difference: Femininity, Feminism and the Histories of Art* (London and New York, NY: Routledge, 1988), pp. 50–90.

3 For a discussion about this, see Laura Meyer, 'A studio of their own: The legacy of the Fresno feminist experiment', in Laura Meyer, ed., *A Studio of Their Own: The Legacy of the Fresno Feminist Experiment* (Fresno: California State University, 2009), pp. 3–5.

4 See: Griselda Pollock, *Differencing the Canon: Feminist Desire and the Writing of Art's Histories* (London and New York, NY: Routledge, 1999); Linda Nochlin, 'Memoirs of an ad hoc art historian', in Linda Nochlin, *Representing Women* (London and New York, NY: Thames & Hudson, 1999), pp. 6–33; Marsha Meskimmon, *Women Making Art: History, Subjectivity, Aesthetics* (London and New York, NY: Routledge, 2003).

5 See Norma Broude and Mary Garrard, 'Introduction: Feminism and art in the twentieth century', in Norma Broude and Mary Garrard, eds, *The Power of Feminist Art: Emergence, Impact and Triumph of the American Feminist Art Movement* (London: Thames & Hudson, 1994), p. 16.

6 See this essay and others in Linda Nochlin, *Women, Art and Power* (London: Thames & Hudson, 1989), pp. 145–78. For a useful early bibliography, see Alexis Rafael Krasilovsky, 'Feminism in the arts: An interim bibliography', *Artforum* (June 1972), pp. 72–5.

7 'Why have there been no great women artists?', *Vassar Innovators* [website]. Available at http://innovators.vassar.edu/innovator.html?id=48 (accessed 7 August 2014).

8 Judy Chicago, *Through the Flower: My Struggles as a Woman Artist* (1975; London: Women's Press, 1982), p. 33.

9 Ibid., pp. 34–6.

10 Ibid., pp. 38–41.

11 Meyer, 'A studio of their own', p. 6.

12 Ibid., p. 6.

13 Whitney Chadwick, 'Reflecting on history as histories', in Diana Burgess Fuller and Daniela Salvioni, eds, *Art/Women/California 1950–2000: Parallels and Intersections* (Berkeley, CA, and London: University of California Press, 2002), p. 21.

14 Daniela Salvioni, 'Introduction: Art in context', in Diana Burgess Fuller and Daniela

Salvioni, eds, *Art/ Women/ California 1950–2000: Parallels and Intersections* (Berkeley, CA, and London: University of California Press, 2002), pp. 3–4.

15 Ibid., p. 5.

16 Benjamin Buchloh, 'A Conversation with Martha Rosler', in Catherine de Zegher, ed., *Martha Rosler: Positions in the Life World* (Cambridge, MA, and London: MIT Press, 1998), p. 25.

17 Betty Friedan, *The Feminine Mystique* (Harmondsworth: Penguin, 1963), pp. 1–16.

18 Ibid., p. 91 ff.

19 Quoted in Whitney Chadwick, *Women, Art, and Society* (1990; 4th edn, London: Thames & Hudson, 2007), p. 339.

20 Hannah Arendt, *The Human Condition* (Chicago, IL, and London: University of Chicago Press, 1958), pp. 22–30. Hannah Arendt was broadly a phenomenologist who had encountered the writings and lectures of Martin Heidegger while a student at Marburg. She was particularly impressed with his ideas about Aristotle and Plato. See Dermot Moran, 'Introduction', in Dermot Moran and Timothy Mooney, eds, *The Phenomenology Reader* (London and New York, NY: Routledge, 2002), p. 19.

21 Arendt, *The Human Condition*, pp. 36–7.

22 See for instance Robin Morgan, ed., *Sisterhood Is Global: The International Women's Movement Anthology* (Harmondsworth: Penguin, 1984), which includes essays from 70 different countries, together with introductions to each that contain statistics relating to demography, politics, the economy, gynography, herstory and mythography.

23 See for instance: Sherry B. Ortner, 'Is female to male as nature is to culture?', in Michelle Zimbalist Rosaldo and Louise Lamphere, eds, *Woman, Culture and Society* (Stanford, CA: California University Press, 1974), pp. 67–87; Claude Lévi-Strauss, *The Elementary Structures of Kinship*, trans. James Harle Bell, ed. John Richard von Sturmer and Rodney Needham (Boston, MA: Beacon, 1969); Anthony Giddens *et al.*, eds, *The Polity Reader in Gender Studies* (Cambridge: Polity Press, 1994).

24 Michelle Zimbalist Rosaldo, 'Woman, culture and society: A theoretical overview', in Michelle Zimbalist Rosaldo and Louise Lamphere, eds, *Woman, Culture and Society* (Stanford, CA: California University Press, 1974), pp. 35–41.

25 Quoted by Carol Small in a review of Lydia Yee *et al.*, *Divisions of Labor: 'Women's Work' in Contemporary Art* [exh. cat.] (New York, NY: Bronx Museum of the Arts, 1995), in *Women's Art Journal* xix/2 (fall/winter 1998), p. 39.

26 Chadwick, 'Reflecting on history as histories', p. 22.

27 'Oral history interview with Eleanor Antin, 2009 May 8–9', *Archives of American Art* [website]. Available at http://www.aaa.si.edu/collections/interviews/oral-history-interview-eleanor-antin-15792 (accessed 7 August 2014).

28 Chadwick, 'Reflecting on history as histories', p. 22.

29 Ibid.

30 'Oral history interview with Eleanor Antin, 2009 May 8–9'.

31 Mikel Dufrenne, 'The world of the aesthetic object', in Clive Cazeaux, ed., *The Continental Aesthetics Reader* (London: Routledge, 2000), pp. 129–50.

32 Victoria Martin, 'A conversation with Eleanor Antin', *Artweek* xxx/7 (July/August 1999), pp. 20–1.

33 Salvioni, 'Introduction: Art in context', p. 2.

34 Faith Wilding, 'The feminist art programs at Fresno and CalArts, 1970–1975', in Norma Broude and Mary Garrard, eds, *The Power of Feminist Art: Emergence, Impact and Triumph of the American Feminist Art Movement* (London: Thames & Hudson, 1994), p. 32.

35 Faith Wilding, 'Gestations in a studio of our own', in Faith Wilding, *By Our Own Hands: The History of the Women Artists' Movement in Southern California, 1970–1977* (Los Angeles, CA: Double X, 1977), pp. 81–2.

36 Meyer, 'A studio of their own', p. 15.

37 Ibid., p. 17.

38 Ibid., p. 7.

39 Wilding, 'Gestations in a studio of our own', p. 98.

40 Daniela Salvioni and Diana Burgess Fuller, 'Burning down the house: Feminist art in California: An interview with Amelia Jones', in Diana Burgess Fuller and Daniela Salvioni, eds, *Art/Women/California 1950–2000: Parallels and Intersections* (Berkeley, CA, and London: University of California Press, 2002), p. 165.

41 Meyer, 'A studio of their own', pp. 7–8.

42 Meredith Brown, 'School is a place to perform: The art and pedagogy of Judy Chicago's Women's Art Program at Fresno State College, 1970–1971', MA dissertation, Courtauld Institute of Art, 2007, p. 7.

43 Chicago, *Through the Flower*, p. 86.

44 Meskimmon, *Women Making Art*, p. 1.

45 Meyer, 'A studio of their own', p. 9.

46 Ibid., p. 8.

47 Ibid., p. 10.

48 Wilding, 'Gestations in a studio of our own', pp. 94–5.

49 Brown, 'School is a place to perform', pp. 12–13.

50 Chicago, *Through the Flower*, p. 98.

51 Andrea Stuart, 'Feminism: Dead or alive?', in Jonathan Rutherford, ed., *Identity: Community, Culture, Difference* (London: Lawrence & Wishart, 1990), p. 36.

52 Chadwick, 'Reflecting on history as histories', p. 25.

53 Miriam Schapiro, 'More on women's art: An exchange', *Art in America* (November/December 1976), p. 17.

54 Meyer, 'A studio of their own', p. 18.

55 Linda Stein, 'Miriam Schapiro: Woman–warrior with lace', *Fiberarts* (March/April, 1998), pp. 35–40.

56 *Womanhouse* was open to the public from 30 January to 28 February 1972. See 'Oral history interview with Miriam Schapiro, 1989 September 10', *Archives of American Art* [website]. Available at http://www.aaa.si.edu/collections/interviews/oral-history-interview-miriam-schapiro-11695 (accessed 7 August 2014).

57 For an interesting discussion, including of why there has been a paucity of attention given to *Womanhouse*, see Temma Balducci, 'Revisiting *Womanhouse*: Welcome to the (deconstructed) dollhouse', *Woman's Art Journal* xxvii/2 (fall/winter 2006), pp. 17–23.

58 'Bad-dream House', *Time* (20 March 1972), p. 77.

59 Faith Wilding, 'Next bodies', in Amelia Jones, *The Feminism and Visual Culture Reader* (London and New York, NY: Routledge, 2003), p. 27.

60 Broude and Garrard, 'Introduction: Feminism and art in the twentieth century', pp. 21–2.

61 Miriam Schapiro, 'The education of women as artists: *Project Womanhouse*', *Art Journal* xxxi/3 (spring 1972), p. 268.

62 Judy Chicago and Miriam Schapiro, *Womanhouse* [exh. cat.] (Valencia, CA: California Institute of the Arts, 1971) [unpaginated]; Schapiro, 'The education of women as artists', p. 268.

63 Chicago and Schapiro, *Womanhouse* [unpaginated]. Unless otherwise stated the details are taken from this catalogue.

64 The environments were made by the following artists: *Personal Environment*: Judy Huddleston; *Leaf Room*: Ann Mills; *Dollhouse Room*: Sherry Brody and Miriam Schapiro; *Dining Room*: Beth Bachenheimer, Sherry Brody, Karen LeCocq, Robin Mitchell, Miriam Schapiro and Faith Wilding; *Nurturant Kitchen*: Susan Frazier, Vicki Hodgetts, Robin Weltsch (including *Aprons in Kitchen* by Susan Frazier and *Eggs to Breasts in Kitchen* by Vicki Hodgetts); *Crocheted Environment*: Faith Wilding; *Menstruation Bathroom*: Judy Chicago; *Bridal Staircase*: Kathy Huberland; *Nursery*: Shawnee Wollenman; *Shoe Closet*: Beth Bachenheimer; *Red Moon Room*: Mira Schor; *Painted Room*: Robin Mitchell; *Nightmare Bathroom*: Robbin Schiff; *Linen Closet*: Sandra Orgel; *Personal Space*: Janice Lester; *Leah's Room from Colette's Chérie*: Karen LeCocq and Nancy Youdelman; *Lipstick Bathroom*: Camille Grey; *Necco Wafers*: Christine Rush; *Garden Jungle*: Paula Longendyke.

65 'Oral history interview with Miriam Schapiro, 1989 September 10'.

66 Arlene Raven, 'Womanhouse', in Norma Broude and Mary Garrard, eds, *The Power of Feminist Art: Emergence, Impact and Triumph of the American Feminist Art Movement* (London: Thames & Hudson, 1994), p. 63.

67 Lucy Lippard, *From the Center: Feminist Essays on Women's Art* (New York, NY: E. P. Dutton, 1976), pp. 81–2.

68 See for instance Tamar Garb, 'Hairlines', in Carol Armstrong and Catherine de Zegher, eds, *Women Artists at the Millennium* (Cambridge, MA, and London: MIT Press, 2006), p. 255.

69 Chicago, *Through the Flower*, p. 113.

70 Ibid.

71 See for instance: *The Quilt Index* [website]. Available at http://www.quiltindex.org (accessed 7 August 2014); Dena S. Katzenberg, *Baltimore Album Quilts* [exh. cat.] (Baltimore, MD: Baltimore Museum of Art, 1980).

72 Imogen Racz, *Contemporary Crafts* (Oxford and New York, NY: Berg, 2009), pp. 6–8, 11–12.

73 Elissa Auther, *String, Felt, Thread: The Hierarchy of Art and Craft in American Art* (Minneapolis, MN, and London: University of Minnesota Press, 2010), pp. xi–xii. For an excellent overview and discussion of fibre art in the 1960s and 1970s, see ch. 1, pp. 1–46.

74 Patricia Malarcher, 'Critical approaches: Fragments from an evolution', in Anna Fariello and Paula Owen, eds, *Objects and Meaning: New Perspectives on Art and Craft* (Lanham, MD: Scarecrow Press, 2004), pp. 36–7. For a discussion that gives good background to the division of the arts, see Rozsika Parker and Griselda Pollock, *Old Mistresses: Women, Art and Ideology* (London: Pandora, 1981), esp. pp. 50–81.

75 See Jon Bird, 'Imagining otherworlds: Connection and difference in the art of Nancy Spero and Kiki Smith', in Jon Bird, ed., *Otherworlds: The Art of Nancy Spero and Kiki Smith* (London: Reaktion and BALTIC, 2003), p. 24.

76 Lippard, *From the Center*, p. 57, quoted in 'Elizabeth A. Sackler Center for Feminist Art: *The Dinner Party*', *Brooklyn Museum* [website]. Available at http://www.brooklynmuseum.org/eascfa/dinner_party/womens_work.php (accessed 7 August 2014).

77 Quoted in Balducci, 'Revisiting *Womanhouse*', p. 18.

78 Schapiro, 'The education of women as artists', p. 269.

79 Balducci, 'Revisiting *Womanhouse*', p. 17.

80 Schapiro, 'The education of women as artists', p. 269.

81 Chicago, *Through the Flower*, p. 113. These curtains had previously been shown in a white-walled gallery, but made more sense in this environment.

82 Balducci, 'Revisiting *Womanhouse*', pp. 17–23.

83 Anna Claypoole Peale was one of the daughters of James Peale, also a miniaturist and still-life painter, and niece of Charles Willson Peale.

84 Gill Valentine, 'Eating in: Home consumption and identity', *Sociological Review* xlvii/3 (1999), pp. 492–4; Deborah Lupton, 'Food, memory and meaning: The symbolic and social nature of food events', *Sociological Review* xlii/4 (1994), p. 679.

85 Meyer, 'A studio of their own', figs 39–43.

86 Balducci, 'Revisiting *Womanhouse*', pp. 17–23.

87 According to feminist literature, battery, sexual harassment and rape were not uncommon. America did not compare favourably with other countries. See for instance Morgan, ed., *Sisterhood Is Global*, p. 706. In 1981 in America, between 2,000 and 4,000 women were battered to death by their husbands, and between 50 per cent and 70 per cent of wives experienced battery. There were 81,536 reported rapes. These were considered conservative statistics.

88 Chicago and Schapiro, quoted in Wilding, 'The feminist art programs at Fresno and CalArts', p. 35.

89 Broude and Garrard, 'Introduction: Feminism and art in the twentieth century', pp. 21–2, 24.

90 Wilding, 'Gestations in a studio of our own', p. 96.

91 Salvioni and Fuller, 'Burning down the house', pp. 167–8.

92 'Oral history interview with Miriam Schapiro, 1989 September 10'.

93 Charles Baudelaire, 'In praise of make-up', in Charles Baudelaire, *Selected Writings on Art and Artists*, trans. P. E. Charvet (Cambridge: Cambridge University Press, 1972), p. 426.

94 'Everything you always wanted to know about perfume but never thought of asking', *Vogue* (November 1970), p. 180, quoted in Katherine Hauser, 'Audrey Flack's still lifes: Between femininity and feminism', *Woman's Art Journal* xxii/2 (fall 2001/winter 2002), pp. 26–30.

95 'Louis Gould faces her face…', *Ms.* (March 1974), p. 81, quoted in Hauser, 'Audrey Flack's still lifes', p. 27.

96 Hauser, 'Audrey Flack's still lifes', pp. 27–8.

97 Ibid., p. 27. See also Salvioni and Fuller, 'Burning down the house', pp. 168–9.

98 John Berger, *Ways of Seeing* (London: BBC and Penguin, 1972), p. 142.

99 Ibid., pp. 36–43.

100 Chicago, *Through the Flower*, pp. 115–17.

101 'Oral history interview with Miriam Schapiro, 1989 September 10'.

102 Schapiro, 'More on women's art', p. 19.

103 For a good discussion, see Joan Gibbons, *Contemporary Art and Memory: Images of Recollection and Remembrance* (London and New York, NY: I.B.Tauris, 2008), pp. 54–8.

104 See for instance: Amelia Jones, ed., *Sexual Politics: Judy Chicago's Dinner Party in Feminist Art History* [exh. cat.] (Berkeley, CA, and London: University of California Press and UCLA, 1996); Judy Chicago, *The Dinner Party* (London: Penguin, 1996).

105 See Salvioni and Fuller, 'Burning down the house', p. 170–2.

106 Auther, *String, Felt, Thread*, p. 120.

107 Ibid., p. 122.

108 Miriam Schapiro, 'Notes from a conversation on art, feminism, and work', in Sara Ruddick and Pamela Daniels, eds, *Working It Out: 23 Women Writers, Artists, Scientists, and Scholars Talk about Their Lives and Work* (New York, NY: Pantheon, 1977), p. 296, quoted in 'Elizabeth A. Sackler Center for Feminist Art: *The Dinner Party*', *Brooklyn Museum* [website]. Available at http://www.brooklynmuseum.org/eascfa/dinner_party/womens_work.php (accessed 7 August 2014).

109 Jeremy Strick, 'Director's foreword', in Lisa Gabrielle Mark, ed., *WACK! Art and the Feminist Revolution* [exh. cat.] (Los Angeles, CA: Museum of Contemporary Art; Cambridge, MA and London: MIT Press, 2007), p. 7.

4. ALIENATION

1 See Alfred Barr, *Fantastic Art: Dada, Surrealism* [exh. cat] (1936; 3rd edn, New York, MA: MoMA, 1946), pp. 53–64, for a prewar chronology.

2 Hanne Bergius, '"Join Dada!" Aspects of Dada's reception since the late 1950s' [lecture, 9 September 2006]. Available at http://www.moma.org/docs/learn/2006_DadaSymp/HanneBergiusDADA.pdf (accessed 7 August 2014).

3 For an interesting discussion about Breton's ideas about the feminine, see Rozsika Parker and Griselda Pollock, *Old Mistresses: Women, Art and Ideology* (London: Pandora, 1981), p. 138.

4 André Breton, 'First manifesto' and 'Second manifesto of surrealism, 1930', in André Breton, *The Manifestoes of Surrealism*, trans. Richard Seaver and Helen R. Lane (Ann Arbor, MI: University of Michigan Press, 1969), pp. 9–11, 161–2. For an interesting discussion, see Briony Fer, David Batchelor and Paul Wood, *Realism, Rationalism, Surrealism: Art between the Wars* (New Haven, CT, and London: Yale University Press and the Open University, 1993), pp. 171–89.

5 Georges Bataille, 'Surrealism' [1948], in Georges Bataille, *The Absence of Myth: Writings*

on Surrealism, ed. and trans. Michael Richardson (London and New York, NY: Verso, 2006), p. 55.

6 Hilde Heynen, 'Modernity and domesticity: Tensions and contradictions', in Hilde Heynen and Gülsüm Baydar, eds, *Negotiating Domesticity: Spatial Productions of Gender in Modern Architecture* (London and New York, NY: Routledge, 2005), p. 2.

7 Jane Alison, 'The surreal house', in Jane Alison, ed., *The Surreal House* [exh. cat.] (New Haven, CT, and London: Barbican Art Gallery and Yale University Press, 2010), p. 14.

8 Ibid., pp. 15–16. See also Walter Benjamin, 'Surrealism: The last snapshot of the European intelligentsia' [1929], in Walter Benjamin, *Reflections: Essays, Aphorisms, Autobiographical Writings*, trans. Edmund Jephcott (New York, NY: Schocken Books, 1986), pp. 178–9.

9 Patricia Allmer, 'Of fallen angels and angels of anarchy', in Patricia Allmer, ed., *Angels of Anarchy: Women Artists and Surrealism* (Munich: Prestel, 2009), p. 14.

10 See Sigmund Freud, *The Uncanny*, trans. David McLintock (London: Penguin, 2003).

11 Nicholas Royle, *The Uncanny* (Manchester: Manchester University Press, 2003).

12 Ibid., pp. 1–4.

13 See for instance: John Jervis, 'Uncanny presences', in Jo Collins and John Jervis, eds, *Uncanny Modernity: Cultural Theories, Modern Anxieties* (Basingstoke and New York, NY: Palgrave, 2008), p. 11; Dylan Trigg, *The Aesthetics of Decay: Nothingness, Nostalgia, and the Absence of Reason* (New York, NY: Peter Lang, 2006), pp. 37–8.

14 Bruce Altshuler, *The Avant-garde in Exhibition: New Art in the 20th Century* (Berkeley and Los Angeles, CA: University of California Press, 1994), pp. 120–2.

15 Ibid., p. 122.

16 Gaston Bachelard, *The Poetics of Space* [1958], trans. Maria Jolas (1964; Boston, MA: Beacon Press, 1994), pp. 4, 39.

17 Trigg, *The Aesthetics of Decay*, p. 24.

18 Belinda Grace Gardner, 'From *Breakfast in Fur* and back again', in Thomas Levy, ed., *Meret Oppenheim: From Breakfast in Fur and Back Again* (Bielefeld: Kerber Verlag, 2003), pp. 11–12.

19 Janine Mileaf, *Please Touch: Dada and Surrealist Objects after the Readymade* (Hanover, NH: Dartmouth College Press, 2010), p. 10.

20 Nathalie Bäschlin, 'Between material and fiction: Aspects of materiality in the works of Meret Oppenheim', in Therese Bhattacharya-Stettler and Matthias Frehner, eds, *Meret Oppenheim Retrospective* [exh. cat.] (Bern: Kunstmuseum and Hatje Cantz, 2006), p. 110.

21 Quoted in Allmer, 'Of fallen angels and angels of anarchy', p. 23.

22 Quoted in Altshuler, *The Avant-garde in Exhibition*, p. 122.

23 Allmer, 'Of fallen angels and angels of anarchy', p. 23.

24 Bäschlin, 'Between material and fiction', p. 150.

25 For an interesting discussion of this, see Daisy Connon, Gillian Jein and Greg Kerr, eds, *Aesthetics of Dislocation in French and Francophone Literature and Art: Strategies of Representation* (Lewiston, NY: Edwin Mellen Press, 2009), pp. 1–2.

26 '*Femme maison*' does not translate literally as 'housewife', but, like the title of Judy Chicago and Miriam Schapiro's work, means 'woman house'.

27 See for instance Louise Bourgeois, 'Interview with Douglas Maxwell', in Marie-Laure Bernadac and Hans-Ulrich Obrist, eds, *Louise Bourgeois: Destruction of the Father. Reconstruction of the Father: Writing and Interviews 1923–1997* (London: Violette Editions, 1998), p. 241. First published in *Modern Painters* (summer 1993), pp. 38–43.

28 Robert Storr, 'A sketch for a portrait: Louise Bourgeois', in Robert Storr and Paulo Herkenhoff, *Louise Bourgeois* (London: Phaidon, 2003), pp. 41–2. During the war Bourgeois visited exiled members of the surrealist group, so knew their ideas. However, she also rebelled against them and their notions of the role of the female.

29 Paulo Herkenhoff, 'Interview with Louise Bourgeois', in Robert Storr and Paulo Herkenhoff, *Louise Bourgeois* (London: Phaidon, 2003), p. 24.

30 Jan Garden Castro, 'Louise Bourgeois: Turning myths inside out', *Sculpture* xx/1 (January/February 2001), p. 17.

31 Michael Fried, 'New York letter', *Art International* 8 (April 1964), p. 58, discussed in E. Speaks, '"We bring our lares with us": Bodies and domiciles in the sculpture of Louise Bourgeois', *Art Journal* lxviii/3 (fall 2009), pp. 88–103.

32 Jan Garden Castro, 'Vital signs: A conversation with Louise Bourgeois', *Sculpture* xxiv/6 (July/August 2005), p. 31.

33 Bernard Blistène, 'J'ai misé sur l'art plutôt que sur la vie', *Beaux Arts* (October 2007), p. 146.

34 Herkenhoff, 'Interview with Louise Bourgeois', p. 22.

35 Quoted in Rainer Crone and Petrus Graf Schaesberg, *Louise Bourgeois: The Secret of the Cells* (Munich: Prestel Verlag, 1998), p. 11. Source unknown, but dated 1979.

36 Louise Bourgeois, 'Taking cover: Interview with Stuart Morgan', in Marie-Laure Bernadac and Hans-Ulrich Obrist, eds, *Louise Bourgeois: Destruction of the Father. Reconstruction of the Father: Writing and Interviews 1923–1997* (London: Violette Editions, 1998), pp. 152–3. First published in *Artscribe* 67 (January 1988), pp. 30–4.

37 Bourgeois, 'Taking cover', p. 155.

38 A photograph of Bourgeois in a studio in Italy in 1968 shows the back wall covered in plaster hands in different expressive gestures. See Crone and Schaesberg, *Louise Bourgeois: The Secret of the Cells*, p. 71.

39 Louise Bourgeois, 'Collecting: An unruly passion', in Marie-Laure Bernadac and Hans-Ulrich Obrist, eds, *Louise Bourgeois: Destruction of the Father: Reconstruction of the Father: Writing and Interviews 1923–1997* (London: Violette Editions, 1998), p. 276.

40 Ann Coxon, *Louise Bourgeois* (London: Tate, 2010), pp. 64–6.

41 Louise Bourgeois, 'A conversation with Bernard Marcadé' [1993], in Marie-Laure Bernadac and Hans-Ulrich Obrist, eds, *Louise Bourgeois: Destruction of the Father: Reconstruction of the Father: Writing and Interviews 1923–1997* (London: Violette Editions, 1998), p. 248.

42 Ibid.

43 Ibid., p. 257.

44 Louise Bourgeois, 'Freud's toys', *Artforum* (January 1990), pp. 111–13.

45 Castro, 'Vital signs', p. 31.

46 Ibid., p. 33.

47 Herkenhoff, 'Interview with Louise Bourgeois', p. 20.

48 Ibid., pp. 20–1.

49 Castro, 'Vital signs', p. 33.

50 Heynen, 'Modernity and domesticity', p. 21.

51 Rachel Taylor, 'Mona Hatoum, *Home* 1999: Summary', *Tate* [website]. Available at http://www.tate.org.uk/art/artworks/hatoum-home-t07918/text-summary (accessed 7 August 2014).

52 Gillian Jein, 'Dislocating travel: New York as anti-domus in Beauvoir's *Amérique au jour le jour*', in Daisy Connon, Gillian Jein and Greg Kerr, eds, *Aesthetics of Dislocation in French and Francophone Literature and Art: Strategies of Representation* (Lewiston, NY: Edwin Mellen Press, 2009), pp. 35–6.

53 Giorgio Verzotti, *Mona Hatoum* [exh. cat.] (Milan: Charta, 1999), p. 7.

54 Trigg, *The Aesthetics of Decay*, pp. 39–40.

55 Jein, 'Dislocating travel', p. 34.

56 Jo Collins and John Jervis, eds, *Uncanny Modernity: Cultural Theories, Modern Anxieties* (Basingstoke and New York, NY: Palgrave, 2008), pp. 1–2; Daisy Connon, *Subjects Not-at-home: Forms of the Uncanny in the Contemporary French Novel: Emmanuel Carrère, Marie NDiaye, Eugène Savitzkaya* (Amsterdam and New York, NY: Rodopi, 2010), p. 78.

57 Rachel Taylor, 'Mona Hatoum, *Home* 1999: Summary'.

58 See for instance Connon, *Subjects Not-at-home*, p. 15.

59 Ursula Panhans-Bühler, 'Being involved', in Christopher Heinrich, ed., *Mona Hatoum* [exh. cat.] (Ostfildern-Ruit: Hatje Cantz, 2004), p. 21.

60 Chiara Bertola, 'Mona Hatoum: Unstable, living, organic and moving forms', in Chiara Bertola, *Mona Hatoum: Interior Landscape* (Milan: Charta, 2009), p. 23.

61 Panhans-Bühler, 'Being involved', p. 24.

62 Email from Mona Hatoum to the author, January 2014.

63 For an interesting discussion of memory, displacement and the sense of self, see Trigg, *The Aesthetics of Decay*, esp. pp. 23–40.

64 For a discussion of this, see Dan Cameron, 'Boundary issues', in *Mona Hatoum* [exh. cat.] (Chicago, IL: Museum of Contemporary Art, 1997), p. 26.

65 Adolph Volker, 'The body and the world', in Christopher Heinrich, ed., *Mona Hatoum* [exh. cat.] (Ostfildern-Ruit: Hatje Cantz, 2004), p. 43.

66 Natalie Rudd, 'From here to infinity and back', in *Size Matters: Exploring Scale in the Arts Council Collection* (London: Hayward Gallery, 2005), pp. 8–15.

67 For an interesting discussion of this see Rachel Wells, 'Scale in contemporary sculpture: The enlargement, the miniature, the life size', PhD thesis, Courtauld Institute of Art, 2008.

68 Volker, 'The body and the world', p. 43.

69 Susan Stewart, 'Prologue: From the museum of touch', in Marius Kwint, Christopher Breward and Jeremy Aynsley, *Material Memories: Design and Evocation* (*Materializing Culture)* (Oxford: Berg, 1999), p. 32.

70 See: Jessica Morgan, 'The poetics of uncovering: Mona Hatoum in and out of perspective', in *Mona Hatoum* [exh. cat.] (Chicago, IL: Museum of Contemporary Art, 1997), p. 1; Andrew Renton, 'Objects encountered along the way…', in Andrew Renton, *Mona Hatoum* [exh. cat.] (London: Jay Jopling and White Cube, 2006), p. 29.

71 Jean-François Lyotard, 'Domus and the megalopolis', in Jean-François Lyotard, *The Inhuman: Reflections on Time* (Cambridge: Polity Press, 1988), discussed in Neil Leach, 'The dark side of the domus', in Andrew Ballantyne, ed., *What Is Architecture?* (London: Routledge, 2002), p. 92.

72 Anthony Vidler, *Warped Space: Art, Architecture, and Anxiety in Modern Culture* (Cambridge, MA, and London: MIT Press, 2000), p. 148.

73 For an interesting discussion about the haptic in art and life, see Steen Eiler Rasmussen, *Experiencing Architecture* (Cambridge, MA: MIT Press, 1962), esp. p. 24. See also Renton, 'Objects encountered along the way…', pp. 9–13.

74 Paul Schimmel, 'Life's echo: Gregor Schneider's *Dead House ur*', in *Gregor Schneider* [exh. cat.] (Milan: Charta, 2003), p. 103. The 'u' and 'r' in the work's title refer to the location of the house: Unterheydener Straße, Rheydt.

75 Gregor Schneider and Ulrich Loock, 'I never throw anything away, I just go on…', in *Gregor Schneider* [exh. cat.] (Milan: Charta, 2003), p. 68.

76 Udo Kittelmann, ed., *Haus ur, Rheydt versus Totes Haus ur, Venice* (Ostfildern-Ruit: Hatje Cantz, 2001), pp. 11–13.

77 Schneider and Loock, 'I never throw anything away', p. 66.

78 Schimmel, 'Life's echo', pp. 106–7.

79 Gary Dufour, *Bruce Nauman* [exh. pamphlet] (Vancouver: Vancouver Art Gallery, 1993). Available in the National Art Library's Information File on Bruce Nauman.

80 Janet Kraynak, 'Bruce Nauman's words', in Janet Kraynak, ed., *Please Pay Attention Please: Bruce Nauman's Words* (Cambridge, MA: MIT Press, 2003), p. 1.

81 Brigitte Kölle, *Totes Haus ur* (Frankfurt: Alfried Krupp von Bohlen und Halbach-Stiftung, 1997), p. 93.

82 Schimmel, 'Life's echo', p. 107.

83 Claire Bishop, *Installation Art: A Critical History* (London: Tate, 2005), pp. 41–2.

84 Schimmel, 'Life's echo', pp. 114–15.

85 Ibid., p. 107.

86 Royle, *The Uncanny*; Trigg, *The Aesthetics of Decay*.

87 Available in the National Art Library's Information File on Gregor Schneider.

88 'Gregor Schneider: *Die Familie Schneider*, October 2004', *Artangel* [website]. Available at http://www.artangel.org.uk/projects/2004/die_familie_schneider (accessed 7 August 2014).

89 James Lingwood, 'By appointment: Doors and curtains at 14 and 16 Walden Street', *Artangel* [website]. Available at http://www.artangel.org.uk//projects/2004/die_familie_schneider/by_appointment_doors_and_curtains_at_14_and_16_walden_street_by_james_lingwood/by_appointment_doors_and_curtains_at_14_and_16_walden_street_by_james_lingwood (accessed 7 August 2014).

90 'Gregor Schneider: *Die Familie Schneider*, October 2004'.

91 Craig Garrett, 'Die Familie Schneider', *Flash Art International* (November/December 2004), p. 113. See also Gilda Williams, 'Doubling', *Art Monthly* 340 (2010), pp. 1–4.

92 Andrew O'Hagan, 'The living rooms' [essay], *Artangel* [website]. Available at http://www.artangel.org.uk/projects/2004/die_familie_schneider/the_living_rooms_by_andrew_o_hagan/the_living_rooms_by_andrew_o_hagan (accessed 7 August 2014).

93 See for instance Dan Fox, 'Die Familie Schneider', *Frieze* 88 (February 2005).

94 Royle, *The Uncanny*, pp. 14–16.

95 Trigg, *The Aesthetics of Decay*, p. 38.

96 Ibid., p. 29.

97 Ibid.

5. THE UNMADE HOUSE

1 Robert Gober, 'Interview with Richard Flood', in Judith Nesbitt, ed., *Robert Gober* [exh. cat.] (London: Serpentine Gallery, 1993), p. 14.

2 Caspar Pearson, *Humanism and the Urban World: Leon Battista Alberti and the Renaissance City* (University Park, PA: Pennsylvania State University Press, 2011), pp. 172–3.

3 Ibid., pp. 26–7.

4 Leon Battista Alberti, *On the Art of Building, in Ten Books*, trans. Joseph Rykwert, Neil Leach and Robert Tavernor (Cambridge, MA: MIT Press, 1988), p. 320, quoted in Pearson, *Humanism and the Urban World*, p. 29.

5 Pearson, *Humanism and the Urban World*, pp. 42–4.

6 Mario Bevilacqua, 'The Rome of Piranesi: Views of the ancient and modern city', in Mario Bevilacqua, Mario Gori Sassoli and Fabio Barry, eds, *The Rome of Piranesi: The Eighteenth Century City in the Great Vedute* [exh. cat.] (Rome: Museo del Corso, 2007), p. 39.

7 Nicholas Penny, *Piranesi* (London: Oresko Books, 1978), pp. 5–8; Peter Murray, *Piranesi and the Grandeur of Ancient Rome* (London: Thames & Hudson, 1971), pp. 9–20.

8 James Monte, 'Looking at the Guggenheim International', *Artforum* (March 1971), p. 31.

9 Jack Burnham, 'Hans Haacke's cancelled show at the Guggenheim', *Artforum* (June 1971), p. 67.

10 See the arguments in Norman I. Fainstein and Susan S. Fainstein, eds, *Urban Policy under Capitalism* (Beverly Hills, CA: Sage Publications, 1982), pp. 10–11.

11 Burnham, 'Hans Haacke's cancelled show at the Guggenheim', pp. 67–8.

12 Quoted ibid., p. 69.

13 Ibid., p. 70.

14 Quoted ibid.

15 For a good discussion about these and related debates, see Paul Wood *et al.*, *Modernism in Dispute: Art since the Forties* (New Haven, CT, and London: Yale University Press and the Open University, 1993), esp. pp. 121–4.

16 Burnham, 'Hans Haacke's cancelled show at the Guggenheim', p. 71.

17 Timothy Ferris, 'A creepy protest at museum', *Artforum* (February 1971), p. 31.

18 Lawrence Alloway, 'Talking with William Rubin: The museum concept is not infinitely expandable', *Artforum* (October 1974), p. 51.

19 Lebbeus Woods, *Anarchitecture: Architecture Is a Political Act* (London: St Martin's Press, 1992), pp. 8–9.

20 Ibid., pp. 10–11.

21 Harry Francis Mallgrave and Christina Contandriopoulos, eds, *Architectural Theory*, vol. 2: *An Anthology from 1871 to 2005* (Oxford: Blackwell, 2008), p. 335.

22 Mumford and Stein are quoted in Jane Jacobs, *The Life and Death of Great American Cities* (1961), an extract from which appears in Mallgrave and Contandriopoulos, eds, *Architectural Theory*, vol. 2, p. 339.

23 Rem Koolhaas, extract from *Delirious New York* (1978), in Mallgrave and Contandriopoulos, eds, *Architectural Theory*, vol. 2, p. 456. Original in italics.

24 Stephanie T. Edens, 'Alternative spaces – Soho style', *Art in America* (November/December 1973), p. 38.

25 Laurie Anderson, 'About 405 East 13th Street review', *Artforum* (September 1973), p. 88.

26 See 'Review', *Artforum* (February 1973), pp. 83–6.

27 See the description of the exhibition *Laurie Anderson, Trisha Brown, Gordon Matta-Clark: Pioneers of the Downtown Scene, New York 1970s*, which ran from 3 March to 22 May 2011 at the Barbican Art Gallery. Available at http://www.barbican.org.uk/artgallery/event-detail.asp?ID=11398 (accessed 7 August 2014).

28 Bruce Jenkins, *Gordon Matta-Clark: Conical Intersect* (London: Afterall, 2011), pp. 52–4.

29 Stephen Walker, *Gordon Matta-Clark: Art, Architecture and the Attack on Modernism* (London and New York, NY: I.B.Tauris, 2009), p. 135.

30 Ibid., pp. 135–9.

31 Jenkins, *Gordon Matta-Clark: Conical Intersect*, p. 71. Matta-Clark studied architecture at Cornell between 1962 and 1968. One of the projects that he completed there was to make a series of improvised interventions within the Victorian home of an art history professor: LeGrace Benson. See Ibid., p. 47.

32 Quoted in Burnham, 'Hans Haacke's cancelled show at the Guggenheim', p. 70.

33 Performance seen in April 2011 at the exhibition *Laurie Anderson, Trisha Brown, Gordon Matta-Clark: Pioneers of the Downtown Scene, New York 1970s*, which ran from 3 March to 22 May 2011 at the Barbican Art Gallery.

34 Jenkins, *Gordon Matta-Clark: Conical Intersect*, p. 48. See also Tom McDonough, 'How to do things with buildings', *Art in America* xcv/10 (November 2007), p. 166.

35 Rosalind Krauss, 'Sculpture in the expanded field', *October* viii (spring 1979), pp. 30–44.

36 Ibid., pp. 43–4.

37 See Pamela M. Lee, *Object to Be Destroyed: The Work of Gordon Matta-Clark* (Cambridge, MA: MIT Press, 2000), pp. 77, 81.

38 James Attlee and Lisa Le Feuvre, *Gordon Matta-Clark: The Space Between* (Portchester: Nazraeli Press, 2003), p. 73.

39 Lee, *Object to Be Destroyed*, p. 11.

40 For a discussion of the move to suburbia, see M. A. Jones, *The Limits of Liberty: American History 1607–1992* (Oxford: Oxford University Press, 1993), pp. 576–7. For information about the development and history of Englewood, see 'Historic Englewood', *City of Englewood* [website]. Available at http://www.cityofenglewood.org/content/1445/2257/default.aspx (accessed 7 August 2014).

41 See photographs in Gordon Matta-Clark, *Splitting*(New York, NY: Green Street Loft Press, 1974) [unpaginated].

42 Quoted in Jenkins, *Gordon Matta-Clark: Conical Intersect*, p. 63.

43 Lee, *Object to Be Destroyed*, p. 21.

44 Matta-Clark knew Serra and Serra was one of the visitors who saw *Splitting*.

45 'Transcript of the John Tusa interview with Richard Serra', *BBC Radio 3* [website]. Available at http://www.bbc.co.uk/programmes/p00nc9n3 (accessed 7 August 2014).

46 Attlee and Le Feuvre, *Gordon Matta-Clark: The Space Between*, p. 40.

47 Ibid., p. 41.

48 Ibid.

49 Lynn Spigel, 'The suburban home companion: Television and the neighbourhood ideal in postwar America', in Beatriz Colomina, ed., *Sexuality and Space* (New York, NY: Princeton Architectural Press, 1992), p. 186.

50 Quoted in Lee, *Object to Be Destroyed*, p. 239.

51 Matta-Clark, *Splitting* [unpaginated].

52 Richard Serra, 'Statements: On frame', *Artforum* (September 1971) [special film issue], p. 64.

53 Lee, *Object to Be Destroyed*, p. 28.

54 Al Brunelle, 'The great divide: "Anarchitecture" by Matta-Clark', *Art in America* lxii/5 (September/October, 1974), p. 92.

55 Attlee and Le Feuvre, *Gordon Matta-Clark: The Space Between*, p. 40.

56 For an interesting discussion about the performative aspects, see McDonough, 'How to do things with buildings', pp. 164–237.

57 Fainstein and Fainstein, eds, *Urban Policy Under Capitalism*, p. 161.

58 Márcio M. Valença, *The Debate on Equity Withdrawal Versus the Housing-linked Interest Rate Mechanism: A View of the Economics of Housing in Conservative Britain during the 1980s* (Brighton: Centre for Urban and Regional Research, University of Sussex, 1992), pp. 3–4.

59 Valença, *The Debate on Equity Withdrawal*, p. 4. For an overview see Janet Ford, *The Indebted Society: Credit and Default in the 1980s* (London and New York, NY: Routledge, 1988), pp. 3–12, 74–90.

60 Keith Dowding and Desmond King, 'Rooflessness in London', *Policy Studies Journal* xxviii/2 (2000), p. 365.

61 James Hall, 'Architecture that puts painting in its place', *Sunday Correspondent* (24 June 1990), p. 37.

62 Antony Gormley, 'Terracotta and lead works, 1983–1988', *Antony Gormley* [website]. Available at http://www.antonygormley.com/sculpture/item-view/id/228 (accessed 7 August 2014).

63 Whiteread and Matta-Clark have been written about together. See Jenkins, *Gordon Matta-Clark: Conical Intersect*, p. 74. However, I do not wish to make it seem as though Whiteread was reproducing his ideas. For an interesting discussion about precedent, see Lisa Tickner, 'Mediating generation: The mother–daughter plot', *Art History* xxv/1 (February 2002), pp. 23–46.

64 For a discussion about the inside and outside of mental pain, see Elaine Scarry, *The Body in Pain: The Making and Unmaking of the World* (New York, NY: Oxford University Press, 1985), p. 284.

65 Susanna Greeves, 'Stairs into space', in Christiane Schneider, ed., *Rachel Whiteread* [exh. cat.] (London: Haunch of Venison, 2002), p. 38.

66 Quoted in Tickner, 'Mediating generation', p. 32.

67 Nigel Parry, 'Breaking the mould', *Observer* (24 November 1991). See also 'Rachel Whiteread: *Ghost*' [interview, 8 June 1990], in Nicholas Philip James, ed., *Interviews – Artists*, vol. 1: *Recordings from Cv/Visual Arts Research Archive 1988–96* (London: Cv Publications, 2007). She gained funding from the Elephant Trust.

68 'Rachel Whiteread: *Ghost*' [interview, 8 June 1990]. The floor had to be shored up to take the weight of the cast.

69 'Rachel Whiteread in conversation with Iwona Blazwick', in *Rachel Whiteread* [exh. cat.] (Amsterdam: Stedelijk, 1992), p. 14.

70 'Rachel Whiteread: *Ghost*' [interview, 8 June 1990].

71 John McEwen, 'The house that Rachel unbuilt', *Sunday Telegraph* (24 October, 1993).

72 See for instance Alwyn W. Turner, *Rejoice! Rejoice! Britain in the 1980s* (London: Aurum Press, 2010), pp. 225, 233, 242–3.

73 See Chapter 2. For a discussion of this, see Neville Wakefield, 'Rachel Whiteread: Separation anxiety and the art of release', *Parkett* 42 (1994), pp. 80–1.

74 Anthony Vidler, 'Full house: Rachel Whiteread's postdomestic casts', in Anthony Vidler, *Warped Space: Art, Architecture, and Anxiety in Modern Culture* (Cambridge, MA, and London: MIT Press, 2000), pp. 146–7.

75 Jennifer R. Gross, 'Remembrance of things present', in Chris Townsend, ed., *The Art of Rachel Whiteread* (London: Thames & Hudson, 2004), p. 35.

76 'A conversation between Michael Craig-Martin, Lisa Jardine, James Lingwood and Michael Morris', in Gerrie van Noord, ed., *Off Limits: 40 Artangel Projects* (London: Artangel/Merrell, 2002), pp. 10, 19–20.
77 Ibid., p. 11.
78 Ibid., p. 12.
79 Doreen Massey, 'Space–time and the politics of location', in James Lingwood, ed., *Rachel Whiteread House* (London: Phaidon, 1995), p. 36. This book is the most complete overview of the project.
80 David Clapham, *The Meaning of Housing: A Pathways Approach* (Bristol: Policy Press, 2005), p. 155.
81 To view Whiteread's drawings, which include works on graph paper, altered photographs and other materials, see Allegra Pesenti, *Rachel Whiteread: Drawings* [exh. cat.] (Los Angeles, CA: Hammer Museum; Munich and London: DelMonico Books, 2010).
82 Film extract available at http://www.luxonline.org.uk/artists/john_smith/blight.html (accessed 7 August 2014).
83 See the photographs in John Davies, 'A photographic essay: August 1993–March 1994', in James Lingwood, ed., *Rachel Whiteread House* (London: Phaidon, 1995), pp. 73–95.
84 There are images of the lino and wallpaper. See James Lingwood, ed., *Rachel Whiteread House* (London: Phaidon, 1995), pp. 24–5.
85 James Lingwood, 'Introduction', in James Lingwood, ed., *Rachel Whiteread House* (London: Phaidon, 1995), pp. 7–11.
86 Grant H. Kester, *Conversation Pieces: Community and Communication in Modern Art* (Berkeley, CA: University of California Press, 2004), p. 20.
87 Gross, 'Remembrance of things present', p. 41.
88 Massey, 'Space–time and the politics of location', pp. 45–6.
89 Ibid., p. 48.
90 *Time Out* (3–10 November 1993), in Anthony Vidler, 'A dark space', in James Lingwood, ed., *Rachel Whiteread House* (London: Phaidon, 1995), p. 69.
91 'House: A chronology', in James Lingwood, ed., *Rachel Whiteread House* (London: Phaidon, 1995), p. 144.
92 Rosalind Krauss, 'Pictorial space and the question of documentary', *Artforum* (November 1971), pp. 68–71.
93 Ibid., p. 70.
94 'Rachel Whiteread in conversation with Iwona Blazwick', p. 10.
95 Ibid., pp. 10–11.
96 Ibid., p. 15.

97 Talitha Kotzé, 'Steffi Klenz: Nummianus', *The List* [website]. Available at http://www.list.co.uk/article/23651-steffi-klenz-nummianus/ (accessed 7 August 2014).

98 Ibid.

99 David Trigg, 'Steffi Klenz, Nummianus', *Art Review* 37 (December 2009), p. 117.

100 'Conversation between Steffi Klenz, Jennifer Thatcher, Jeremy Till and Jean Wainwright', in Mark Cousins *et al.*, *Polo: Bound for Passaic* [exh. cat.] (Walsall: New Art Gallery, 2009) [unpaginated].

101 'Steffi Klenz discusses Nummianus' [video]. Available at http://www.youtube.com/watch?v=Sl4DcACAdAM (accessed 7 August 2014); John-Paul Stonard, 'Andreas Gursky', *Tate* [website]. Available at http://www.tate.org.uk/art/artists/andreas-gursky-2349 (accessed 7 August 2014).

102 'Conversation between Steffi Klenz, Jennifer Thatcher, Jeremy Till and Jean Wainwright' [unpaginated].

103 'Steffi Klenz discusses Nummianus' [video]. Available at http://www.youtube.com/watch?v=Sl4DcACAdAM (accessed 7 August 2014).

104 'Conversation between Steffi Klenz, Jennifer Thatcher, Jeremy Till and Jean Wainwright' [unpaginated].

6. WITHDRAWAL

1 Ilya Kabakov, 'Introduction', in Ilya Kabakov, *On the Total Installation*, trans. Cindy Martin (Ostfildern: Hatje Cantz, 1995), p. 244.

2 Ilya Kabakov, 'In conversation with Robert Storr (extract), 1995', in Boris Groys, David A. Ross and Iwona Blazwick, *Ilya Kabakov* (London: Phaidon, 1998), p. 125.

3 Kabakov, 'Introduction', pp. 245–6.

4 David Ross, 'Interview with Ilya Kabakov', in Boris Groys, David A. Ross and Iwona Blazwick, *Ilya Kabakov* (London: Phaidon, 1998), pp. 24–6.

5 For a detailed explanation of the factors Kabakov thought essential for a 'total installation', see Ilya Kabakov, 'Time in the "total" installation', in Ilya Kabakov, *On the Total Installation*, trans. Cindy Martin (Ostfildern: Hatje Cantz, 1995), pp. 256–60.

6 Ilya Kabakov, 'What is a communal apartment?', in Ilya Kabakov, *Ten Characters* [exh. cat.] (New York, NY: Ronald Feldman Fine Arts; London: ICA, 1989), pp. 50, 52.

7 Boris Groys, 'Survey: The movable cave, or Kabakov's self-memorials', in Boris Groys, David A. Ross and Iwona Blazwick, *Ilya Kabakov* (London: Phaidon, 1998), pp. 54–63.

8 Kabakov, 'In conversation with Robert Storr', p. 124.

9 Ilya and Emilia Kabakov, *The Palace of Projects: 1995–1998* [exh. cat.] (London: Artangel; Madrid: Museo Nacional Centro de Arte Reina Sofia, 1998).

10 Ilya Kabakov, *16 Installations* [exh. cat.] (Antwerp: Museum van Hedendaagse Kunst, 1998), p. 78. Other details are from pp. 12 and 62. The catalogue is attributed to Ilya Kabakov only.

11 Ibid., p. 96.

12 Kabakov, 'Time in the "total" installation', pp. 281, 283.

13 Ibid., p. 282.

14 Ibid., pp. 283–4.

15 Gaston Bachelard, *The Poetics of Space* [1958], trans. Maria Jolas (1964; Boston, MA: Beacon Press, 1994), pp. 9–10, 14.

16 Helen Chadwick, *Notebook on Ego Geometria Sum*, pp. 74–5. Available at http://www.henry-moore.org/hmi/archive/turning-the-pages--helen-chadwick-notebooks (accessed 7 August 2014).

17 See diagrams ibid., pp. 60–1.

18 I would like to thank Claire Mayoh at the Henry Moore Institute Archive in Leeds for arranging for me to view *The Juggler's Table*, the notebooks and the earlier works. The notebooks are small so easy to carry around, and are full of plans, lists and ideas.

19 Gunnthórunn Gudmundsdóttir, *Borderlines: Autobiography and Fiction in Postmodern Life Writing* (Amsterdam and New York, NY: Rodopi, 2003), p. 11.

20 See Paul John Eakin, *Fictions in Autobiography: Studies in the Art of Self-invention* (Princeton, NJ: Princeton University Press, 1985), p. 3.

21 Helen Chadwick, *Notebook on Ego Geometria Sum*, pp. 4, 5.

22 Ibid., p. 5.

23 Ibid., pp. 8, 17–18, 64–7.

24 Ibid., pp. 7–8.

25 Pierre Nora, 'Between memory and history: *Les lieux de mémoire*', *Representations* 26 (spring 1989), p. 13.

26 Mark Sladen, 'A red mirror', in Mark Sladen, ed., *Helen Chadwick* [exh. cat.] (London: Barbican Art Gallery and Hatje Cantz, 2004), p. 15.

27 Helen Chadwick, *Notebook on Ego Geometria Sum*, pp. 100–1. See also the notes on Arthur Koestler, *The Sleepwalkers: A History of Man's Changing Vision of the Universe* (1959; London: Penguin Arkana, 1989), in Helen Chadwick, *Notebook on Ego Geometria Sum*, pp. 102–11. This is also discussed in the short essay by Eva Martischnig in Stephen Feeke *et al.* *'My Personal Museum': Ego Geometria Sum* [exh. leaflet] (Leeds: Henry Moore Institute, 2004).

28 Helen Chadwick, *Notebook on Ego Geometria Sum*, pp. 70–1, 74–5.

29 Ibid., pp. 16–17.

30 Ibid., p. 81.

31 Marina Warner, 'Preface', in Mark Sladen, ed., *Helen Chadwick* [exh. cat.] (London: Barbican Art Gallery and Hatje Cantz, 2004), p. 11.

32 Helen Chadwick, *Notebook on Ego Geometria Sum*, p. 9.

33 Ibid., p. 12.

34 Ibid., pp. 98–9.

35 Lynn Barber, 'In a private world of interiors', *Observer* (1 September 1996).

36 Bachelard, *Poetics of Space*, pp. 78–9.

37 Gaston Bachelard, *The Poetics of Reverie: Childhood, Language, and the Cosmos*, trans. Daniel Russell (Boston, MA: Beacon Press, 1960), pp. 99–100, 102–3.

38 See for instance Natalie Rudd, 'From here to infinity and back', in *Size Matters: Exploring Scale in the Arts Council Collection* (London: Hayward Gallery, 2005), pp. 8–15.

39 Patrick Elliott, 'Sculpting nothing: An introduction to the work of Rachel Whiteread', in Lisa G. Corrin, Patrick Elliott and Andrea Schlieker, *Rachel Whiteread* [exh. cat.] (Edinburgh: Scottish National Gallery of Modern Art; London: Serpentine Gallery, 2001), p. 16.

40 Barber, 'In a private world of interiors'.

41 Bachelard, *The Poetics of Reverie*, p. 99.

42 Jennifer R. Gross, 'Remembrance of things present', in Chris Townsend, ed., *The Art of Rachel Whiteread* (London: Thames & Hudson, 2004), p. 38.

43 Bachelard, *The Poetics of Reverie*, p. 102.

44 Quoted in Mary Lynn Kotz, *Rauschenberg: Art and Life* (New York, NY: Harry N. Abrams, 1990), p. 85.

45 Quoted in Alan Solomon, 'The new art' [1963], in Carol Anne Mahsun, ed., *Pop Art: The Critical Dialogue* (Ann Arbor, MI: UMI Research Press, 1989), p. 54. See Chapter 2.

46 Alexandra Schantl, 'About the love of objects', in Alexandra Schantl, ed., *The Love of Objects: Aspects of Contemporary Sculpture* (Vienna: Springer Verlag, 2008), p. 21.

47 Quoted in Démosthènes Davvetas, 'Jasper Johns et sa famille d'objets', in Kirk Varnedoe, ed., *Jasper Johns: Writings, Sketchbook Notes, Interviews* (New York, NY: MoMA, 1996), p. 219.

48 See Charlotte Klonk, *Spaces of Experience: Art Gallery Interiors from 1800–2000* (New Haven, CT, and London: Yale University Press, 2009), p. 194.

49 Quoted in Jonathan Fineberg, 'To sleep, perchance to dream: *The House of Dreams*', in Jonathan Fineberg, *Ilya and Emilia Kabakov: The House of Dreams* [exh. cat.] (London: Serpentine Gallery, 2005), p. 50.

50 Ibid., p. 51.

51 Rod Mengham, 'Agents and penitents', in Jonathan Fineberg, *Ilya and Emilia Kabakov: The House of Dreams* [exh. cat.] (London: Serpentine Gallery, 2005), p. 22.

52 Brian O'Doherty, 'Inside the white cube, part II: The eye and the spectator', *Artforum* (April 1976), p. 32.

53 'Oral history interview with George Segal, 1973 November 26', *Archives of American Art* [website]. Available at http://www.aaa.si.edu/collections/interviews/oral-history-interview-george-segal-12613 (accessed 7 August 2014).

54 George Segal, taped conversation with José L. Barrio-Garay in 1972, quoted in José L. Barrio-Garay, *George Segal: Environments* [exh. cat.] (Philadelphia, PA: Institute of Contemporary Arts, 1976) [unpaginated].

55 Henry Geldzahler, 'An interview with George Segal', *Artforum* (November 1964), p. 29.

56 Jan van der Marck, *George Segal* (New York, NY: Harry N. Abrams, 1979), p. 16.

57 Quoted in Sheena Wagstaff, 'The elation of sunlight', in Sheena Wagstaff, *Edward Hopper* [exh. cat.] (London: Tate, 2004), p. 16.

58 Gregory Minissale, *Framing Consciousness in Art: Transcultural Perspectives* (Amsterdam and New York, NY: Rodopi, 2009), pp. 68–71.

59 Elizabeth Legge, 'Reinventing derivation: Roles, stereotypes, and "Young British Art"', *Representations* 71 (summer 2000), pp. 4–6, 9–14.

60 John A. Walker, *Cultural Offensive: America's Impact on British Art since 1945* (London and Sterling, VA: Pluto Press, 1998), p. 245. See also Adrian Searle, 'Letter from London: Turner again', *Artforum* (February 1995), p. 27.

61 Karsten Schubert quoted in discussion, in Liam Gillick and Andrew Renton, eds, *Technique Anglaise: Current Trends in British Art* (London: Thames & Hudson, 1991), p. 37.

62 Michael Corris, 'British? Young? Invisible? W/attitude?', *Artforum* (May 1992), p. 106.

63 For an interesting discussion of British and American youth culture overlaps, see Jon Savage, 'Museum piece: Anarchy in the V&A', *Artforum* (February 1995), pp. 29–30.

64 Quoted in Rosemary Betterton, 'Why is my art not as good as me? Femininity, feminism and life-drawing in Tracey Emin's art', in Mandy Merck and Chris Townsend, eds, *The Art of Tracey Emin* (London: Thames & Hudson, 2002), p. 36.

65 Ibid., p. 23.

66 Ibid., p. 30.

67 Quoted in Patrick Elliott, 'Becoming Tracey Emin', in Patrick Elliott and Julian Schnabel, *Tracey Emin: 20 Years* (Edinburgh: National Galleries of Scotland, 2008), p. 28.

68 Ibid., p. 25.

69 Betterton, 'Why is my art not as good as me?', p. 37.

70 Elliott, 'Becoming Tracey Emin', pp. 18, 20.

71 Jean Wainwright, 'Interview with Tracey Emin', in Mandy Merck and Chris Townsend, eds, *The Art of Tracey Emin* (London: Thames & Hudson, 2002), pp. 204–5.

72 Rebecca Fortnum, 'Interview with Tracey Emin', in Rebecca Fortnum, *Contemporary British Women Artists: In Their Own Words* (London and New York, NY: I.B.Tauris, 2007), p. 57.

73 Ibid.

74 Elliott, 'Becoming Tracey Emin', p. 18.

75 Fortnum, 'Interview with Tracey Emin', p. 60.

76 Ibid., p. 61.

77 Deborah Cherry, 'On the move: *My Bed* 1998–1999', in Mandy Merck and Chris Townsend, eds, *The Art of Tracey Emin* (London: Thames & Hudson, 2002), pp. 136–8.

78 Wainwright, 'Interview with Tracey Emin', p. 209.

79 Quoted in Cherry, 'On the move', p. 146.

80 See for instance Wainwright, 'Interview with Tracey Emin', pp. 195–6.

81 Rudi Fuchs, 'Tracey Emin: A particular honesty' [essay] (2005). Available at http://whitecube.com/artists/tracey_emin/text/tracey_emin_a_particular_honesty/ (accessed 7 August 2014).

82 Ibid.

83 Fortnum, 'Interview with Tracey Emin', p. 62.

84 Ibid., p. 61.

85 'Debate: Would you show your bed to the public?', *Independent* (24 October 1999).

86 Matthew Collings, 'You've made your bed; and if you are Tracey Emin, you might just win the Turner Prize with it. But can anyone's bed be a work of art?', *Observer* (24 October 1999).

87 This mattress will always remain the same for this work. This detail and those regarding the fruit and vegetables come from a discussion in July 2012 between the author and Lisa Le Feuvre, head of sculptural studies at the Henry Moore Institute, Leeds, and curator of the exhibition *Sarah Lucas: Ordinary Things*, held at the Henry Moore Institute from 18 July to 21 October 2012.

88 Amna Malik, *Sarah Lucas: Au naturel* (London: Afterall, 2009), p. 23. Malik provides a useful discussion about the destabilising of feminist narratives in this work – see pp. 18–23.

89 Pryle Behrman, 'Öyvind Fahlström and Sarah Lucas', *Contemporary Visual Arts* 32 (2000), p. 63.

90 I would like to thank the staff at the Henry Moore Institute, Leeds, who allowed me to go back after the doors were closed to look again at the work.

91 Behrman, 'Öyvind Fahlström and Sarah Lucas', p. 63.

92 Discussion with Lisa Le Feuvre. In Jerry Saltz, ed., *An Ideal Syllabus: Artists, Critics and Curators Choose the Books We Need to Read* (London: Frieze, 1998), Lucas selects Andrea Dworkin, *Intercourse* (1987; New York, NY: Free Press, 1997) as one of her choices.

93 Dworkin, *Intercourse*, pp. 3–12.

94 Quoted ibid., p. 40.

95 Elizabeth Manchester, 'Sarah Lucas, *Sod You Gits* 1991: Summary', *Tate* [website]. Available at http://www.tate.org.uk/art/artworks/lucas-sod-you-gits-p78205/text-summary (accessed 7 August 2014).

96 Ibid.

7. OBJECTS, SENTIMENT AND MEMORY

1 Judy Attfield, *Wild Things: The Material Culture of Everyday Life* (Oxford and New York, NY: Berg, 2000), pp. 12–16. This is an excellent discussion about the things that surround us.

2 Toby Israel, *Some Place like Home: Using Design Psychology to Create Ideal Places* (Chichester: John Wiley, 2003), pp. 113–14.

3 Daniel Miller, *The Comfort of Things* (Cambridge and Malden, MA: Polity Press, 2008), pp. 1–2.

4 Doreen Massey, 'A place called home?', *New Formations* 17 (1992), p. 7; Alison Ravetz with Richard Turkington, *The Place of Home: The English Domestic Environment 1914–2000* (London: E. & F. N. Spon, 1995), pp. 206–8.

5 Miller, *The Comfort of Things*, pp. 287, 293, 296.

6 Ibid., p. 8.

7 Ibid., pp. 57–66.

8 Ibid., pp. 18–31.

9 Tony Godfrey, 'The identity of the sculptor 1975–2000', in Penelope Curtis, ed., *Sculpture in 20th-Century Britain*, vol. 1 (Leeds: Henry Moore Institute, 2003), p. 227.

10 Andrea Tarsia, 'Conditions of display 1975–2000', in Penelope Curtis, ed., *Sculpture in 20th-century Britain*, vol. 1 (Leeds: Henry Moore Institute, 2003), p. 253.

11 Christopher Frayling, *The Royal College of Art: 150 Years of Art and Design* (London: Barrie & Jenkins, 1987), pp. 144, 156.

12 Stephen Cohen, 'Editorial', *Ark* 30 (1961) [unpaginated].

13 See for instance: Glynn Williams, 'Defining sculpture', *Art Monthly* 29 (September 1979), pp. 4–7; Peter Fuller, 'Stockwell depot', *Art Monthly* 30 (October 1979), pp. 14–16; and the reply, Anthony Caro, 'Stockwell depot', *Art Monthly* 32 (December 1979/January, 1980), p. 27.

14 See *Art Monthly* between 1978 and 1982. For instance: John Elsom, 'Whose side are you on? A review of the 1979/89 Arts Council report: *Progress and Renewal*,' *Art Monthly* 42 (December 1980/January 1981), pp. 3–6; Pat Gilmour, 'Page two: Talking the Tate round', *Art Monthly* 30 (October 1979), pp. 2–3; Lawrence Alloway, 'The support system and art galleries', *Art Monthly* 53 (February 1982), pp. 2–3.

15 Richard Cork, *New Spirit, New Sculpture, New Money: Art in the 1980s* (New Haven, CT: Yale University Press, 2003), pp. 8–10.

16 Lynne Cooke, 'Between image and object: The "New British Sculpture"', in Terry A. Neff, ed., *A Quiet Revolution: British Sculpture since 1965* (London: Thames & Hudson, 1987), p. 39; Penelope Curtis, *Modern British Sculpture from the Collection* (London: Tate, 1988), pp. 129–30.

17 Cooke, 'Between image and object', pp. 34–6; Lewis Biggs, Iwona Blaszczyk and Sandy Nairne, 'Introduction', in Lewis Biggs, Iwona Blaszczyk and Sandy Nairne, *Objects and Sculpture* [exh. cat.] (London and Bristol: ICA and Arnolfini, 1981), p. 5. *Objects and Sculpture* was held at the ICA, London, and the Arnolfini, Bristol, between May and August 1981. It included work by Edward Allington, Richard Deacon, Antony Gormley, Anish Kapoor, Margaret Organ, Peter Randall-Page, Jean Luc Vilmouth and Bill Woodrow.

18 See the 'Biography' section of Tony Cragg's website. Available at http://tony-cragg.com/ (accessed 7 August 2014).

19 'Writings by Tony Cragg', in *Tony Cragg: Winner of the 1988 Turner Prize* (London: Tate Gallery & Patrons of New Art, 1989), p. 11.

20 Helmut Friedel, ed., *Anthony Cragg: Material_Object_Form* (Munich: Hatje Cantz, 1995), p. 60.

21 Germano Celant, 'Tony Cragg and industrial Platonism', in Tony Cragg *et al.*, *Tony Cragg: Signs of Life* (Düsseldorf: Richter Verlag, 2003), pp. 23–4.

22 'Writings by Tony Cragg', pp. 14–15.

23 Tony Cragg, *In and Out of Material* [interview with Jon Wood] (Cologne: Walther König, 2006), pp. 81, 121.

24 Ibid., p. 18.

25 'Tony Cragg talks to Barry Schwabsky', *Artforum* (April 2003), p. 200.

26 Harold Bloom, *The Anxiety of Influence: A Theory of Poetry* (London: Oxford University Press, 1997), p. 14.

27 Peter Schjeldahl, 'Cragg's big bang', in Tony Cragg *et al.*, *Tony Cragg: Signs of Life* (Düsseldorf: Richter Verlag, 2003), pp. 86–7.
28 See Attfield, *Wild Things*, p. 174.
29 'Tony Cragg talks to Barry Schwabsky', p. 200.
30 Michael Bracewell, '"So much depends": An introduction to the art of Richard Wentworth', *Richard Wentworth* [exh. cat.] (Liverpool and London: Tate, 2005), p. 6.
31 Marina Warner, 'Richard Wentworth: A sense of things', in Marina Warner, *Richard Wentworth* [exh. cat.] (London: Thames & Hudson and Serpentine Gallery, 1993), p. 12. The whole text is an excellent discussion of Wentworth's ideas.
32 Attfield, *Wild Things*, p. 238; Bracewell, '"So much depends"', p. 7.
33 See the occasional series of photographs that he has developed over the decades entitled Making Do and Getting By.
34 Warner, 'Richard Wentworth: A sense of things', pp. 12–13.
35 Richard Cork, 'British sculpture in the late twentieth century', in Catherine Marshall, ed., *Breaking the Mould: British Art of the 1980s and 1990s* (London: Lund Humphries and Dublin: Irish Museum of Modern Art, 1997), p. 15.
36 Julia Kelly, 'Sculpture, bricolage and the art of Bill Woodrow', in *Bill Woodrow: Sculptures 1981–1988* [exh. cat.] (London: Waddington Custot Galleries, 2011), p. 6.
37 Ibid.
38 Waldemar Januszczak, 'Bill Woodrow, Waddington Galleries', *Waldemar Januszczak* [website] (27 March 2011). Available at http://www.waldemar.tv/2011/03/bill-woodrow-waddington-galleries/ (accessed 7 August 2014).
39 Claire Bishop, *Installation Art: A Critical History* (London: Tate, 2005), p. 41.
40 Tomás Maldonado, 'The idea of comfort', in Victor Margolin and Richard Buchanan, eds, *The Idea of Design* (Cambridge, MA: MIT Press, 1995), p. 248.
41 Ibid., p. 248.
42 Mihaly Csikszentmihalyi, 'Design and order in everyday life', in Victor Margolin and Richard Buchanan, eds, *The Idea of Design* (Cambridge, MA: MIT Press, 1995), p. 126.
43 Ibid., pp. 119–21.
44 Chris Gosden, 'Making and display: Our aesthetic appreciation of things and objects', in Colin Renfrew, Chris Gosden and Elizabeth DeMarrais, eds, *Memory, Display, Archaeology and Art* (Cambridge: McDonald Institute for Archaeological Research, 2004), pp. 35–6.
45 The exhibition ran from 26 November 1988 to 7 January 1989. I would like to thank the Ikon Gallery for sending me a catalogue. For a more complete discussion of this work and other works by Parker involving the destruction of objects, see Imogen

Racz, 'Cornelia Parker's *Thirty Pieces of Silver*', in Jenny Walden ed., *Art and Destruction* (Newcastle: Cambridge Scholars Press, 2013), pp. 45–56.

46 For a discussion of this, see Antonia Payne, 'Neither from nor towards', in G. Brett *et al.*, *Cornelia Parker: Avoided Object* [exh. cat.] (Cardiff: Chapter, 1996), pp. 39–50.

47 Leddy's argument is summarised in Yuriko Saito, *Everyday Aesthetics* (Oxford: Oxford University Press, 2007), p. 153.

48 Ibid., pp. 154–5.

49 See for instance: Gaston Bachelard, *The Poetics of Space* [1958], trans. Maria Jolas (1964; Boston, MA: Beacon Press, 1994); Maurice Merleau-Ponty, *Phenomenology of Perception* (London and New York, NY: Routledge, 2002); and Edmund Husserl, *Ideas: General Introduction to Pure Phenomenology*, trans. W. R. Boyce Gibson (London: Allen & Unwin; New York, NY: Humanities Press, 1931).

50 Jessica Morgan, 'Matter and what it means', in *Cornelia Parker* [exh. cat.] (Boston, MA: ICA, 2000), p. 16.

51 Darian Leader, 'The double life of objects', in Andrea Jahn, ed., *Cornelia Parker: Perpetual Canon* [exh. cat.] (Stuttgart: Kerber Verlag, 2004), p. 74.

52 I would like to thank Helen Makin at Coventry University for explaining the processes to me.

53 See 'Cornelia Parker' [video]. Available at http://www.bing.com/videos/search?q=Cornelia+parker+youtube&docid=4545218974846847&mid=BC014589B5713201C062BC014589B5713201C062&view=detail&FORM=VIRE3 (accessed 7 August 2014).

54 See Norman Bryson, *Looking at the Overlooked: Four Essays on Still Life Painting* (London: Reaktion, 1990), pp. 96–8.

55 See 'Cornelia Parker', in Virginia Button *et al.*, *The Turner Prize 1997* (London: Tate, 1997) [unpaginated]; Morgan, 'Matter and what it means', p. 16.

56 Lisa Tickner, 'A strange alchemy: Cornelia Parker', *Art History* xxvi/3 (2003), p. 372.

57 The link to Monet's paintings has been made by a number of art historians including Tickner, 'A strange alchemy', p. 371.

58 Cornelia Parker has discussed this in relation to the instability of meaning in life. See Lisa G. Corrin, *Cornelia Parker* [exh. cat.] (London: Serpentine Gallery, 1998) [unpaginated].

59 Email from Tamar Maor, sculpture conservator at Tate Britain, to the author, 9 March 2012. I would like to thank Tamar Maor for explaining to me the processes of hanging and caring for the objects in this work.

60 Bachelard, *Poetics of Space*, pp. xxxiv–xxxv.

61 Corrin, *Cornelia Parker* [unpaginated].

62 Email from Tamar Maor to the author, 9 March 2012; Tickner, 'A strange alchemy', p. 375.
63 Tickner, 'A strange alchemy', p. 375.
64 For an interesting discussion about viewing and displacement, see Bishop, *Installation Art*, pp. 128–33.
65 Bryson, *Looking at the Overlooked*, p. 61.
66 Laura Tansini, 'Sculpture to enlarge our reality: A conversation with Tony Cragg', *Sculpture* xxiii/4 (May 2004), p. 36.
67 Bryson, *Looking at the Overlooked*, pp. 63–9.
68 Quoted in Friedel, ed., *Anthony Cragg: Material_Object_Form*, p. 57.
69 Quoted in Ina Cole, 'Mapping traces: Rachel Whiteread', in Glenn Harper and Twylene Moyer, eds, *Conversations on Sculpture* (Hamilton, NJ: ISC Press, 2007), p. 197.
70 Ibid., pp.199–200.
71 Juhani Pallasmaa, 'Petrified silence', in Eckhard Schneider, ed., *Rachel Whiteread: Walls, Doors, Floors and Stairs* (Cologne: Walther König, 2005), p. 22.
72 James Lawrence, 'Sculptural common sense', in *Rachel Whiteread* [exh. cat.] (Beverly Hills, CA: Gagosian Gallery, 2008), p. 10.
73 Alexandra Parigoris, 'Truth to material: Bronze, on the reproducibility of truth', in Anthony Hughes and Erich Ranfft, eds, *Sculpture and Its Reproductions* (London: Reaktion, 1997), p. 147.
74 For an interesting discussion, see Natasha Daintry, 'The essential vessel', in Rob Barnard, Natasha Daintry and Clare Twomey, eds, *Breaking the Mould: New Approaches to Ceramics* (London: Black Dog, 2007), pp. 6–15.
75 Tanya Harrod, *The Crafts in Britain in the Twentieth Century* (New Haven, CT: Yale University Press, 1999), p. 373.
76 David Hamilton, 'No man's land', *Crafts* (July/August 1975), p. 42; Imogen Racz, *Contemporary Crafts* (Oxford and New York, NY: Berg, 2009), pp. 50, 66–8, 95–100.
77 Alison Britton, 'The manipulation of skill on the outer limits of function', in Crafts Council, *Beyond the Dovetail* [exh. cat.] (London: Crafts Council, 1991) [unpaginated].
78 'Ceramic points of view: "Big White Jug", by Alison Britton', *V&A* [website]. Available at http://www.vam.ac.uk/content/articles/c/ceramics-points-of-view-alison-britton-big-white-jug/ (accessed 7 August 2014).
79 John Houston, *The Abstract Vessel* (London: Bellew Publishing, 1991), p. 53.
80 Richard Cork, 'Art as vessel', in Richard Cork, *New Spirit, New Sculpture, New Money: Art in the 1980s* (New Haven, CT: Yale University Press, 2003), pp. 109–10.
81 Martina Margetts, 'Metamorphosis: The culture of ceramics', in David Elliott, ed., *The Raw and the Cooked: New Work in Clay in Britain* [exh. cat.] (London: Crafts Council; Oxford: MoMA, 1993), pp. 13–15.

82 For a discussion about this, see Imogen Racz, 'Sculptural vessels across the great divide: Tony Cragg's *Laibe* and the metaphors of clay', *Journal of Visual Art Practice* viii/3 (2009), pp. 215–28.

83 Bryson, *Looking at the Overlooked*, p. 61.

84 See Simon Groom, ed., *A Secret History of Clay: From Gauguin to Gormley* [exh. cat.] (London: Tate, 2004).

85 'Cindy Sherman (b.1954): *Madame de Pompadour (née Poisson) Soup Tureen and Saucer*, 1990', *Pulitzer Foundation for the Arts* [website]. Available at http://www.portrait.pulitzerarts.org/entrance-gallery/pompadour/ (accessed 7 August 2014).

86 Marjan Boot *et al.*, *Grayson Perry: Guerrilla Tactics* [exh. cat.] (Rotterdam: NAi Uitgevers, 2002), p. 23.

87 For a discussion of Perry's work in relation to Bernard Leach's ideas, see J. Jones, 'Grayson Perry: The pot is the man', in Julian Stair, ed., *The Body Politic: The Role of the Body and Contemporary Craft* (London: Crafts Council, 2000), pp. 96–101.

88 Boot *et al.*, *Grayson Perry: Guerrilla Tactics*, p. 24.

89 Quoted in Louisa Buck, 'The personal political pots of Grayson Perry', in Marjan Boot *et al.*, *Grayson Perry: Guerrilla Tactics* [exh. cat.] (Rotterdam: NAi Uitgevers, 2002), p. 100.

90 Deborah Stevenson, *Cities and Urban Cultures* (Maidenhead and Philadelphia, PA: Open University Press, 2003), pp. 20–1; Charles Baudelaire, 'Au lecteur', in Charles Baudelaire, *Complete Poems*, trans. Walter Martin (Manchester: Carcanet, 1997), pp. 2–5.

91 'Ask this year's Turner Prize winner' [interview with Grayson Perry], *BBC News* [website] (7 December 2003). Available at http://news.bbc.co.uk/1/hi/talking_point/3291691.stm (accessed 7 August 2014).

92 Maria Alvarez, 'The provocative potter', *Telegraph Magazine* (14 April 2001).

93 Ibid.

94 Boot *et al.*, *Grayson Perry: Guerrilla Tactics*, p. 8.

95 Hugo Williams, 'Commentary', *Times Literary Supplement* (26 June 1998), p. 18.

SELECT BIBLIOGRAPHY

PRINT SOURCES

Alberti, Leon Battista, *On Painting and On Sculpture*, trans. Cecil Grayson (London: Phaidon, 1972).

Alison, Jane, ed., *The Surreal House* [exh. cat.] (New Haven, CT, and London: Barbican Art Gallery and Yale University Press, 2010).

Allmer, Patricia, 'Of fallen angels and angels of anarchy', in Patricia Allmer, ed., *Angels of Anarchy: Women Artists and Surrealism* (Munich: Prestel, 2009), pp. 12–27.

Alloway, Lawrence, 'Talking with William Rubin: The museum concept is not infinitely expandable', *Artforum* (October 1974), pp. 51–7.

Altshuler, Bruce, *The Avant-garde in Exhibition: New Art in the 20th Century* (Berkeley and Los Angeles, CA: University of California Press, 1994).

Anderson, Laurie, 'About 405 East 13th Street review', *Artforum* (September 1973), pp. 88–90.

Arendt, Hannah, *The Human Condition* (Chicago, IL, and London: University of Chicago Press, 1958).

Attfield, Judy, *Wild Things: The Material Culture of Everyday Life* (Oxford and New York, NY: Berg, 2000).

Attlee, James, and Lisa Le Feuvre, *Gordon Matta-Clark: The Space Between* (Portchester: Nazraeli Press, 2003).

Auther, Elissa, *String, Felt, Thread: The Hierarchy of Art and Craft in American Art* (Minneapolis, MN, and London: University of Minnesota Press, 2010).

Bachelard, Gaston, *The Poetics of Space* [1958], trans. Maria Jolas (1964; Boston, MA: Beacon Press, 1994).

——— *The Poetics of Reverie: Childhood, Language, and the Cosmos*, trans. Daniel Russell (Boston, MA: Beacon Press, 1960).

Balducci, Temma, 'Revisiting *Womanhouse*: Welcome to the (deconstructed) dollhouse', *Woman's Art Journal* xxvii/2 (fall/winter 2006), pp. 17–23.

Baldwin, Carl R., 'On the nature of pop', *Artforum* (June 1974), pp. 34–7.

Ballantyne, Andrew, ed., *What Is Architecture?* (London: Routledge, 2002).

Barrio-Garay, José L., *George Segal: Environments* [exh. cat.] (Philadelphia, PA: Institute of Contemporary Arts, 1976).

Bäschlin, Nathalie, 'Between material and fiction: Aspects of materiality in the works of Meret Oppenheim', in Therese Bhattacharya-Stettler and Matthias Frehner, eds, *Meret Oppenheim Retrospective* [exh. cat.] (Bern: Kunstmuseum and Hatje Cantz, 2006), pp. 107–21.

Bataille, Georges, *The Absence of Myth: Writings on Surrealism*, ed. and trans. Michael Richardson (London and New York, NY: Verso, 2006).

Baudelaire, Charles, 'The painter of modern life', in Charles Baudelaire, *Selected Writings on Art and Artists*, trans. P. E. Charvet (Cambridge: Cambridge University Press, 1972), pp. 390–435.

Behrman, Pryle, 'Öyvind Fahlström and Sarah Lucas', *Contemporary Visual Arts* 32 (2000), pp. 62–3.

Benjamin, Walter, 'Surrealism: The last snapshot of the European intelligentsia' [1929], in Walter Benjamin, *Reflections: Essays, Aphorisms, Autobiographical Writings*, trans. Edmund Jephcott (New York, NY: Schocken Books, 1986), pp. 177–92.

——— 'A Berlin chronicle', in Walter Benjamin, *One Way Street*, trans. Edmund Jephcott and Kingsley Shorter (London and New York, NY: Verso, 2000), pp. 294–346.

Bertola, Chiara, 'Mona Hatoum: Unstable, living, organic and moving forms', in Chiara Bertola, *Mona Hatoum: Interior Landscape* (Milan: Charta, 2009), pp. 19–33.

Betterton, Rosemary, 'Why is my art not as good as me? Femininity, feminism and life-drawing in Tracey Emin's art', in Mandy Merck and Chris Townsend, eds, *The Art of Tracey Emin* (London: Thames & Hudson, 2002), pp. 23–38.

Bevilacqua, Mario, 'The Rome of Piranesi: Views of the ancient and modern city', in Mario Bevilacqua, Mario Gori Sassoli and Fabio Barry, eds, *The Rome of Piranesi: The Eighteenth Century City in the Great Vedute* [exh. cat.] (Rome: Museo del Corso, 2007), pp. 39–60.

Białostocki, Jan, 'The eye and the window: Realism and symbolism of light reflections in the art of Albrecht Dürer and his predecessors', in Jan Białostocki, *The Message of Images: Studies in the History of Art* (Vienna: Irsa Verlag, 1988), pp. 77–92.

Bishop, Claire, *Installation Art: A Critical History* (London: Tate, 2005).

Blistène, Bernard, 'J'ai misé sur l'art plutôt que sur la vie', *Beaux Arts* (October 2007), pp. 144–51.

Bloemink, Barbara J., 'Interview with the artist', in Thomas McEvilley, *James Croak* (New York, NY: Harry N. Abrams, 1998), pp. 97–110.

Bloom, Harold, *The Anxiety of Influence: A Theory of Poetry* (London: Oxford University Press, 1997).

Blum, Shirley Neilsen, 'The open window: A Renaissance view', in Suzanne Delehanty, ed., *The Window in Twentieth-century Art* [exh. cat.] (New York, NY: Neuberger Museum, 1986), pp. 9–16.

Blunt, Alison, and Robyn Dowling, *Home* (London and New York, NY: Routledge, 2006).

Boot, Marjan, *et al.*, *Grayson Perry: Guerrilla Tactics* [exh. cat.] (Rotterdam: NAi Uitgevers, 2002).

Bourgeois, Louise, 'Freud's toys', *Artforum* (January 1990), pp. 111–13.

——— 'Interview with Douglas Maxwell', in Marie-Laure Bernadac and Hans-Ulrich Obrist, eds, *Louise Bourgeois: Destruction of the Father: Reconstruction of the Father: Writing and Interviews 1923–1997* (London: Violette Editions, 1998), pp. 239–47.

Bracewell, Michael, '"So much depends": An introduction to the art of Richard Wentworth', *Richard Wentworth* [exh. cat.] (Liverpool and London: Tate, 2005), pp. 6–8.

Breton, André, 'Artistic genesis and perspective of surrealism' [1941], in André Breton, *Surrealism and Painting*, trans. Simon Watson Taylor (Paris and London: Macdonald, 1972), pp. 51–82.

——— *The Manifestoes of Surrealism*, trans. Richard Seaver and Helen R. Lane (Ann Arbor, MI: University of Michigan Press, 1969).

Britton, Alison, 'The manipulation of skill on the outer limits of function', in Crafts Council, *Beyond the Dovetail* [exh. cat.] (London: Crafts Council, 1991) [unpaginated].

Broude, Norma, and Mary Garrard, eds, *The Power of Feminist Art: Emergence, Impact and Triumph of the American Feminist Art Movement* (London: Thames & Hudson, 1994).

Brown, Meredith, 'School is a place to perform: The art and pedagogy of Judy Chicago's Women's Art Program at Fresno State College, 1970–1971', MA dissertation, Courtauld Institute of Art, 2007.

Brown, Roni, 'Identity and narrativity in homes made by amateurs', *Home Cultures* iv/3 (2007), pp. 213–38.

Brunelle, Al, 'The great divide: "Anarchitecture" by Matta-Clark', *Art in America* lxii/5 (September/October, 1974), pp. 92–3.

Bryson, Norman, *Looking at the Overlooked: Four Essays on Still Life Painting* (London: Reaktion, 1990).

Burnett, John, *A Social History of Housing, 1815–1985* (1978; 2nd edn, Newton Abbot: David & Charles, 1986).

Burnham, Jack, 'Hans Haacke's cancelled show at the Guggenheim', *Artforum* (June 1971), pp. 67–71.

Cage, John, 'Rhythm etc.', in Gyorgy Kepes, ed., *Module, Proportion, Symmetry, Rhythm* (New York, NY: George Braziller, 1966), pp. 194–203.

——— *A Room: For Piano (with or without Preparations) Solo* (New York, NY: Henmar Press, 1968).

——— 'Experimental music', in John Cage, *Silence: Lectures and Writings* (London: Marion Boyars, 1978), pp. 7–12.

——— 'The future of music: Credo', in John Cage, *Silence: Lectures and Writings* (London: Marion Boyars, 1978), pp. 3–6.

——— 'On Robert Rauschenberg, artist, and his work', in John Cage, *Silence: Lectures and Writings* (London: Marion Boyars, 1978), pp. 98–108.

Cameron, Dan, 'Boundary issues', in *Mona Hatoum* [exh. cat.] (Chicago, IL: Museum of Contemporary Art, 1997), pp. 25–33.

Celant, Germano, 'Tony Cragg and industrial Platonism', in Tony Cragg *et al., Tony Cragg: Signs of Life* (Düsseldorf: Richter Verlag, 2003), pp. 20–8.

Chadwick, Whitney, *Women, Art, and Society* (1990; 4th edn, London: Thames & Hudson, 2007).

Chicago, Judy, *Through the Flower: My Struggles as a Woman Artist* (1975; London: Women's Press, 1982).

Chicago, Judy, and Miriam Schapiro, *Womanhouse* [exh. cat.] (Valencia, CA: California Institute of the Arts, 1971).

Clapham, David, *The Meaning of Housing: A Pathways Approach* (Bristol: Policy Press, 2005).

Cohn, Robert, 'Mallarmé's windows', *Yale French Studies* 54 (1977), pp. 23–31.

Collins, Jo, and John Jervis, eds, *Uncanny Modernity: Cultural Theories, Modern Anxieties* (Basingstoke and New York, NY: Palgrave, 2008).

Connon, Daisy, *Subjects Not-at-home: Forms of the Uncanny in the Contemporary French Novel: Emmanuel Carrère, Marie NDiaye, Eugène Savitzkaya* (Amsterdam and New York, NY: Rodopi, 2010).

Connon, Daisy, Gillian Jein and Greg Kerr, eds, *Aesthetics of Dislocation in French and Francophone Literature and Art: Strategies of Representation* (Lewiston, NY: Edwin Mellen Press, 2009).

'A conversation between Michael Craig-Martin, Lisa Jardine, James Lingwood and Michael Morris', in Gerrie van Noord, ed., *Off Limits: 40 Artangel Projects* (London: Artangel/Merrell, 2002), pp. 10–20.

'Conversation between Steffi Klenz, Jennifer Thatcher, Jeremy Till and Jean Wainwright', in Mark Cousins *et al.*, *Polo: Bound for Passaic* [exh. cat.] (Walsall: New Art Gallery, 2009) [unpaginated].

Cooke, Lynne, 'Between image and object: The "New British Sculpture"', in Terry A. Neff, ed., *A Quiet Revolution: British Sculpture since 1965* (London: Thames & Hudson, 1987), pp. 34–53.

——— 'Disputed terrain', in Judith Nesbitt, ed., *Robert Gober* [exh. cat.] (London: Serpentine Gallery, 1993), pp. 16–24.

Cork, Richard, 'British sculpture in the late twentieth century', in Catherine Marshall, ed., *Breaking the Mould: British Art of the 1980s and 1990s* (London: Lund Humphries and Dublin: Irish Museum of Modern Art, 1997), pp. 13–29.

——— *New Spirit, New Sculpture, New Money: Art in the 1980s* (New Haven, CT: Yale University Press, 2003).

Corrin, Lisa G., *Cornelia Parker* [exh. cat.] (London: Serpentine Gallery, 1998).

——— 'A conversation with Rachel Whiteread, March 2001', in Lisa G. Corrin, Patrick Elliott and Andrea Schlieker, *Rachel Whiteread* [exh. cat.] (Edinburgh: Scottish National Gallery of Modern Art; London: Serpentine Gallery, 2001).

Corrin, Lisa G., Patrick Elliott and Andrea Schlieker, *Rachel Whiteread* [exh. cat.] (Edinburgh: Scottish National Gallery of Modern Art; London: Serpentine Gallery, 2001).

Cox, Rosie, 'Dishing the dirt: Dirt in the home', in Nadine Monem, ed., *The Filthy Reality of Everyday Life: Dirt* (London: Profile, 2011), pp. 37–64.

Coxon, Ann, *Louise Bourgeois* (London: Tate, 2010).

Cragg, Tony, *Tony Cragg: In and Out of Material* [interview with Jon Wood] (Cologne: Walther König, 2006).

Crone, Rainer, and Petrus Graf Schaesberg, *Louise Bourgeois: The Secret of the Cells* (Munich: Prestel Verlag, 1998).

Csikszentmihalyi, Mihaly, 'Design and order in everyday life', in Victor Margolin and Richard Buchanan, eds, *The Idea of Design* (Cambridge, MA: MIT Press, 1995), pp. 118–26.

Cullinan, Nicholas, 'To exist in passing time', in Susan Davidson and David White, eds, *Robert Rauschenberg: Photographs, 1949–1962* (London: Thames & Hudson, 2011), pp. 13–37.

Curtis, Penelope, *Modern British Sculpture from the Collection* (London: Tate, 1988).

Davidson, Susan, and David White, eds, *Robert Rauschenberg: Photographs, 1949–1962* (London: Thames & Hudson, 2011).

Davvetas, Démosthènes, 'Jasper Johns et sa famille d'objets', in Kirk Varnedoe, ed., *Jasper Johns: Writings, Sketchbook Notes, Interviews* (New York, NY: MoMA, 1996), pp. 217–20.

Delehanty, Suzanne, 'The artist's window', in Suzanne Delehanty, ed., *The Window in Twentieth-century Art* [exh. cat.] (New York, NY: Neuberger Museum, 1986), pp. 17–28.

Dowding, Keith, and Desmond King, 'Rooflessness in London', *Policy Studies Journal* xxviii/2 (2000), pp. 365–81.

Dripps, R. D., *The First House: Myth, Paradigm and the Task of Architecture* (Cambridge, MA, and London: MIT Press, 1997).

Driscoll, Catherine, 'The moving ground: Locating everyday life', in Ian Buchanan, ed., *Michel de Certeau: In the Plural* [*South Atlantic Quarterly* c/2 (spring 2001)], pp. 381–98.

Dufrenne, Mikel, 'The world of the aesthetic object', in Clive Cazeaux, ed., *The Continental Aesthetics Reader* (London: Routledge, 2000), pp. 129–50.

Dworkin, Andrea, *Intercourse* (1987; New York, NY: Free Press, 1997).

Eakin, Paul John, *Fictions in Autobiography: Studies in the Art of Self-invention* (Princeton, NJ: Princeton University Press, 1985).

Eckmann, Sabine, 'Seeing and performing', in Sabine Eckmann and Lutz Koepnick, eds, *Window/Interface* (St Louis, MO: Mildred Lane Kemper Art Museum, 2006), pp. 61–86.

Edens, Stephanie T., 'Alternative spaces – Soho style', *Art in America* (November/December 1973), pp. 38–9.

Elliott, Patrick, 'Sculpting nothing: An introduction to the work of Rachel Whiteread', in Lisa G. Corrin, Patrick Elliott and Andrea Schlieker, *Rachel Whiteread* [exh. cat.] (Edinburgh: Scottish National Gallery of Modern Art; London: Serpentine Gallery, 2001), pp. 9–15.

——— 'Becoming Tracey Emin', in Patrick Elliott and Julian Schnabel, *Tracey Emin: 20 Years* (Edinburgh: National Galleries of Scotland, 2008), pp. 17–33.

Fainstein, Norman I., and Susan S. Fainstein, eds, *Urban Policy under Capitalism* (Beverly Hills, CA: Sage Publications, 1982).

Fariello, Anna, and Paula Owen, eds, *Objects and Meaning: New Perspectives on Art and Craft* (Lanham, MD: Scarecrow Press, 2004).

Fineberg, Jonathan, 'To sleep, perchance to dream: *The House of Dreams*', in Jonathan Fineberg, *Ilya and Emilia Kabakov: The House of Dreams* [exh. cat.] (London: Serpentine Gallery, 2005), pp. 43–54.

Ford, Janet, *The Indebted Society: Credit and Default in the 1980s* (London and New York, NY: Routledge, 1988).

Fortnum, Rebecca, 'Interview with Tracey Emin', in Rebecca Fortnum, *Contemporary British Women Artists: In Their Own Words* (London and New York, NY: I.B.Tauris, 2007), pp. 55–63.

Foster, Hal, 'An art of missing parts', *October* 92 (spring 2000), pp. 128–56.

Frayling, Christopher, *The Royal College of Art: 150 Years of Art and Design* (London: Barrie & Jenkins, 1987).

Freud, Sigmund, *The Uncanny*, trans. David McLintock (London: Penguin, 2003).

Fried, Michael, 'Art and objecthood', in Charles Harrison and Paul Wood, eds, *Art in Theory, 1900–2000: An Anthology of Changing Ideas* (Oxford: Blackwell, 2003), pp. 835–49.

Friedan, Betty, *The Feminine Mystique* (Harmondsworth: Penguin, 1963).

Friedel, Helmut, ed., *Anthony Cragg: Material_Object_Form* (Munich: Hatje Cantz, 1995).

Friedman, Martin, 'George Segal: Proletarian mythmaker', in Martin Friedman and Graham W. J. Beal, *George Segal: Sculptures* [exh. cat.] (Minneapolis, MN: Walker Art Gallery, 1979), p. 18.

Fuller, Diana Burgess, and Daniela Salvioni, eds, *Art/Women/California 1950–2000: Parallels and Intersections* (Berkeley, CA, and London: University of California Press, 2002).

Gardner, Belinda Grace, 'From *Breakfast in Fur* and back again', in Thomas Levy, ed., *Meret Oppenheim: From Breakfast in Fur and Back Again* (Bielefeld: Kerber Verlag, 2003), pp. 7–23.

Gayford, Martin, 'Starting at zero: Black Mountain College 1933–1957: Kettle's Yard', *Modern Painters* (March 2006), p. 123.

Geldzahler, Henry, 'An interview with George Segal', *Artforum* (November 1964), pp. 26–9.

Gibbons, Joan, *Contemporary Art and Memory: Images of Recollection and Remembrance* (London and New York, NY: I.B.Tauris, 2008).

Giddens, Anthony, *et al.*, eds, *The Polity Reader in Gender Studies* (Cambridge: Polity Press, 1994).

Gilbert and George, 'Interview with Mark Francis' [1981], in Robert Violette and Hans-Ulrich Obrist, eds, *The Words of Gilbert and George: With Portraits of the Artists from 1968 to 1997* (London: Thames & Hudson in association with Violette Editions, 1997), pp. 115–19.

Gilbert and George, 'The fabric of their world: From interviews with Carter Ratcliff' [1986], in Robert Violette and Hans-Ulrich Obrist, eds, *The Words of Gilbert and George: With Portraits of the Artists from 1968 to 1997* (London: Thames & Hudson in association with Violette Editions, 1997).

Gillick, Liam, and Andrew Renton, eds, *Technique Anglaise: Current Trends in British Art* (London: Thames & Hudson, 1991).

Gober, Robert, 'Interview with Richard Flood', in Judith Nesbitt, ed., *Robert Gober* [exh. cat.] (London: Serpentine Gallery, 1993), pp. 8–14.

Godfrey, Tony, 'The identity of the sculptor 1975–2000', in Penelope Curtis, ed., *Sculpture in 20th-century Britain*, vol. 1 (Leeds: Henry Moore Institute, 2003), pp. 221–30.

Goodchild, Anne, *Without from Within* [exh. cat.] (Nottingham: Djanogly Art Gallery, 2010).

Gosden, Chris, 'Making and display: Our aesthetic appreciation of things and objects', in Colin Renfrew, Chris Gosden and Elizabeth DeMarrais, eds, *Memory, Display, Archaeology and Art* (Cambridge: McDonald Institute for Archaeological Research, 2004), pp. 35–45.

Greenberg, Clement, 'Modernist painting', in Charles Harrison and Paul Wood, eds, *Art in Theory, 1900–2000: An Anthology of Changing Ideas* (Oxford: Blackwell, 2003), pp. 773–9.

Greeves, Susanna, 'Stairs into space', in Christiane Schneider, ed., *Rachel Whiteread* [exh. cat.] (London: Haunch of Venison, 2002), pp. 37–52.

Gris, Juan, *The Letters of Juan Gris 1913–1927*, ed. and trans. Douglas Cooper (London: privately published, 1956).

Gross, Jennifer R., 'Remembrance of things present', in Chris Townsend, ed., *The Art of Rachel Whiteread* (London: Thames & Hudson, 2004), pp. 35–50.

Groys, Boris, 'Survey: The movable cave, or Kabakov's self-memorials', in Boris Groys, David A. Ross and Iwona Blazwick, *Ilya Kabakov* (London: Phaidon, 1998), pp. 30–78.

Gudmundsdóttir, Gunnthórunn, *Borderlines: Autobiography and Fiction in Postmodern Life Writing* (Amsterdam and New York, NY: Rodopi, 2003).

Harrod, Tanya, *The Crafts in Britain in the Twentieth Century* (New Haven, CT: Yale University Press, 1999).

Hauser, Katherine, 'Audrey Flack's still lifes: Between femininity and feminism', *Woman's Art Journal* xxii/2 (fall 2001/winter 2002), pp. 26–30.

Heidegger, Martin, 'Building, dwelling, thinking', in Martin Heidegger, *Poetry, Language, Thought*, trans. Albert Hofstadter (New York, NY: Harper & Row, 1971), pp. 143–62.

Herbert, Martin, 'It never starts from meaning', *Art Review* 12 (June 2007), pp. 56–63.

Herkenhoff, Paulo, 'Interview with Louise Bourgeois', in Robert Storr and Paulo Herkenhoff, *Louise Bourgeois* (London: Phaidon, 2003), pp. 8–25.

Heynen, Hilde, 'Modernity and domesticity: Tensions and contradictions', in Hilde Heynen and Gülsüm Baydar, eds, *Negotiating Domesticity: Spatial Productions of Gender in Modern Architecture* (London and New York, NY: Routledge, 2005), pp. 1–29.

Hilty, Greg, 'Seeing and breathing', in Ann Jones, ed., *Recent British Sculpture* (London: Arts Council, 1993), pp. 9–12.

Holstein, Jonathan, *American Pieced Quilts* (Lausanne: Éditions des Massons S.A., 1972).

Hopps, Walter, *Robert Rauschenberg: The Early 1950s* (Houston, TX: Fine Art Press, 1991).

Houston, John, *The Abstract Vessel* (London: Bellew Publishing, 1991).

Husserl, Edmund, *Ideas: General Introduction to Pure Phenomenology*, trans. W. R. Boyce Gibson (London: Allen & Unwin; New York, NY: Humanities Press, 1931).

Israel, Toby, *Some Place like Home: Using Design Psychology to Create Ideal Places* (Chichester: John Wiley, 2003).

Januszczak, Waldemar, 'Room for reflection', *Sunday Times* (21 May 1995).

Jein, Gillian, 'Dislocating travel: New York as anti-domus in Beauvoir's *Amérique au jour le jour*', in Daisy Connon, Gillian Jein and Greg Kerr, eds, *Aesthetics of Dislocation in*

French and Francophone Literature and Art: Strategies of Representation (Lewiston, NY: Edwin Mellen Press, 2009), pp. 33–52.

Jenkins, Bruce, *Gordon Matta-Clark: Conical Intersect* (London: Afterall, 2011).

Jodidio, Philip, *Architecture: Art* (Munich: Prestel, 2005).

Jones, J., 'Grayson Perry: The pot is the man', in Julian Stair, ed., *The Body Politic: The Role of the Body and Contemporary Craft* (London: Crafts Council, 2000), pp. 96–101.

Jones, M. A., *The Limits of Liberty: American History 1607–1992* (Oxford: Oxford University Press, 1993).

Joseph, Branden W., 'John Cage and the architecture of silence', *October* (summer 1997), pp. 81–104.

Judd, Donald, 'Specific objects', in Charles Harrison and Paul Wood, eds, *Art in Theory, 1900–2000: An Anthology of Changing Ideas* (Oxford: Blackwell, 2003), pp. 824–8.

Kabakov, Ilya, 'What is a communal apartment?', in Ilya Kabakov, *Ten Characters* [exh. cat.] (New York, NY: Ronald Feldman Fine Arts; London: ICA, 1989), pp. 50–2.

——— 'Introduction', in Ilya Kabakov, *On the Total Installation*, trans. Cindy Martin (Ostfildern: Hatje Cantz, 1995), pp. 243–9.

——— 'Time in the "total" installation', in Ilya Kabakov, *On the Total Installation*, trans. Cindy Martin (Ostfildern: Hatje Cantz, 1995), pp. 281–8.

——— *16 Installations* [exh. cat.] (Antwerp: Museum van Hedendaagse Kunst, 1998).

——— 'In conversation with Robert Storr (extract), 1995', in Boris Groys, David A. Ross and Iwona Blazwick, *Ilya Kabakov* (London: Phaidon, 1998), pp. 124–9.

Kaprow, Allan, 'Performing life', in Jeff Kelley, ed., *Allan Kaprow: Essays on the Blurring of Art and Life* (Berkeley, CA: University of California Press, 2003), pp. 195–8.

——— 'The real experiment', in Jeff Kelley, ed., *Allan Kaprow: Essays on the Blurring of Art and Life* (Berkeley, CA: University of California Press, 2003), pp. 201–18.

Kelly, Julia, 'Sculpture, bricolage and the art of Bill Woodrow', in *Bill Woodrow: Sculptures 1981–1988* [exh. cat.] (London: Waddington Custot Galleries, 2011), pp. 5–13.

Kittelmann, Udo, ed., *Haus ur, Rheydt versus Totes Haus ur, Venice* (Ostfildern-Ruit: Hatje Cantz, 2001).

Klonk, Charlotte, *Spaces of Experience: Art Gallery Interiors from 1800–2000* (New Haven, CT, and London: Yale University Press, 2009).

Koepnick, Lutz, *Framing Attention: Windows on Modern German Culture* (Baltimore, MD: John Hopkins University Press, 2007).

Kölle, Brigitte, *Totes Haus ur* (Frankfurt: Alfried Krupp von Bohlen und Halbach-Stiftung, 1997).

Kotz, Mary Lynn, *Rauschenberg: Art and Life* (New York, NY: Harry N. Abrams, 1990).

Krauss, Rosalind, 'Pictorial space and the question of documentary', *Artforum* (November 1971), pp. 68–71.

——— 'Rauschenberg and the materialised image' [1974], in Branden W. Joseph, ed., *Robert Rauschenberg* (Cambridge, MA: MIT Press, 2002), pp. 39–55.

Kraynak, Janet, 'Bruce Nauman's words', in Janet Kraynak, ed., *Please Pay Attention Please: Bruce Nauman's Words* (Cambridge, MA: MIT Press, 2003), pp. 1–45.

Krivitsky, Kristy, 'Apocalyptic wallpaper', *Art Papers* xxi/6 (1997), p. 60.

Kwint, Marius, Christopher Breward and Jeremy Aynsley, *Material Memories: Design and Evocation (Materializing Culture)* (Oxford: Berg, 1999).

Lawrence, James, 'Sculptural common sense', in *Rachel Whiteread* [exh. cat.] (Beverly Hills, CA: Gagosian Gallery, 2008), pp. 7–18.

Leach, Neil, 'The dark side of the domus', in Andrew Ballantyne, ed., *What Is Architecture?* (London: Routledge, 2002), pp. 88–101.

Leader, Darian, 'The double life of objects', in Andrea Jahn, ed., *Cornelia Parker: Perpetual Canon* [exh. cat.] (Stuttgart: Kerber Verlag, 2004), pp. 72–9.

Lee, Pamela M., *Object to Be Destroyed: The Work of Gordon Matta-Clark* (Cambridge, MA: MIT Press, 2000).

Legge, Elizabeth, 'Reinventing derivation: Roles, stereotypes, and "Young British Art"', *Representations* 71 (summer 2000), pp. 1–23.

Lévi-Strauss, Claude, *The Elementary Structures of Kinship*, trans. James Harle Bell, ed. John Richard von Sturmer and Rodney Needham (Boston, MA: Beacon, 1969);

Lingwood, James, ed., *Rachel Whiteread House* (London: Phaidon, 1995).

Lippard, Lucy, *From the Center: Feminist Essays on Women's Art* (New York, NY: E. P. Dutton, 1976).

Livingstone, Marco, *Jim Dine: The Alchemy of Images* (New York, NY: Monacelli Press, 1998).

Lodge, Robert C., *Plato's Theory of Art* (London: Routledge & Kegan Paul, 1953).

McAllester Jones, Mary, *Gaston Bachelard, Subversive Humanist: Texts and Readings* (Madison, WI: University of Wisconsin Press, 1991).

McDonough, Tom, 'How to do things with buildings', *Art in America* xcv/10 (November 2007), pp. 164–237.

McEvilley, Thomas, 'The sculpture of James Croak', in Thomas McEvilley, *James Croak* (New York, NY: Harry N. Abrams, 1998), pp. 10–31.

Maldonado, Tomás, 'The idea of comfort', in Victor Margolin and Richard Buchanan, eds, *The Idea of Design* (Cambridge, MA: MIT Press, 1995), pp. 248–56.

Malik, Amna, *Sarah Lucas: Au naturel* (London: Afterall, 2009).

Mallgrave, Harry Francis, and Christina Contandriopoulos, eds, *Architectural Theory*, vol. 2: *An Anthology from 1871 to 2005* (Oxford: Blackwell, 2008).

Marck, Jan van der, 'Introduction', in *George Segal: 12 Human Situations* [exh. cat.] (Chicago, IL: Museum of Contemporary Art, 1968) [unpaginated].

——— *George Segal* (New York, NY: Harry N. Abrams, 1979).

Margetts, Martina, 'Metamorphosis: The culture of ceramics', in David Elliott, ed., *The Raw and the Cooked: New Work in Clay in Britain* [exh. cat.] (London: Crafts Council; Oxford: MoMA, 1993), pp. 13–15.

Mark, Lisa Gabrielle, ed., *WACK! Art and the Feminist Revolution* [exh. cat.] (Los Angeles, CA: Museum of Contemporary Art; Cambridge, MA and London: MIT Press, 2007).

Martin, Victoria, 'A conversation with Eleanor Antin', *Artweek* xxx/7 (July/August 1999), pp. 20–1.

Massey, Doreen, 'A place called home?', *New Formations* 17 (1992), pp. 3–15.

Masters, Christopher, *Windows in Art* (New York, NY, and London: Merrell, 2011).

Matta-Clark, Gordon, *Splitting* (New York, NY: Green Street Loft Press, 1974).

Mengham, Rod, 'Agents and penitents', in Jonathan Fineberg, *Ilya and Emilia Kabakov: The House of Dreams* [exh. cat.] (London: Serpentine Gallery, 2005), pp. 19–30.

Merck, Mandy, and Chris Townsend, eds, *The Art of Tracey Emin* (London: Thames & Hudson, 2002).

Merleau-Ponty, Maurice, *Phenomenology of Perception* (London and New York, NY: Routledge, 2002).

Meskimmon, Marsha, *Women Making Art: History, Subjectivity, Aesthetics* (London and New York, NY: Routledge, 2003).

Meyer, Laura, 'A studio of their own: The legacy of the Fresno feminist experiment', in Laura Meyer, ed., *A Studio of Their Own: The Legacy of the Fresno Feminist Experiment* (Fresno: California State University, 2009), pp. 3–34.

Meyer-Hermann, Eva, *Carl Andre Sculptor, 1996: Krefeld at Home, Wolfsburg at Large* (Stuttgart: Oktagon, 1996).

Miller, Daniel, *The Comfort of Things* (Cambridge and Malden, MA: Polity Press, 2008).

Minissale, Gregory, *Framing Consciousness in Art: Transcultural Perspectives* (Amsterdam and New York, NY: Rodopi, 2009).

Monem, Nadine, ed., *The Filthy Reality of Everyday Life: Dirt* (London: Profile, 2011).

Monte, James, 'Looking at the Guggenheim International', *Artforum* (March 1971), pp. 28–32.

Morgan, Jessica, 'The poetics of uncovering: Mona Hatoum in and out of perspective', in *Mona Hatoum* [exh. cat.] (Chicago, IL: Museum of Contemporary Art, 1997), pp. 1–23.

——— 'Matter and what it means', in *Cornelia Parker* [exh. cat.] (Boston, MA: ICA, 2000), pp. 11–39.

Morgan, Robin, ed., *Sisterhood Is Global: The International Women's Movement Anthology* (Harmondsworth: Penguin, 1984).

Morris, Robert, *Continuous Project Altered Daily: The Writings of Robert Morris* (Cambridge, MA: October Books, MIT Press, 1995).

Murray, Peter, *Piranesi and the Grandeur of Ancient Rome* (London: Thames & Hudson, 1971).
Nesbitt, Judith, ed., *Robert Gober* [exh. cat.] (London: Serpentine Gallery, 1993).
Nochlin, Linda, *Women, Art and Power* (London: Thames & Hudson, 1989).
——— *The Body in Pieces: The Fragment as a Metaphor of Modernity* (London: Thames & Hudson, 1994).
——— 'Memoirs of an ad hoc art historian', in Linda Nochlin, *Representing Women* (London and New York, NY: Thames & Hudson, 1999), pp. 6–33.
Nora, Pierre, 'Between memory and history: *Les lieux de mémoire*', *Representations* 26 (spring 1989), pp. 7–25.
O'Doherty, Brian, 'Inside the white cube, part II: The eye and the spectator', *Artforum* (April 1976), pp. 26–34.
Ortner, Sherry B., 'Is female to male as nature is to culture?', in Michelle Zimbalist Rosaldo and Louise Lamphere, eds, *Woman, Culture and Society* (Stanford, CA: California University Press, 1974), pp. 67–87.
Pallasmaa, Juhani, 'Identity, intimacy and domicile: Notes on the phenomenology of home', in David N. Benjamin, ed., *The Home: Words, Interpretations, Meanings and Environments* (Aldershot: Avebury, 1995), pp. 131–47.
——— 'Petrified silence', in Eckhard Schneider, ed., *Rachel Whiteread: Walls, Doors, Floors and Stairs* (Cologne: Walther König, 2005), pp. 22–30.
Panhans-Bühler, Ursula, 'Being involved', in Christopher Heinrich, ed., *Mona Hatoum* [exh. cat.] (Ostfildern-Ruit: Hatje Cantz, 2004), pp. 13–40.
Parry, Nigel, 'Breaking the mould', *Observer* (24 November 1991).
Payne, Antonia, 'Neither from nor towards', in G. Brett *et al.*, *Cornelia Parker: Avoided Object* [exh. cat.] (Cardiff: Chapter, 1996), pp. 39–50.
Pearson, Caspar, *Humanism and the Urban World: Leon Battista Alberti and the Renaissance City* (University Park, PA: Pennsylvania State University Press, 2011).
Penny, Nicholas, *Piranesi* (London: Oresko Books, 1978).
Perry, Gill, 'Introduction: Visibility, difference and excess', *Art History* xxvi/3 (June 2003), pp. 319–39.
Pollock, Griselda, *Vision and Difference: Femininity, Feminism and the Histories of Art* (London and New York, NY: Routledge, 1988).
——— *Differencing the Canon: Feminist Desire and the Writing of Art's Histories* (London and New York, NY: Routledge, 1999).
Potts, Alex, *The Sculptural Imagination: Figurative, Modernist, Minimalist* (New Haven, CT: Yale University Press, 2000).
——— 'Installation and sculpture', *Oxford Art Journal* xxiv/2 (2001) [special issue on installation], pp. 5–24.

——— 'Robert Rauschenberg and David Smith: Compelling contiguities', *Art Bulletin* lxxxix/1 (March 2007), pp. 148–59.

Powell, Helen, 'Time, television, and the decline of DIY', *Home Cultures* vi/1 (March 2009), pp. 89–108.

Prince, Mark, 'Waiting game', *Art Monthly* 355 (April 2012), pp. 1–4.

Pritchett, James, *The Music of John Cage* (Cambridge: Cambridge University Press, 1993).

Racz, Imogen, 'Juan Gris: The uncompromising cubist', MA thesis, University of Central England, 1993.

——— 'Sculptural vessels across the great divide: Tony Cragg's *Laibe* and the metaphors of clay', *Journal of Visual Art Practice* viii/3 (2009), pp. 215–28.

——— *Contemporary Crafts* (Oxford and New York, NY: Berg, 2009).

——— 'Michael Landy's *Semi-detached* and the art of making', *Journal of Visual Art Practice* x/3 (2011), pp. 231–43.

Rapoport, Amos, 'A critical look at the concept "home"', in David N. Benjamin, ed., *The Home: Words, Interpretations, Meanings and Environments* (Aldershot: Avebury, 1995), pp. 25–55.

Rasmussen, Steen Eiler, *Experiencing Architecture* (Cambridge, MA: MIT Press, 1962).

Ravetz, Alison, with Richard Turkington, *The Place of Home: The English Domestic Environment 1914–2000* (London: E. & F. N. Spon, 1995).

Reijnders, Anton, *The Ceramic Process: A Manual and Source of Inspiration of Ceramic Art and Design* (London: A & C Black; Philadelphia, PA: University of Pennsylvania Press, 2005).

Renton, Andrew, *Mona Hatoum* [exh. cat.] (London: Jay Jopling and White Cube, 2006).

Robicsek, Hyla, '"You give us this and we give you that": The British response to the legacy of American minimalism in the 1990s', MA dissertation, Courtauld Institute of Art, 2003.

Rosaldo, Michelle Zimbalist, 'Woman, culture and society: A theoretical overview', in Michelle Zimbalist Rosaldo and Louise Lamphere, eds, *Woman, Culture and Society* (Stanford, CA: California University Press, 1974), pp. 35–41.

Rose, Barbara, 'Robert Rauschenberg', *Art and Antiquities* xxx/6 (June 2007), pp. 111–13.

Rosenberg, Karin, ed., *George Segal* [exh. cat.] (Chicago, IL: Museum of Contemporary Art, 1968).

Royle, Nicholas, *The Uncanny* (Manchester: Manchester University Press, 2003).

Rudd, Natalie, 'From here to infinity and back', in *Size Matters: Exploring Scale in the Arts Council Collection* (London: Hayward Gallery, 2005), pp. 8–15.

Saito, Yuriko, *Everyday Aesthetics* (Oxford: Oxford University Press, 2007).

Saunders, Gill, 'How wallpaper left home and made an exhibition of itself', in Gill Saunders, *Walls Are Talking: Wallpaper, Art and Culture* [exh. cat.] (Manchester: Whitworth Art Gallery, 2010), pp. 27–95.

Savage, Jon, 'Museum piece: Anarchy in the V&A', *Artforum* (February 1995), pp. 29–30.

Scarry, Elaine, *The Body in Pain: The Making and Unmaking of the World* (New York, NY: Oxford University Press, 1985).

Schantl, Alexandra, 'About the love of objects', in Alexandra Schantl, ed., *The Love of Objects: Aspects of Contemporary Sculpture* (Vienna: Springer Verlag, 2008), pp. 18–24.

Schapiro, Miriam, 'The education of women as artists: *Project Womanhouse*', *Art Journal* xxxi/3 (spring 1972), pp. 268–70.

——— 'More on women's art: An exchange', *Art in America* (November/December 1976), p. 17.

Schimmel, Paul, 'Life's echo: Gregor Schneider's *Dead House ur*', in *Gregor Schneider* [exh. cat.] (Milan: Charta, 2003), pp. 103–18.

——— 'Autobiography and self-portraiture in Rauschenberg's *Combines*', in Paul Schimmel, ed., *Robert Rauschenberg: Combines* [exh. cat.] (New York, NY: MoMA, 2005), pp. 211–28.

Schjeldahl, Peter, 'Cragg's big bang', in Tony Cragg *et al.*, *Tony Cragg: Signs of Life* (Düsseldorf: Richter Verlag, 2003), pp. 86–93.

Schneider, Eckhard, 'Constructing the ephemeral', in Eckhard Schneider, ed., *Rachel Whiteread: Walls, Doors, Floors and Stairs* (Cologne: Walther König, 2005), pp. 7–11.

Schneider, Gregor, and Ulrich Loock, 'I never throw anything away, I just go on…', in *Gregor Schneider* [exh. cat.] (Milan: Charta, 2003), pp. 35–68.

Schwarzbauer, Franz, 'Intensified perception: Artificial quotation in the work of Tom Wesselmann', in Nicole Fritz and Franz Schwarzbauer, eds, *Tom Wesselmann und die Pop Art* [exh. cat.] (Ravensburg: Städtische Galerie, 2008), pp. 107–13.

Segal, George, 'Commentaries on six sculptures', in Martin Friedman and Graham W. J. Beal, *George Segal: Sculptures* [exh. cat.] (Minneapolis, MN: Walker Art Gallery, 1979), p. 55

Serra, Richard, 'Statements: On frame', *Artforum* (September 1971) [special film issue], p. 64.

Sladen, Mark, 'A red mirror', in Mark Sladen, ed., *Helen Chadwick* [exh. cat.] (London: Barbican Art Gallery and Hatje Cantz, 2004), pp. 13–32.

Slyce, John, 'Temporary monumental: Visibility, labour, value and procedure in the projects of Michael Landy', in Judith Nesbitt and John Slyce, *Michael Landy: Semi-detached* [exh. cat.] (London: Tate, 2004), pp. 50–63.

Solomon, Alan, 'The new art' [1963], in Carol Anne Mahsun, ed., *Pop Art: The Critical Dialogue* (Ann Arbor, MI: UMI Research Press, 1989), pp. 49–60.

Spate, Virginia, *Orphism: The Evolution of Non-figurative Painting in Paris 1910–1914* (New York, NY: Oxford University Press, 1979).

Speaks, E., '"We bring our lares with us": Bodies and domiciles in the sculpture of Louise Bourgeois', *Art Journal* lxviii/3 (fall 2009), pp. 88–103.

Spigel, Lynn, 'The suburban home companion: Television and the neighbourhood ideal in postwar America', in Beatriz Colomina, ed., *Sexuality and Space* (New York, NY: Princeton Architectural Press, 1992), pp. 185–217.

Stein, Linda, 'Miriam Schapiro: Woman–warrior with lace', *Fiberarts* (March/April, 1998), pp. 35–40.

Stevenson, Deborah, *Cities and Urban Cultures* (Maidenhead and Philadelphia, PA: Open University Press, 2003).

Storr, Robert, 'A sketch for a portrait: Louise Bourgeois', in Robert Storr and Paulo Herkenhoff, *Louise Bourgeois* (London: Phaidon, 2003), pp. 28–93.

Tansini, Laura, 'Sculpture to enlarge our reality: A conversation with Tony Cragg', *Sculpture* xxiii/4 (May 2004), pp. 34–41.

Tarsia, Andrea, 'Conditions of display 1975–2000', in Penelope Curtis, ed., *Sculpture in 20th-century Britain*, vol. 1 (Leeds: Henry Moore Institute, 2003), pp. 253–63.

Thorns, David C., *The Transformation of Cities: Urban Theory and Urban Life* (Basingstoke and New York, NY: Palgrave Macmillan, 2002).

Tickner, Lisa, 'A strange alchemy: Cornelia Parker', *Art History* xxvi/3 (2003), pp. 364–91.

'Tony Cragg talks to Barry Schwabsky', *Artforum* (April 2003), pp. 200–1, 253.

Tony Cragg: Winner of the 1988 Turner Prize (London: Tate Gallery & Patrons of New Art, 1989).

Trigg, David, 'Steffi Klenz, Nummianus', *Art Review* 37 (December 2009), p. 117.

Trigg, Dylan, *The Aesthetics of Decay: Nothingness, Nostalgia, and the Absence of Reason* (New York, NY: Peter Lang, 2006).

Turner, Alwyn W., *Rejoice! Rejoice! Britain in the 1980s* (London: Aurum Press, 2010).

Valença, Márcio M., *The Debate on Equity Withdrawal Versus the Housing-linked Interest Rate Mechanism: A View of the Economics of Housing in Conservative Britain during the 1980s* (Brighton: Centre for Urban and Regional Research, University of Sussex, 1992).

Verzotti, Giorgio, *Mona Hatoum* [exh. cat.] (Milan: Charta, 1999).

Vickery, Amanda, *Behind Closed Doors: At Home in Georgian England* (New Haven, CT, and London: Yale University Press, 2009).

Vidler, Anthony, 'Full house: Rachel Whiteread's postdomestic casts', in Anthony Vidler, *Warped Space: Art, Architecture, and Anxiety in Modern Culture* (Cambridge, MA, and London: MIT Press, 2000).

Volker, Adolph, 'The body and the world', in Christopher Heinrich, ed., *Mona Hatoum* [exh. cat.] (Ostfildern-Ruit: Hatje Cantz, 2004), pp. 43–59.

Wagstaff, Sheena, *Edward Hopper* [exh. cat.] (London: Tate, 2004).

Wakefield, Neville, 'Rachel Whiteread: Separation anxiety and the art of release', *Parkett* 42 (1994), pp. 76–82.

Walker, John A., *Cultural Offensive: America's Impact on British Art since 1945* (London and Sterling, VA: Pluto Press, 1998).

Walker, Stephen, *Gordon Matta-Clark: Art, Architecture and the Attack on Modernism* (London and New York, NY: I.B.Tauris, 2009).

Warner, Marina, 'Richard Wentworth: A sense of things', in Marina Warner, *Richard Wentworth* [exh. cat.] (London: Thames & Hudson and Serpentine Gallery, 1993), pp. 9–16.

Wells, Rachel, 'Scale in contemporary sculpture: The enlargement, the miniature, the life size', PhD thesis, Courtauld Institute of Art, 2008.

Wilding, Faith, 'Gestations in a studio of our own', in Faith Wilding, *By Our Own Hands: The History of the Women Artists' Movement in Southern California, 1970–1977* (Los Angeles, CA: Double X, 1977)

——— 'The feminist art programs at Fresno and CalArts, 1970–1975', in Norma Broude and Mary Garrard, eds, *The Power of Feminist Art: Emergence, Impact and Triumph of the American Feminist Art Movement* (London: Thames & Hudson, 1994), pp. 32–47.

——— 'Next bodies', in Amelia Jones, *The Feminism and Visual Culture Reader* (London and New York, NY: Routledge, 2003), pp. 26–9.

Williams, Gilda, 'Doubling', *Art Monthly* 340 (2010), pp. 1–4.

Wood, Paul, *et al.*, *Modernism in Dispute: Art since the Forties* (New Haven, CT, and London: Yale University Press and the Open University, 1993).

Woods, Christine, 'Introduction: It's the background that explains the foreground', in Gill Saunders, *Walls Are Talking: Wallpaper, Art and Culture* [exh. cat.] (Manchester: Whitworth Art Gallery, 2010), pp. 10–25.

Woods, Lebbeus, *Anarchitecture: Architecture Is a Political Act* (London: St Martin's Press, 1992).

Young, Pamela, 'Off the wall', *Applied Arts* xxv/1 (February/March 2010), pp. 20–22.

Zegher, Catherine de, ed., *Martha Rosler: Positions in the Life World* (Cambridge, MA, and London: MIT Press, 1998).

ONLINE SOURCES

'Ask this year's Turner Prize winner' [interview with Grayson Perry], *BBC News* [website] (7 December 2003). Available at http://news.bbc.co.uk/1/hi/talking_point/3291691.stm (accessed 7 August 2014).

Bergius, Hanne, '"Join Dada!" Aspects of Dada's reception since the late 1950s' [lecture, 9 September 2006]. Available at http://www.moma.org/docs/learn/2006_DadaSymp/HanneBergiusDADA.pdf (accessed 7 August 2014).

'Ceramic points of view: "Big White Jug", by Alison Britton', *V&A* [website]. Available at http://www.vam.ac.uk/content/articles/c/ceramics-points-of-view-alison-britton-big-white-jug/ (accessed 7 August 2014).

Chadwick, Helen, *Notebook on Ego Geometria Sum.* Available at http://www.henry-moore.org/hmi/archive/turning-the-pages--helen-chadwick-notebooks (accessed 7 August 2014).

'Cindy Sherman (b.1954): *Madame de Pompadour (née Poisson) Soup Tureen and Saucer*, 1990', *Pulitzer Foundation for the Arts* [website]. Available at http://www.portrait.pulitzerarts.org/entrance-gallery/pompadour/ (accessed 7 August 2014).

Croak, James, 'Summer reading: Body and soil', *Artnet* [website]. Available at http://www.artnet.com/magazineus/books/croak/summer-reading-6-18-12.asp (accessed 7 August 2014).

'Elizabeth A. Sackler Center for Feminist Art: *The Dinner Party*', *Brooklyn Museum* [website]. Available at http://www.brooklynmuseum.org/eascfa/dinner_party/womens_work.php (accessed 7 August 2014).

Fuchs, Rudi, 'Tracey Emin: A particular honesty' [essay] (2005). Available at http://whitecube.com/artists/tracey_emin/text/tracey_emin_a_particular_honesty/ (accessed 7 August 2014).

Gormley, Antony, 'Terracotta and lead works, 1983–1988', *Antony Gormley* [website]. Available at http://www.antonygormley.com/sculpture/item-view/id/228 (accessed 7 August 2014).

'Gregor Schneider: *Die Familie Schneider*, October 2004', *Artangel* [website]. Available at http://www.artangel.org.uk/projects/2004/die_familie_schneider (accessed 7 August 2014).

Januszczak, Waldemar, 'Bill Woodrow, Waddington Galleries', *Waldemar Januszczak* [website] (27 March 2011). Available at http://www.waldemar.tv/2011/03/bill-woodrow-waddington-galleries/ (accessed 7 August 2014).

'Jerwood Artists Platform', *Mary Maclean* [website]. Available at http://www.marymaclean.org.uk/?page_id=786 (accessed 7 August 2014).

John Smith [website]. Available at http://www.johnsmithfilms.com/texts/sf2.html# (accessed 7 August 2014).

'Laurie Anderson, Trisha Brown, Gordon Matta-Clark: Pioneers of the Downtown Scene, New York 1970s', *Barbican* [website]. Available at http://www.barbican.org.uk/artgallery/event-detail.asp?ID=11398 (accessed 7 August 2014).

'London Toile', *Timorous Beasties* [website]. Available at http://www.timorousbeasties.com/shop/wallcoverings/85/london-toile/ (accessed 7 August 2014).

Manchester, Elizabeth, 'Sarah Lucas, *Sod You Gits* 1991: Summary', *Tate* [website]. Available at http://www.tate.org.uk/art/artworks/lucas-sod-you-gits-p78205/text-summary (accessed 7 August 2014).

O'Hagan, Andrew, 'The living rooms' [essay], *Artangel* [website]. Available at http://www.artangel.org.uk//projects/2004/die_familie_schneider/the_living_rooms_by_andrew_o_hagan/the_living_rooms_by_andrew_o_hagan (accessed 7 August 2014).

'Oral history interview with Eleanor Antin, 2009 May 8–9', *Archives of American Art* [website]. Available at http://www.aaa.si.edu/collections/interviews/oral-history-interview-eleanor-antin-15792 (accessed 7 August 2014).

'Oral history interview with Robert Rauschenberg, 1965 Dec. 21', *Archives of American Art* [website]. Available at http://www.aaa.si.edu/collections/interviews/oral-history-interview-robert-rauschenberg-12870 (accessed 7 August 2014).

'Oral history interview with Miriam Schapiro, 1989 September 10', *Archives of American Art* [website]. Available at http://www.aaa.si.edu/collections/interviews/oral-history-interview-miriam-schapiro-11695 (accessed 7 August 2014).

'Oral history interview with George Segal, 1973 November 26', *Archives of American Art* [website]. Available at http://www.aaa.si.edu/collections/interviews/oral-history-interview-george-segal-12613 (accessed 7 August 2014).

'Rachel Whiteread, *Walls, Doors, Floors and Stairs*', *Kunsthaus Bregenz* [website]. Available at http://www.kunsthaus-bregenz.at/ehtml/ewelcome00.htm?aus_whiteread.htm (accessed 7 August 2014).

'Richard Billingham', *Saatchi Gallery* [website]. Available at http://www.saatchi-gallery.co.uk/artists/richard_billingham.htm (accessed 7 August 2014).

Taylor, Rachel, 'Mona Hatoum, *Home* 1999: Summary', *Tate* [website]. Available at http://www.tate.org.uk/art/artworks/hatoum-home-t07918/text-summary (accessed 7 August 2014).

'Transcript of the John Tusa interview with Richard Serra', *BBC Radio 3* [website]. Available at http://www.bbc.co.uk/programmes/p00nc9n3 (accessed 7 August 2014).

'Why have there been no great women artists?', *Vassar Innovators* [website]. Available at http://innovators.vassar.edu/innovator.html?id=48 (accessed 7 August 2014).

ARCHIVE MATERIAL

'Michael Landy: Judith Nesbitt discusses the artist in relation to his work *Semi-detached*, 15/10/04', Tate Archive audio-visual collection, Tate Britain [tape TAV 2865A].

Email from Carolyn Kerr to Judith Nesbitt and Lizzie Carey-Thomas, 12 September 2003, Tate Archive, Tate Britain [EX 121.0, A13841].

INDEX

References to images are in *italic*.